Felix Leif Keppmann

Decentralized Control and Adaptation in Distributed Applications via Web and Semantic Web Technologies

Decentralized Control and Adaptation in Distributed Applications via Web and Semantic Web Technologies

by
Felix Leif Keppmann

KIT Scientific Publishing

Decentralized Control and Adaptation in Distributed Applications via Web and Semantic Web Technologies

Zur Erlangung des akademischen Grades eines Doktor der Ingenieurwissenschaften (Dr.-Ing.) von der KIT-Fakultät für Wirtschaftswissenschaften des Karlsruher Instituts für Technologie (KIT) genehmigte Dissertation

von M.Sc. Felix Leif Keppmann

Tag der mündlichen Prüfung: 03. September 2018
Hauptreferent: Prof. Dr. Rudi Studer
Korreferent: Prof. Dr. Oscar Corcho

Impressum

Karlsruher Institut für Technologie (KIT)
KIT Scientific Publishing
Straße am Forum 2
D-76131 Karlsruhe

KIT Scientific Publishing is a registered trademark of Karlsruhe Institute of Technology.
Reprint using the book cover is not allowed.

www.ksp.kit.edu

Print on Demand 2020 – Gedruckt auf FSC-zertifiziertem Papier

ISBN 978-3-7315-0966-0
DOI 10.5445/KSP/1000097534

Acknowledgments

My work on this doctoral thesis has been supported by several people. They provided me with research opportunities, motivated me, kept me focused, and supported me both in my professional and private life.

I thank my doctorate supervisor, Prof. Dr. Rudi Studer, the second doctorate supervisor, Prof. Dr. Andreas Harth, and the reviewer of my thesis, Prof. Dr. Oscar Corcho. All three are respected researcher and well-known in the research community. Rudi Studer provided me with the opportunity to work as a research associate at the Institute of Applied Informatics and Formal Description Methods (AIFB) of the Karlsruher Institute of Technology (KIT). His guidance, experience, and notable leadership style provided me with both the freedom of researching my own topics and the opportunity to take over responsibility in projects and management. Andreas Harth guided and challenged my research in close collaboration, enabling me to benefit from his founded knowledge in this research area. Oscar Corcho provided me with valuable feedback on my thesis and was a integral member of the examining board.

I thank my wife, Dr. Maria Maleshkova, for her strong support in both my professional and private life. In our professional life, we collaborated on different research topics and on hosting events for the research community. But especially in my private life, Maria has been always supporting and motivating me to stay focused and to complete my research. Without her support, my work on this doctoral thesis would have not been finished with the same success.

I thank my parents, Vera and Dr. Hans Adolf Burbach, for their strong support during all chapters of my life. They always encouraged me to keep on my journey through bachelor, master, and doctoral studies.

Finally, I would like to thank all people that have been supporting me but have not been mentioned here.

Abstract

Current developments in multiple domains are characterized by the increased use of mobile devices, wearables, and sensors. In this context, the visions of the IoT, the WoT, and the SWoT as well as related visions such as the I4.0 promise the interconnection and collaboration between billions of "things". Still, what we are currently witnessing is the proliferation of isolated islands of custom solutions, which support a restricted set of protocols and devices, and cannot be easily integrated or extended. In general, these visions mark a shift towards more modularized and distributed application designs, in which applications are composed of several smaller, virtually or even physically separated, components with distinct domain-specific capabilities that communicate via a network to provide value-added functions.

The design of distributed applications, built on top of a diverse landscape of components with a multitude of involved stakeholders, poses a number of challenges. These include overcoming the data and communication heterogeneity of the involved components, dealing with requirements of multi-stakeholder scenarios, where a priori we hardly know the needs and constraints of all possible integration scenario, and enabling decentralized control in distributed applications that are composed of several distinct developed components.

To this end, this thesis aims to benefit from the basic interoperability provided by the Web stack and relies on semantic technologies for enabling data integration to provide an approach and an implementation for enabling decentralized control in distributed applications composed of heterogeneous components. In particular, we introduce the novel concept of Smart Components, which enable adaptability at run-time through an adaptation layer, and give a reference architecture with a specific prototypical implementation. The presented solutions are thoroughly evaluated in terms of function, performance, and scalability. For the scalability tests, we design and implement a benchmark environment that enables us to easily evaluate use cases with only a few or multiple components.

Contents

Figures

Tables

Listings

Algorithms

Equations

1 Introduction

Recent technology developments are characterized by the increased use of mobile devices, wearables, and sensors as well as the modularization and distribution of formerly monolithic applications. In this context, the visions of the Internet of Things (IoT) [66, 9], the Web of Things (WoT) [167, 72, 70, 68], and the Semantic Web of Things (SWoT) [143, 128] as well as related visions such as the Industry 4.0 (I4.0) [109, 86] promise the interconnection and collaboration between billions of "things". Furthermore, the Web [18, 25, 28], the Semantic Web (SW) [30, 29, 146], and the Web of Data (WoD) [33, 32] evolved from a Web of static interlinked documents for humans to a Web that is enriched with a vast, continuously increasing amount of machine-readable, semantically annotated, and interlinked data, which is openly available for consumption and integration as part of applications, or is part of commercial offers. In addition, the capabilities provided by the Web and Semantic Web Technologies (SWT) [49] with respect to the integration of heterogeneous communication approaches and data find their way from the classical client-server based provisioning of information to the integration of components, which have several different roles as part of distributed composite applications, e.g., being both a server and a client.

In general, these visions mark a shift towards more modularized and distributed solutions design, in which applications are composed of several small, virtually or physically separated components with distinct domain-specific capabilities, which communicate via networks to provide the value-added functions of these applications. These distributed applications are built by either decomposing formerly monolithic systems into smaller components or by being aligned from scratch with the visions.

The applications, which are built in this distributed and highly modularized manner, offer several advantages that are dependent on the requirements of the actual specific application use cases. Some examples of these advantages are listed in the following.

- The complexity of individual components is reduced due to their independent development and focus on specific domains.
- The distributed applications become more scalable, since workloads can be addressed by adding or removing components.
- The value-added functions of distributed applications are backed-up by redundancy to avoid business-critical failures and to provide robustness against errors.
- The pervasiveness and geographical distribution of applications are increased by integrating all kinds of "things" as components, e.g., mobile devices and sensors.
- The stakeholders that operate distributed applications gain independence and can avoid vendor lock-ins by depending on multiple suppliers.

1.1 Challenges

The design of distributed applications, built on a heterogeneous landscape of components with a multitude of involved stakeholders, requires the addressing of several challenges. In integration scenarios, distributed applications are composed out of a landscape of components with diverse characteristics. These components may represent, e.g., sensors and apps, stationary and mobile devices, low-cost embedded computers and high-end servers, or user information and encyclopedia data. Furthermore, the distributed applications, which are composed of these components, expose their own heterogeneous properties. These are characterized by, e.g., single-location and multi-location distribution, centralized and decentralized control, public or private availability, or low-latency and high-payload data processing. Furthermore, multiple stakeholders are involved in the development of the components, their provisioning, and their integration into distributed applications. In the following, we elaborate on some of these problem areas and their challenges.

Integration of Distributed Components The development of composite distributed applications, in the context of IoT, WoT, or SWoT, requires that a heterogeneous landscape of components is able to collaborate. During the integration of a plenitude of distinct components, which are developed by different stakeholders, we face *Communication Heterogeneity* in terms of the different interaction mechanisms and interfaces used for communication. The communication between components is required to establish data flows and, thereby, exchange messages that embody the collaboration for providing the value-added functions of the applications. Components must either passively expose interfaces or actively execute interactions to communicate. Related to the aforementioned challenge, the *Information Heterogeneity* of the communicated messages is another integration challenge. On the one hand, this heterogeneity appears in terms of different data formats and models, i.e., the way, in which data is encoded, and, on the other hand, in terms of non-existing or diverging data semantics, i.e., the meaning of data across a heterogeneous landscape of components.

Unspecific Development Needs There is an almost endless number of possible integration scenarios for components within distributed applications. In such multi-stakeholder scenarios, in which components are built by different manufacturers and developers, in which these components are integrated and used by other stakeholders, and in which we hardly know the requirements of all possible integration scenarios during the design time of the components, we face the challenge of *Requirements Unawareness*. Consequently, we can only provide default interfaces and interactions and are not able to design the components that provide the optimal solutions for all specific use cases. Even if we would know all current and future integration scenarios, we also face *Development Inefficiency* as a challenge. The design and development of the same component in multiple adapted versions for every possible use case do not only lead to very complex and inefficient development, i.e., the development is time-consuming, but, in consequence, may also be inefficient in terms of business requirements, i.e., the development is not profitable.

Control of Distributed Applications The integration of several components into a distributed application requires collaboration based on the components' individual functions in an application-specific manner. This application-specific control logic includes, e.g., the required interaction needed to establish data flows, the selection of data and its formatting as the payload of interactions, or the decisions that overreach the function of individual components. The most basic control pattern is based on a single component that controls the distributed application in a centralized manner. However, integration scenarios for emerging application use cases as well as the provisioning of some of the aforementioned advantages, e.g., replication for performance or redundancy, require the decentralized handling of the control logic. Enabling *Decentralized Control* in distributed applications, which are composed of several distinct and independently developed components, is challenging. The control logic that is specific to a distributed application needs to be handled by the participating components themselves. In addition, hybrid control patterns that include partially centralized and decentralized control are valid integration patterns. Related to the aforementioned challenge, we also face *Control Deployment* as a challenge. The control logic must be deployed at the components after their development and with respect to the specific requirements of the distributed application use cases. Since the requirements of every possible future use case cannot be known, we can, in general, not integrate this application logic during the design of components.

Interaction in Distributed Applications Providing support for the interaction between components within distributed applications is also challenging. Components realize data flows between each other through different interaction patterns, e.g., by pushing information, or by pulling information. The use of different interaction patterns can lead to *Interaction Inefficiency*. The selected interaction patterns may not be optimal in every case, e.g., due to bandwidth limitations, or due to latency requirements. This is especially true if components are supplied by several independent stakeholders and are not well attuned a priori. If, in addition, the factors that influence the optimal selection of interaction patterns change over time, we are challenged with *Meta-interaction Patterns*, which are required for enabling the automatic optimization of interactions. These meta-interactions enable components to communicate with respect to the actual interaction patterns for realizing data flows within distributed applications and to enable their adjustment.

Integration of Non-compliant Components The IoT, WoT, and SWoT all promote cross-domain application use cases. Consequently, the architectures that support their integration must, to a certain extent, be domain independent. However, with respect to the requirements of individual domains, established specialized architectures, i.e., domain-specific architectures, provide optimized solutions. In addition, the implementation of a domain-independent integration architecture at every specialized component may not be feasible. As a result, we are challenged with typical integration problems on the architectural level. In particular, we face *Non-compliant Communication* as a challenge, which is focused on the realization of data flows between components that assume different interactions. In addition, we face *Non-compliant Representation* as a challenge, which relates to having different representations and semantic meaning of the exchanged data, due to dealing with heterogeneous architectures.

Data for Distributed Benchmarks Independently of the solutions provided for the aforementioned challenges, the comparison of different versions of the same solution as well as the comparison of different solutions for the same problem require a common benchmark evaluation with respect to functional and performance characteristics. However, the nature of distributed applications – a composition of components that collaborate through interactions via connecting networks, is particularly challenging for performance benchmarks. On the one hand, we face the *Data Generation* as a challenge. Distributed benchmarks must provide settings for generating and handling data not only for single components but also for sets of components. On the other hand, we face the *Dataset Distribution* as a challenge. Distributed benchmarks must support the data distribution, the required data flows between components, as well as the interaction mechanisms for data access and modification.

Provisioning of Distributed Benchmarks Providing benchmarks for distributed architectures is challenging not only because of the aforementioned data distribution but also because of the communication and component distribution setup. In particular, benchmarks for distributed applications need to be able to support the creating and handling of a multitude of components, their connection through networks, as well as the supply with appropriate computing resources. Hereby, we face *Deployment Complexity* as a challenge. The complexity related to deploying distributed benchmarks goes beyond the sole generation of datasets for the evaluation of individual components. In addition, we face *Difficult*

Reproducibility as a challenge. The aforementioned generation and distribution of the benchmarks, as well as the handling of their deployment, must be reproducible to enable the repetitive comparison of different solutions with respect to distributed application settings with the same characteristics.

1.2 Hypothesis

In this thesis, given the context of the work set in the introduction and focusing on the aforementioned challenges, we aim to investigate the following hypothesis:

Hypothesis *Web and Semantic Web concepts and technologies enable at runtime 1) the adaptation of components for their integration into distributed applications, 2) their control in centralized, decentralized, or hybrid manner, and 3) the deployment of this control.*

We believe that the combination and extension of established, standardized, and publicly available Web and Semantic Web concepts and technologies can pave the way for coping with the challenges that accompany emerging IoT, WoT, and SWoT visions. In particular, we aim to address the heterogeneous landscape of components and multiple involved stakeholders, thus counteracting the emergence of isolated, proprietary, non-standardized islands of components, which support only the integration of applications fitting the specific ecosystem.

1.3 Research Questions

We define the scope of our work and approach the analysis of the hypothesis by examining the following research questions:

Research Question 1 *How can we design an architecture for distributed applications, based on Web and Semantic Web concepts and technologies, that enables the adaptation of components at runtime, supporting both their integration and the deployment of control logic?*

By relying on Web and SW concepts and technologies, we aim to reuse and extend existing solutions in order to address the challenges related to *Communication Heterogeneity* and *Information Heterogeneity*. By following the approach of building on established technologies, we ensure the interoperability and incorporation of already broadly applied standards and technologies, which have proven to provide means to cope with the given challenges.

The focus on enabling adaptation for integration at runtime is especially important for being able to address the challenges related to *Requirements Unawareness* and *Development Inefficiency* with respect to the design of individual components. Thus we aim to support the adaptability of individual components during their runtime in terms of adapting their interfaces and interactions, and in terms of enabling the processing, which is required to update the interfaces or to execute the interactions with other components.

Being able to deploy control logic on behalf of the distributed applications at runtime, is crucial for addressing the challenges related to *Decentralized Control* and *Control Deployment* with respect to the integration of multiple components in the compositions of distributed applications. We aim to provide support for distributing control logic, which is specific to individual distributed applications and to the components in their compositions.

Research Question 2 *How can we enable the optimization of interactions between components, which are based on our architecture, and enable the integration of components, which are based on other specialized architectures?*

Providing a method for optimizing the interactions between components is an important part of tackling the challenges related to *Interaction Inefficiency* and *Meta-interaction Patterns*. We aim to investigate suitable means for optimizing the data flows between components within distributed applications, which are based on the architecture developed in the context of the first research question. In addition, we aim to enable the autonomous optimization of interactions of components during their runtime.

For supporting the integration of components from specialized architectures, we advocate an approach based on creating mappings between the individual architectures and our architecture, thus addressing the challenges related to *Non-compliant Communication* and *Non-compliant Representation*. Similarly to the integration of individual components, we aim to provide support for the integration of interfaces and interactions, as well as the representation of information but, in contrast, on the level of architectures.

Research Question 3 *How can we support the evaluation of distributed applications, based on our architecture, in terms of generating distributed benchmarks and in terms of providing these benchmarks as distributed environments?*

Benchmarks that are specifically designed for evaluating distributed applications need to focus on the challenges related to *Data Generation* and *Dataset Distribution*. In particular, this means that it is insufficient to support only the generation of datasets, which serve as the basis for the evaluation of requests against the data that is provided by components. Instead, the distribution of datasets, which emulates the distribution of the data on several components within distributed applications, also needs to be enabled.

By providing benchmarks as distributed environments, we focus on addressing the challenges related to *Deployment Complexity* and *Difficult Reproducibility*. In addition to the dataset generation and distribution, it is also necessary to provide means for the setup and deployment of the actually distributed environments, which contain the generated and distributed datasets. Furthermore, to enable true benchmarking, we also need to ensure the reproducibility of the setup and the deployment of the benchmark, and of the correspondingly produced evaluation results.

1.4 Methodology

We follow a hybrid and iterative methodology. In particular, we combine methodologies, which are specific to one of the three main research areas that we investigate (c.f., Figure 1.1). Furthermore, each of the developed contributions has undergone a number of cycles of improvement and refinement, based on requirements-compliance checks, evaluation of implemented prototypes and use case tests.

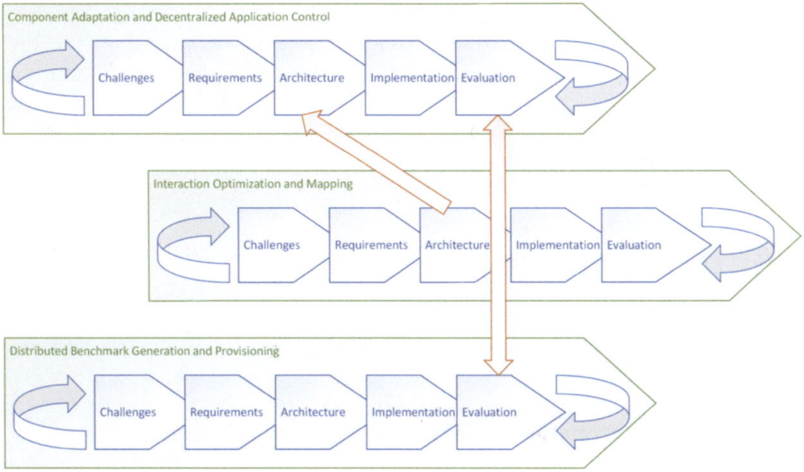

Figure 1.1: Methodology

In Figure 1.1 we give an overview of the research methodology that we use to approach the research questions. We define our research work within the scope of three larger areas, each of which is aligned with one of the research questions. The investigated research areas are interconnected and co-dependent – visualized in Figure 1.1 via the two connecting arrows, but at the same time maintain their interdependencies – visualized as enclosing arrows. The research areas are tracked by following different approaches for each of the research questions, which, however, all include the same steps – the detailed description of challenges, requirements, architecture, implementation, and evaluation. In the research on *Component Adaptation and Decentralized Application Control* (c.f., Chapter 3), we focus on the first research question, in the research on *Interaction Optimization and Mapping* (c.f., Chapter 4), we focus on the second research question, and finally in the research on *Distributed Benchmark Generation and Provisioning* (c.f., Chapter 5), we focus on the third research question. In some cases, the approaches are interconnected with the other research areas. For example, the approach for component adaptation and decentralized control is reused in the evaluation of the approach for distributed benchmark generation and provisioning, and the architecture of the approach for interaction optimization and mapping partially depends on the architecture of the first approach.

As already mentioned, due to the nature of the research field, we use an iterative method. We back up our requirements and conceptional solutions with implementations and evaluations and, subsequently, interactively refine the approach by adjusting the requirements and the conceptual solution. In this thesis, we present the refined state of our research.

1.5 Contributions

With respect to the three research questions, we make the following contributions.

Component Adaptation and Decentralized Application Control In Chapter 3, we present our approach and contributions for the adaptation of components and the decentralized control of distributed applications. First, we elaborate in more detail on the challenges related to *Communication Heterogeneity*, *Information Heterogeneity*, *Requirements Unawareness*, *Development Inefficiency*, *Control Deployment*, and *Control Deployment*. Subsequently, we analyze these challenges and derive requirements for an integration architecture in general and, in particular, for an architecture that supports component adaptation. We present the first main contribution of this chapter – an integration architecture that unifies heterogeneous communication and information, based on established principles and technologies. Afterward, we present the second main contribution – an architectural approach for component design and implementation, which enables the adaptation of interfaces, interaction, and processing as well as the deployment of application-specific control logic at runtime. We provide a prototypical implementation of our approach that supports the aforementioned adaptability as a standalone component, as a wrapper, or by directly integrating it with the domain-specific function of components. The generic implementation is accompanied by the implementation of a domain-specific component, which provides adaptability based on the integrated generic implementation. We evaluate our approach and implementation with respect to the supported functionality and with respect to the performance overhead of the implementation.

Interaction Optimization and Mapping In Chapter 4, we present our approach and contributions on the optimization of interactions and the mapping of interactions between specialized, domain-specific architectures and our integration architecture. First, we elaborate in more detail on the challenges related to *Interaction Inefficiency*, *Meta-interaction Patterns*, *Non-compliant Communication*, and *Non-compliant Representation*. Subsequently, we analyze these challenges and derive requirements for our approaches on optimizing interactions and on mapping interactions between architectures. We present the first main contribution of this chapter – our network model and algorithm for frequency-based optimization of pull- and push-based interaction between components. The second main contribution of this chapter is the mapping of concepts and interactions between a domain-specific architecture from the field of robotics and our integration architecture. For the approach on interaction mapping, we provide a proof-of-concept implementation, which demonstrates the feasibility and applicability of the developed solution. Finally, we evaluate our approach on frequency-based interaction optimization by applying the algorithm to a given optimization scenario.

Distributed Benchmark Generation and Provisioning In Chapter 5, we present our approach on generating distributed benchmarks as well as their highly automated and reproducible deployment. First, we elaborate in more detail on the challenges related to *Data Generation*, *Dataset Distribution*, *Deployment Complexity*, and *Difficult Reproducibility*. Subsequently, we analyze these challenges and derive requirements for the architecture of a distributed benchmark environment. The architecture, which is the main contribution of this chapter, is independent of specific dataset generators, provides a pervasive declaration, utilizes container-based visualization for automation, and supports reproducibility based on a small set of parameters. As the implementation of our architecture, we provide a domain-specific distributed benchmark that is deployable on local computers, private clouds, or publicly available computing resources. Finally, we evaluate our approach and implementation by utilizing instances of our distributed benchmark environment to evaluate centralized as well as decentralized query evaluation scenarios. The latter evaluation is realized by integrating the implementation of our approach for component adaptation.

1.6 Outline

In Chapter 2, we introduce the foundations of our work, providing details on relevant high-level visions, paradigms, architectures, and technologies, as well as concepts and terminology. In Chapter 3, we present our approach for component adaptation and decentralized control of distributed applications. Afterward, in Chapter 4, we describe our approaches for optimizing the interactions in distributed applications as well as for mapping interactions between domain-specific architectures and our integration architecture. In Chapter 5, we elaborate on our approach for the generation and provisioning of distributed benchmarks. Finally, we summarize our work, highlight the thesis contributions, and point out prospective future work in Chapter 6.

1.7 Publications

The aforementioned contributions are backed up by a number of publications, which serve as the basis for this thesis. The relevant publications are listed below.

- Conferences
  - Keppmann, F.L., Maleshkova, M., Harth, A.: **Adaptable interfaces, interactions, and processing for Linked Data Platform components**. In: Proceedings of the International Conference on Semantic Systems (SEMANTiCS) (2017) [103]
  - Keppmann, F.L., Maleshkova, M., Harth, A.: **DLUBM: A benchmark for distributed linked data knowledge base systems**. In: Proceedings of the On the Move to Meaningful Internet Systems Conferences (OTM) (2017) [104]

- Keppmann, F.L., Maleshkova, M.: **Smart components for enabling intelligent Web of Things applications**. In: Proceedings of the International Conference on Intelligent Systems and Applications (INTELLI) (2016) [99]
- Keppmann, F.L., Maleshkova, M., Harth, A.: **Semantic technologies for realising decentralised applications for the Web of Things**. In: Proceedings of the International Conference on Engineering of Complex Computer Systems (ICECCS) (2016) [102]
- Harth, A., Käfer, T., Keppmann, F.L., Rubinstein, D., Schubotz, R., Vogelgesang, C.: **Industrielle VT-Anwendungen auf Basis von Web-Technologien**. In: Proceedings of the VDE-Kongress - Internet der Dinge (2016) [84]

• Workshops

- Bader, S., Wolf, A., Keppmann, F.L.: **Evaluation environment for Linked Data web services**. In: Proceedings of the Workshop on Services and Applications over Linked APIs and Data (SALAD) at the International Conference on Semantic Systems (SEMANTiCS) (2017) [11]
- Keppmann, F.L., Maleshkova, M., Harth, A.: **Building REST APIs for the Robot Operating System - mapping concepts and interaction**. In: Proceedings of the Workshop on Services and Applications over Linked APIs and Data (SALAD) at the European Semantic Web Conference (ESWC) (2015) [100]
- Keppmann, F.L., Maleshkova, M., Harth, A.: **Towards optimising the data flow in distributed applications**. In: Proceedings of the Workshop on Web APIs and RESTful Design Workshop (WS-REST) at the International World Wide Web Conference (WWW) (2015) [101]
- Keppmann, F.L., Maleshkova, M.: **Towards pervasive Web API-based systems**. In: Proceedings of the Research Workshop at the Karlsruhe Service Summit (KSS) (2015) [98]
- Keppmann, F.L., Stadtmüller, S.: **Semantic RESTful APIs for dynamic data sources**. In: Proceedings of the Workshop on Services and

Applications over Linked APIs and Data (SALAD) at the European Semantic Web Conference (ESWC) (2014) [105]

- Demos
  - Keppmann, F.L., Käfer, T., Stadtmüller, S., Schubotz, R., Harth, A.: **High performance Linked Data processing for Virtual Reality environments**. In: Proceedings of the International Semantic Web Conference (ISWC) [Demo] (2014) [96]
  - Keppmann, F.L., Käfer, T., Stadtmüller, S., Schubotz, R., Harth, A.: **Integrating highly dynamic RESTful Linked Data APIs in a Virtual Reality environment**. In: Proceedings of the International Symposium on Mixed and Augmented Reality (ISMAR) [Demo] (2014) [97]
- Book Chapters
  - Antakli, A., Alvarado Moya, P., Brüderlin, B., Canzler, U., Dammertz, H., Enderlein, V., Grüninger, J., Harth, A., Hoffmann, H., Jundt, E., Keitler, P., Keppmann, F.L., Krzikalla, R., Lampe, S., Löffler, A., Meder, J., Otto, M., Pankratz, F., Pfützner, S., Roth, M., Sauerbier, R., Schreiber, W., Stechow, R., Tümler, J., Vogelgesang, C., Wasenmüller, O., Weinmann, A., Willneff, J., Wirsching, H.J., Zinnikus, I., Zürl, K.: **Virtuelle Techniken und Semantic-Web**. In: Web-basierte Anwendungen Virtueller Techniken: Das ARVIDA-Projekt – Dienstebasierte Software-Architektur und Anwendungsszenarien für die Industrie (2017) [5]
  - Behr, J., Blach, R., Bockholt, U., Harth, A., Hoffmann, H., Huber, M., Käfer, T., Keppmann, F.L., Pankratz, F., Rubinstein, D., Schubotz, R., Vogelgesang, C., Voss, G., Westner, P., Zürl, K.: **ARVIDA-Referenzarchitektur**. In: Web-basierte Anwendungen Virtueller Techniken: Das ARVIDA-Projekt – Dienste-basierte Software-Architektur und Anwendungsszenarien für die Industrie (2017) [16]

2 Foundations

In the following, we contextualize and back up our work with relevant foundations. In Section 2.1, we present a selection of Web-related visions that accompany and drive current trends towards highly modularized and distributed applications. These visions highlight the broader context of this work, introduce certain requirements, paradigms, as well as technologies, and outline some of the application fields for our contributions. In Section 2.2, we present different architectural paradigms and introduce per paradigm a set of technologies that are commonly utilized for its realization. These paradigms and their technologies comprise the conceptional and technological foundation of our work and are each partially related to one or more visions. In Section 2.3, we define a coherent set of concepts, which we refer to and incorporate in the remainder of this work. These concepts introduce a consistent wording, foster a common understanding, and detail our view on the elements of distributed applications.

2.1 The Web and Related Visions

This thesis is embedded in a field of broad and long-term Web-related visions that emerged over time from the appearance of the Internet, to the human-readable and machine-readable Web, to more recent developments, including the modularization and distribution of applications, driven by the increasing miniaturization and computing power as well as availability of Internet connectivity of almost every newly developed device.

In Figure 2.1, we give an overview of relevant, related visions that augment this thesis in the research field, indicate their occurrence over time, and their relation to each other. We talk about *Web visions*, in order to explicitly refer to the underlying conceptualization and fundamental principles, rather than to the direct technology implementations. The origin is the appearance of the Internet in the 1960s, which we date to the first work on packet switching in 1974 by Cerf and Kahn [44], leading among others to the specification of the Internet Protocol (IP) [129, 87]. In the following, we present in short the vision of the Web, the SW, the WoD, the IoT, the WoT, the SWoT, name further related visions, and elaborate on the relation between the visions and on the relation to this thesis.

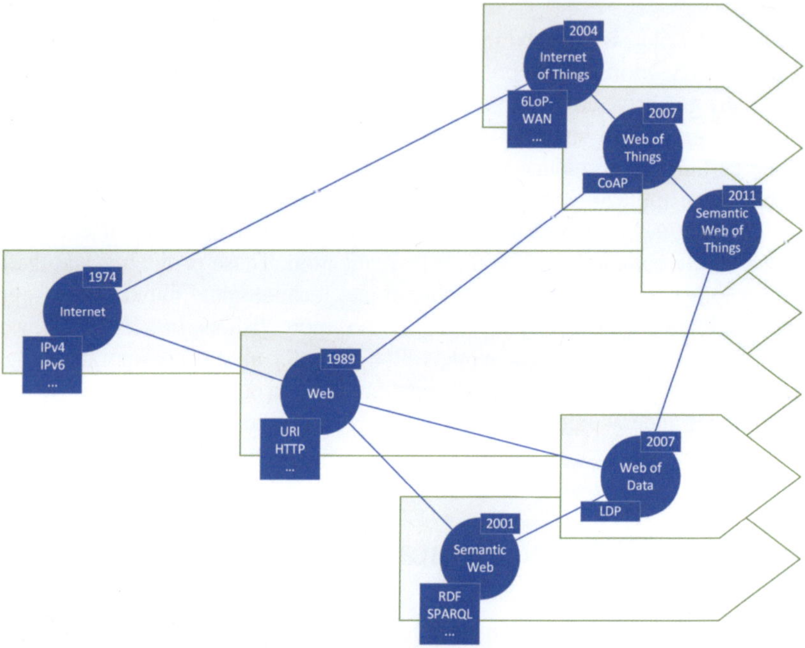

Figure 2.1: The Web and Related Visions

2.1.1 World Wide Web (WWW)

The vision of the World Wide Web (WWW) [18, 25, 28], commonly called *the Web*, as originally conceptualized is a Web of decentralized published and interlinked documents that are primarily targeting the human user. Proposed in 1989 by Berners-Lee [18] for the management of information about technical systems and experiments at the European Organization for Nuclear Research (CERN), it subsequently evolved to an initiative for an organization-independent global WWW [25]. The focus of this Web is a global repository of documents with simple means for accessing, publishing, and interlinking these documents [50], independent from specific computing platforms. Therefore, the proposal and later-developed specifications introduce a global addressing scheme with unique identifiers, i.e., Uniform Resource Identifiers (URIs) (c.f., Section 2.2.1.1), a common transport protocol, i.e., Hypertext Transfer Protocol (HTTP) (c.f., Section 2.2.1.2), the relation of documents with links, i.e., Link Relation (LR) (c.f., Section 2.2.1.3), the negotiation of formats, and a platform-independent format for hypertext documents, i.e., Hypertext Markup Language (HTML). During the standardization process of the involved technologies by the World Wide Web Consortium (W3C), the underlying architectural principles, that paved the way for broad application and success of the Web, synthesized to what is known as Representational State Transfer (REST) (c.f., Section 2.2.1).

2.1.2 Semantic Web (SW)

The goal of the Semantic Web (SW) [30, 29, 146] vision is a machine-readable Web. Introduced in 2001 by Berners-Lee et al. [30], the mission of the SW is complementary to the Web for humans, which consists of human-readable and interlinked documents. The SW focuses on machines that use and act on the SW in order to realize machine-to-machine communication and, therefore, must be provided with the explicit semantics of the data without the need for human interpretation. In the end, they may serve as agents for human users that delegate tasks to these machines as part of human-machine interaction [50]. Thereby, the SW is not meant to be a replacement of the Web but rather enhance it.

> "The Semantic Web is not a separate Web but an extension of the current one, in which information is given well-defined meaning, better enabling computers and people to work in cooperation." [30]

In particular, the standard Web technologies for unique identification are used to identify semantic concepts, and Web protocols for data transport are incorporated for the access and manipulation of semantically enriched data. This enrichment of data is achieved by annotating included entities and relations with the help of ontologies [67] that in turn may be shared via means provided by the Web and, thereby, contribute to shared, machine-readable knowledge about the semantics of data exchanged between the involved parties [50]. In addition to the core characteristics of the Web, the SW vision includes several technologies, i.e., Semantic Web Technologies (c.f., Section 2.2.2), that are in principle not bound to the Web. These include among others, for example, graph-based representation of semantically annotated data, i.e., Resource Description Framework (RDF) (c.f., Section 2.2.2.1), means for querying this data, i.e., SPARQL Protocol and RDF Query Language (SPARQL) (c.f., Section 2.2.2.2), or logic for inferencing and learning on top of this data, e.g., Notation3 (N3) (c.f., Section 2.2.2.3).

2.1.3 Web of Data (WoD)

The Web of Data (WoD) [33, 32], as a spin-off or a sub-vision, and sometimes even used as a synonym for the Semantic Web, is focused on the publishing and consuming of semantically enriched and interlinked data on the Web. While the term *Web of Data* has been used before, the Linking Open Data community project [31], initiated by the Semantic Web Education and Outreach (SWEO) interest group of the W3C, started in 2007 a broader initiative for the promotion of the WoD. In particular, the initiative promoted the term *Linked Data* (c.f., Section 2.2.3), the Linked Data (LD) principles [33] as an underlying paradigm, and provided a set of interlinked datasets on the Web as a starting point for the WoD.

In Figure 2.2, the Linked Open Data Cloud (LODC) from 2007 shows this initial WoD consisting of nine interlinked datasets, which include the DBpedia [10, 34] as the central provider of concepts that are derived from structured data available in the Wikipedia. This WoD grew since its initiation by magnitudes in scale and number of datasets, as shown, e.g., by the LODC diagram from April 2018 [112] with 1184 datasets and 15993 connections, i.e., sets of connecting links, between these datasets that qualified for the inclusion in the diagram due to their size and degree of interlinking with other datasets.

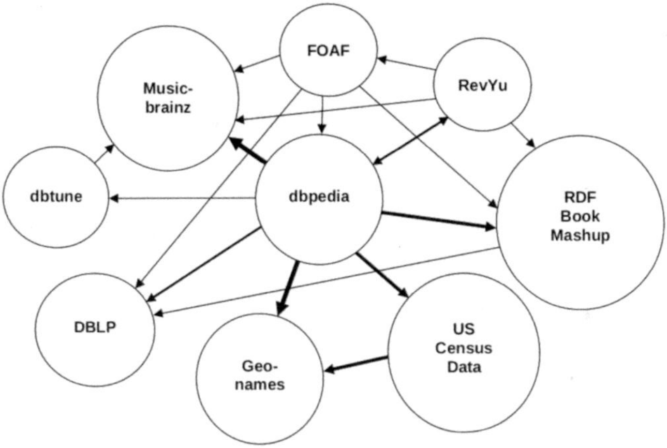

Figure 2.2: Linked Open Data Cloud 2007 [31]

While in the beginning, the WoD started with read-only interlinked datasets, several approaches [162, 157, 152, 163, 108] extended the LD principles by combining these with the further elements of the REST architectural style, i.e., establishing Read-Write Linked Data (RWLD). The LD principles as well as the approaches for RWLD lead to the Linked Data Platform (LDP) specification of the W3C (c.f., Section 2.2.3.1), that provides for the first time the combination of both paradigms in a formalized manner. While there have been discussions on whether the SW and WoD are complementary or contrary visions with overlapping goals, we use in this thesis the SW as the broader and long-term vision that includes all kinds of research fields related to semantics, and the WoD as the pragmatic approach on realizing an actual Web of machine-readable and interlinked semantic data that is a true extensions of the WWW. In other words, we see the realization of the WoD as a major building block in the realization of the more comprehensive SW.

2.1.4 Internet of Things (IoT)

The Internet of Things (IoT) vision has gained increased popularity in the last decade, among others, driven by the broader integration of Internet technologies such as the IP in all kinds of devices as well as the increasing modularization and miniaturization of these devices. As a term already being used earlier [8], the idea of an "Internet-0" was proposed in 2004 by Gershenfeld et al. [66] to the broader research community. However, while the underlying paradigm remains untouched, i.e., interconnecting a tremendous amount of heterogeneous virtual and physical things in a common network, the vision itself is manifold [9]. The aforementioned vision represents only one variation of a diverse collection of alternative viewpoints on the IoT, driven by different fields in industry and research. Atzori et al. [9] name three major perspectives on the vision as well as on their main concepts and technologies, both visualized in Figure 2.3. As it can be seen, these can sometimes differ substantially.

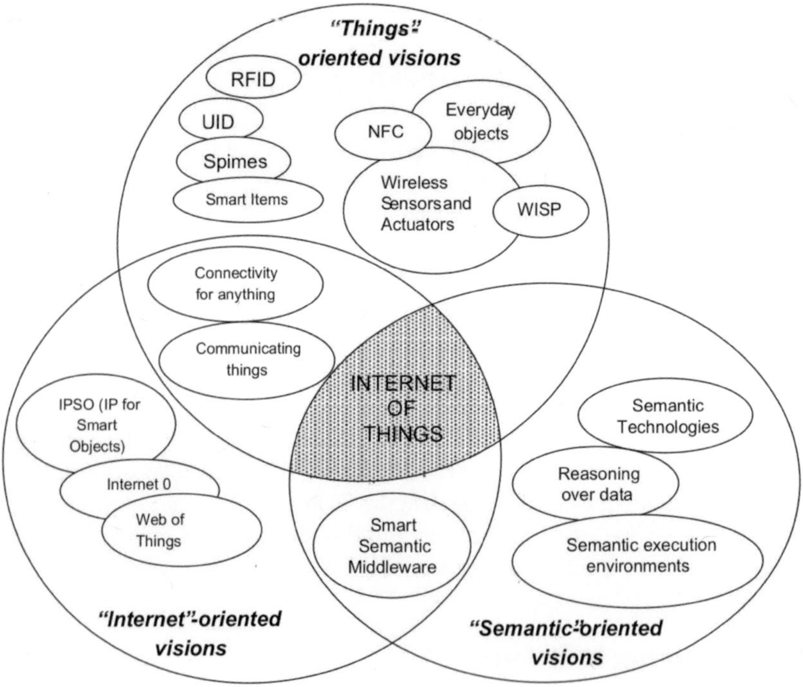

Figure 2.3: Internet of Things Visions [9]

Things-oriented The IoT vision has been driven by and is originating from the development and application of Radio-Frequency IDentification (RFID) technologies. This technological direction primarily enables the identification and traceability of objects and has strong support both in business and industry. Thereby, the border between the physical, real world and the virtual computing and networking merges and becomes blurred. In addition to RFID, this perspective on IoT includes considerably more technologies and concepts, going beyond the pure identification and traceability, e.g., Near Field Communications (NFC), or Wireless Sensor and Actuator Network (WSAN), that are supposed to be built upon more basic elements, leading to interconnected things, which may also act actively on their own. In the end, the physical thing is the focus of the *Things-oriented perspective* on the IoT vision.

Internet-oriented The more broadly interpreted Things-oriented perspective leads to the *Internet-oriented perspective* on the IoT vision, in which the IP plays a major role. For example, the aforementioned idea of an "Internet-0" [66] promotes the extension of the principles, that are the underlying success factor for the Internet, to each and every device. In particular, packet switching, i.e., the data is split independently from specific data types in packets that are individually routed from the data source to the data sink, and end-to-end connections, i.e., connections are initiated from data sources to data sinks without the need for managing the details of networks involved in establishing the connection. These principles are used in the "Internet-0" independently from the actual modulation of the signals that are used to transmit the packages. In other words, also very slow- and high-latency types of transmission may be used, which do not necessarily have to be based on the current physical mediums used for IP. Several other paradigms and technologies are part of this perspective [2], that simplify the IP technology for application also on the smallest devices, e.g., IPv6 over Low power Wireless Personal Area Network (6LoWPAN). In addition, the application of Web paradigms and technologies, i.e., the WoT vision (c.f., Section 2.1.5), is part of this broader perspective. In the end, the interconnection of virtual and physical things based on IP is the focus of the Internet-oriented perspective on the IoT.

Semantic-oriented The potentially tremendously high amount of things in the IoT leads to a *Semantic-oriented perspective*. In contrast to both other perspectives, that focus on the things and their interconnection respectively, the management and collaboration of the heterogeneous landscape of things is taken into account. This involves, for example, the interpretation of data communicated between things, the representation of things, the discovery of things, or the search for things. Semantic technologies may provide means for coping with different challenges that arise in these fields. In the end, the annotation and interpretation of data provided and consumed by things is the focus of the Semantic-oriented perspective on the IoT.

2.1.5 Web of Things (WoT)

The Web of Things (WoT) [167, 72, 70, 68] vision combines the IoT and the Web visions by enabling improved interoperability of things through Web technologies. As a term already used earlier [160, 133], the WoT vision, in which the paradigms and technologies that lead to the success of the Web play a key role, has been introduced to the broader research community by Wilde [167] in 2007. The emerging vision has been driven from the very beginning by use cases from related research areas, e.g., related to Sensors and Actuator Networks (SAN) [159], Geographic Information System (GIS) [168], Wireless Sensor Network (WSN) [69, 71], embedded web servers [54], and search engines [122]. The WoT vision builds, as part of the "Internet-oriented" perspective on the IoT (c.f., Section 2.1.4), on top of the basic interconnection of things and focuses on the interaction at the level of applications.

> "In the Web of Things (WoT), we are considering smart things as first-class citizens of the Web. We position the Web of Things as a refinement of the Internet of Things by integrating smart things not only into the Internet (the network), but into the Web (the application layer)." [72]

The approaches of the "Thing-oriented" and classical "Internet-oriented" perspectives (c.f., Section 2.1.4) embed Information Technology (IT) in the physical world or augment physical objects with IT to establish connectivity by providing network infrastructure. Unfortunately, applications built on top of this network infrastructure form small islands of incompatible things that are only connected within their islands of proprietary interfaces and software [72]. However, these applications commonly constitute some kind of information system that conceptually contains resources and means for accessing resources. These characteristics meet the assumptions and constraints of the already established REST architectural style (c.f., Section 2.2.1). Therefore, the realization of the IoT may profit from unique identifiers, uniform interfaces, and stateless communication of representations, leading to a loosely-coupled WoT that enables the composition of applications in the IoT.

> "[...] we argue that the goals of pervasive and ubiquitous computing should be to provide loose coupling and that there should be a low barrier-to-entry for interacting with resources that are made accessible through the 'Internet of Things'". [167]

Thereby, the aforementioned "smart things", i.e., all kinds digitalized devices and objects that are able to communicate on a network and thus connect the physical and virtual worlds, provide their internal state as resources. In particular, they enable the identification of these resources by URIs (c.f., Section 2.2.1.1), provide a uniform HTTP (c.f., Section 2.2.1.2) interface for them, and permit the access and, optionally, the manipulation of their state by exchanging their representation, supported by content negotiation. In addition to these core REST characteristics, the WoT vision introduces means for syndication and callbacks. Syndication enables the support for interacting with collections of resources. Callbacks enable things, which provide data, to actively push new data to things, which consume data, once these have registered their information needs, i.e., the communication switches from pull-based to push-based interaction.

Another concern of the WoT vision is the Web-enabling of devices, in particular, of constraint devices with low power or computing resources. Figure 2.4 shows two ways of integrating devices on the Web that are practicable. On the one hand, devices may be directly integrated on the Web, thus provide their own Web server that exposes resources at the network. On the other hand, for example in the case of specialized protocols for certain use cases or existing platform-depended protocols, the deployment of "smart gateways" [161] may be feasible. These gateways act as intermediates in the REST architectural style, i.e., as proxies or reverse proxies, and enable the mapping between specialized protocols and the Web.

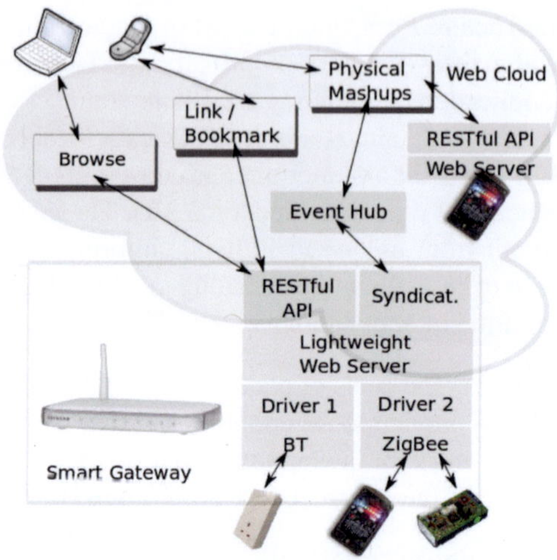

Figure 2.4: Web of Things Integration [72, 70]

2.1.6 Semantic Web of Things (SWoT)

The Semantic Web of Things (SWoT) [143, 128] vision combines elements from the IoT vision and the SW vision to enable embedded semantically annotated data on things, in particular, on constraint devices with low energy or computing power. As a term already used before in the SW community [38], the SWoT has been introduced in 2009 by Scioscia and Ruta [143] as part of an approach for the compression of semantic annotations that retain the support for querying.

> "The goal of the Semantic Web of Things is to embed semantically rich and easily accessible information into the physical world. To this aim, Knowledge Representation tools and technologies must be adapted to functional and non-functional requirements of mobile computing applications." [143]

In general, the SWoT outlines the next evolutionary step after the IoT and the WoT, as visualized in Figure 2.5. While the IoT, in particular, in the "Internet-oriented" viewpoint (c.f., Section 2.1.4), focuses on a common network protocol and the WoT focuses on a common applications protocol, the

SWoT builds on top and focuses on the abstraction from devices and common descriptions. With respect to the "classical" Internet, Web, and SW/WoD, the evolution in the "* of Things" domain shows significant analogies. The IoT, WoT, and SWoT represent similar steps in the evolution, but, in contrast, taking into account the restrictions imposed by small, mobile devices with low energy and computing power.

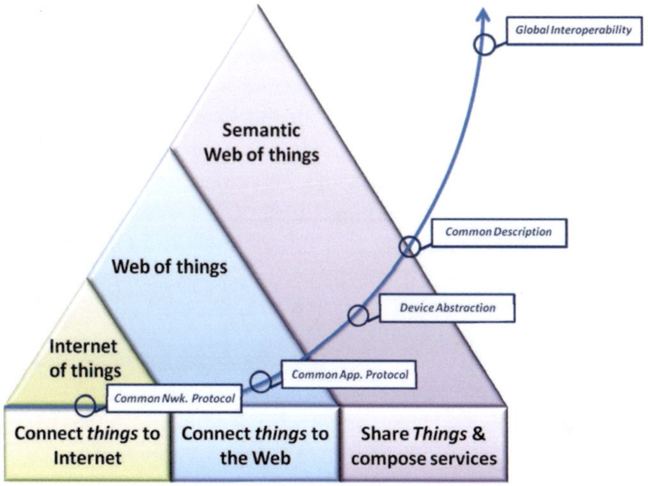

Figure 2.5: Semantic Web of Things Evolution [91, 92]

In contrast to the Web for humans, that evolved around human-readable documents, the "* of Things" domain has never been intended to be used by humans directly, but through appropriate user interfaces and agents. Therefore, machine-readable, shared, and semantically enriched information can be seen as an obligatory evolutionary step to reach the underlying goal of connecting all kinds of devices and to build applications as compositions on top, which are independent of domains, manufacturers, or physical environments. In other words, the evolution from the IoT, over the WoT, to the SWoT must pave the way for evolving from vertically connected deployments that are specific to devices, scenarios, and vendors, to applications that integrate horizontally, thereby, integrating multiple capabilities from different domains towards a larger ecosystem [91]. However, unfortunately, no single methodology and no fixed set of technologies and standards have been, at the time of writing, standardized and converged to a common SWoT architecture.

> "The SWoT is, on the one hand, the fusion of the trends of the IoT for moving towards the web technologies with protocols such as CoAP, REST architecture and the Web of Things concept, and, on the other hand, the evolution of the web with the semantic web technologies." [91]

Different research projects have contributed to the research field, e.g., the project UBIWARE [95], focused on a smart semantic middleware for the IoT, the project Integrating the Physical with the Digital World of the Network of the Future (SENSEI) [130], with the Sense2Web [14] platform focused on publishing sensor data as LD in the WoD, the project SPITFIRE [128], focused on abstractions for things, on fundamental services for search and annotation, as well as on integrating sensors and things into the LODC, or the project OpenIoT [149], focused on IoT services with semantic interoperability in the cloud.

In addition, several approaches emphasize the need for semantics in the IoT for horizontal integration, with or without identifying the need for abstracting from individual devices and the generalization at the application level, i.e., the WoT. Ruta et al. [143, 135, 134, 136, 137] present an approach and architecture for a SWoT framework based on an extension of the Internet Engineering Task Force (IETF) Request for Comments (RFC) 7252 on the Constrained Application Protocol (CoAP) [147] and of the IETF RFC 6690 on the Constrained RESTful Environments (CoRE) [148] link format in combination with the LD principles to enable resource discovery and semantic descriptions without breaking backward compatibility of the protocol. Gyrard et al. [79, 74, 75, 80] present an approach and architecture for a SWoT framework influenced by the ontology engineering domain to support the complete workflow of building SWoT applications. Java et al. [91, 92] evaluate the different methodologies, technologies, and standards that can be subsumed under the SWoT vision. On the one hand, these methodologies, technologies, and standards are introduced in the area of cellular networks, i.e., broadly available long-range networks, and connected capillary networks [138, 121], i.e., short-range, low-energy, and low-cost networks. On the other hand, these methodologies, technologies, and standards are introduced in the area of the Web and the SW.

Furthermore, several technologies have been proposed or developed with reference to the SWoT, e.g., the Semantic Smart Gateway Framework (SSGF) [107], the Extended Global Sensor Network (XGSN) [39], the Machine-to-Machine Measurement (M3) framework [77, 78], the Micro-Ontology Context-Aware Protocol (MOCAP) [139], the Linked Open Vocabularies for Internet of Things (LOV4IoT) [76], the Web of Things Semantic Search Engine (WOTS2E) [94], or the Semantic Web of Things Suite (SWoTSuite) [124].

2.1.7 Positioning of the Thesis

The core research of this thesis is placed in the context of the overall vision of the Web, at the intersection of the Semantic Web and WoD with the WoT and SWoT.

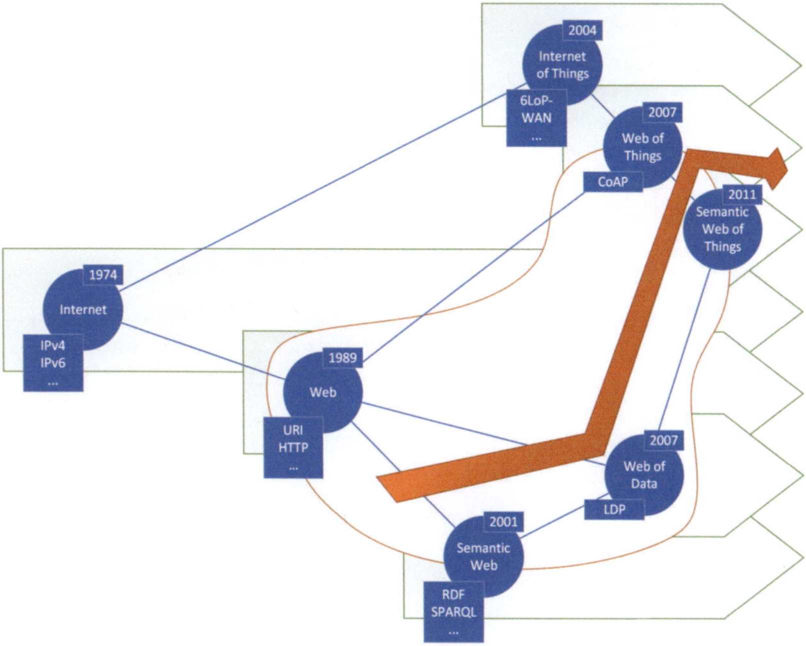

Figure 2.6: Relation of Visions and Thesis

In Figure 2.6, we mark the on-topic relationship of this thesis with respect to the relevant visions (orange area) and indicate the direction of exploration (orange arrow). The thesis is grounded on the generic architectural style and technologies of the Web (c.f., Section 2.2.1), takes advantage of different technologies from the Semantic Web (c.f., Section 2.2.2), and is strongly related to the WoD enabling principles (c.f., Section 2.2.3) as well as to the WoT vision, while seeking, promoting, and pushing the synergies of these visions and their realizing technologies in the same way as the SWoT vision.

Thus, the work presented in this thesis contributes directly to the state of the art and the evolution of the WoT and SWoT.

2.2 Paradigms, Architectures, and Technologies

In the following, we present a selection of architectural paradigms that comprise the conceptual foundation of our work. In addition, we introduce a set of technologies that are commonly used to realize these paradigms, are broadly available, and are supported by large communities. These paradigms and their technologies comprise the technological foundation of our work.

2.2.1 Representational State Transfer (REST)

The Representational State Transfer (REST) introduced by Fielding [64] as an architectural style describes the constraints of a Resource-Oriented Architecture (ROA) [123] for large-scale network-based distributed hypermedia applications. In general, REST is technology-agnostic but most prominently realized with Web technologies. Starting in October 1994, the architectural style has been iteratively developed over several years during the standardization efforts on URI [21], HTTP [62], and HTML [56] in several RFCs for different Internet Standards (STDs) by the IETF in cooperation with the – at that time – newly founded W3C.

> "The name 'Representational State Transfer' is intended to evoke an image of how a well-designed Web application behaves: a network of web pages (a virtual state-machine), where the user progresses through the application by selecting links (state transi-

> tions), resulting in the next page (representing the next state of the application) being transferred to the user and rendered for their use." [64, p. 109]

Therefore, REST has not been the subject of standardization efforts itself, but guided the development of major Web standards and, in principle, can be applied to other application areas as well. In its core, REST consists of a set of constraints that have been derived from and optimized for the common case of distributed hypermedia applications at web-scale and incorporates or is based on several preexisting network-based architectural styles, e.g., client-server, or layered system. Major Web standards, e.g., URI, or HTTP, are designed to cover and to adhere to the REST constraints but may have further non-REST use cases.

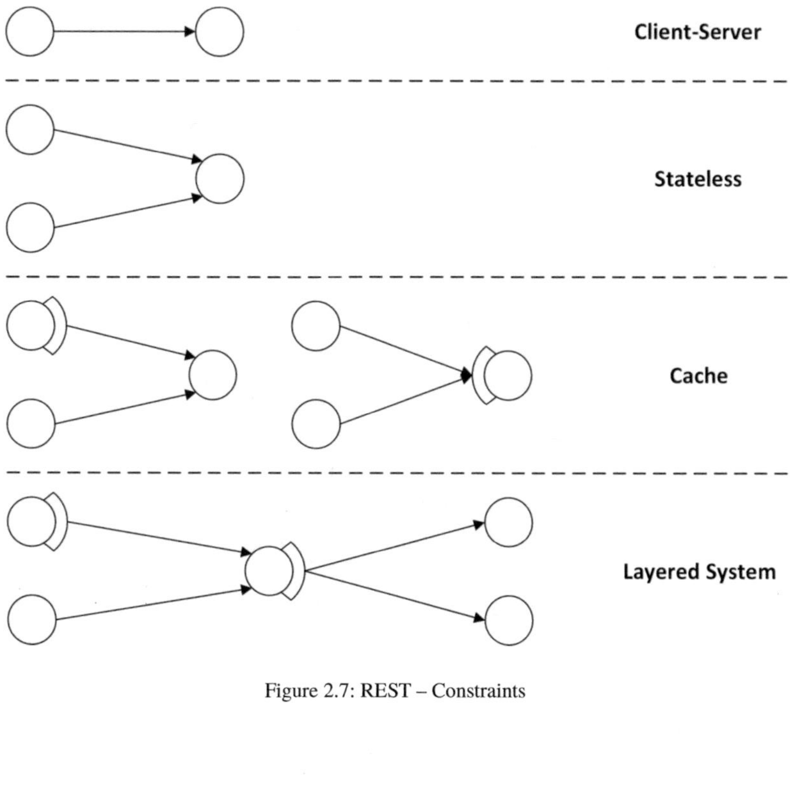

Figure 2.7: REST – Constraints

On the one hand, the REST constraints limit the degrees of freedom for designing elements within architectures. In particular, the means for exposing function and for communication between components of architectures are restricted in specific ways, still without limiting their function to any particular domain. On the other hand, the REST constraints – by limiting the degrees of freedom – ease the integration within architectures and foster scalability, performance, and robustness for the common Web-scale case. Starting with a large distributed hypermedia system as a black box, i.e., the WWW, the constraints distinguish the involved components and their interactions. In the following, we first present these guiding constraints (c.f., Figure 2.7) and afterward elaborate on major Web standards that are relevant in the context of this work, i.e., on URI in Section 2.2.1.1, on HTTP in Section 2.2.1.2, and on LR in Section 2.2.1.3.

Client-Server The *client-server constraint* – as the most basic constraint – is the distinction between components and, in the context of communication between components, the distinction between clients and servers [64]. The interaction between clients and servers follows a request-response pattern, in which clients send requests to servers, and the servers answer to these requests with responses. While a request with its following response is a synchronous interaction, the transferred message within the interaction may be streamed and processed on-the-fly. On the one hand, the constraint enables separation of concerns, e.g., differentiating between components that act in distributed applications as user interfaces for humans, or components that act as data storages. On the other hand, and more importantly in the context of Web-scale, the constraint enables the independent evolving of components and, thereby, fosters scalability as well as support for multiple stakeholders. For example, in the traditional human-oriented Web the Web browsers act as clients that provide user interfaces and that are independently developed from each other and from the Web servers. The Web servers, in contrast, provide as servers the content and business functionalities that can be presented by any Web browser to the human users, and that are independently developed from each other and from the Web browsers.

Stateless The *stateless constraint* imposes statelessness for any interaction between clients and servers. In particular, servers must not be aware of the context of the individual requests of a client with respect to other requests of the same or other clients or manage any kind of session on the server over a series of requests. The overall application state is determined by the state of the participating components. As a consequence, all information for processing messages that are transferred via interactions must be included in the messages themselves. This self-descriptiveness of messages is part of the uniform interface constraint below. The advantages fostered by stateless interactions are 1) visibility, due to self-descriptive messages that may be subject to inspection; 2) reliability, since failing requests are not hampering other requests; and 3) scalability, as requests can be handled in parallel. The advantages are accompanied by the disadvantages of: 1) decreased performance over a series of interactions, since all information required for processing a number of messages must be included in every single message; and 2) reduced control of the client behavior, i.e., the correct interpretation of data semantics must be ensured across all clients, because application state is managed on the clients.

Cache The *cache constraint* prescribes that responses in the request-response interaction between clients and servers must be either marked as cacheable or non-cacheable [64]. This constraint is enabled by the stateless constraint that implies self-descriptive messages. These messages can be cached either on the client-side, to intercept and answer redundant requests to servers and, thereby, reduce the network usage, or on the server-side to directly answer redundant requests by clients and, thereby, reduce the processing to be spent on the generation of responses. The advantages are increased efficiency, scalability, performance – due to reduced processing on the servers, and reduced latency on the network. However, as a disadvantage, caches and, in particular, shared caches, i.e., caches that are shared between a number of different clients, may potentially lead to inconsistencies, if cached responses are not corresponding to the responses that would have been newly generated by the servers.

Layered System The *layered system constraint* targets the complexity and heterogeneity of scenarios with multiple stakeholders and diverting domain functionality of components in Web-scale scenarios. By restricting the depth of interactions executed by individual components in a composition of interacting components to one, the constraint enables hierarchical layers of components, i.e., components may only directly interact with other components but not via the same interaction with subsequent components. These layers may consist each only of a single component or encapsulate as black boxes several other components, without changing the interaction mechanisms, i.e., layers are compositions of components that may take part in further compositions as individual atomic components with a single interface. Layered systems provide as an advantage an overall reduced complexity due to the independence of layers, which can be individually developed and scaled. In addition, layers can serve as means for security, i.e., security measures and actions can be applied and enforced at the border of layers. The constraint, however, introduces as disadvantages an increased overhead and an increased latency, if requests are concentrated at the border of layers and are not executed directly but indirectly through the borders to subsequent hidden components. The impact of these disadvantages can be reduced in certain cases by utilizing shared caches.

Code-on-Demand The *code-on-demand constraint* represents the only optional constraint in the REST architectural style. The constraint enables the extension of client functionality by code downloaded from servers, e.g., by applets, or by scripts [64]. Due to the optionality of the constraint, the advantages and disadvantages of this constraint only apply to parts of distributed applications in an architecture that provides support for this constraint. In combination with the layered system constraint, for example, parts of a distributed application may support this constraint internally but – as a black box – hide the support in the communication with further components. The advantages of this constraint are simpler clients and improved system extensibility since existing clients can be extended on-the-fly and not all functionality that is potentially required must be implemented by the clients in advanced. The disadvantage is reduced visibility.

Uniform Interface The *uniform interface constraint* represents the most significant REST constraint and restricts the access to components to interfaces that are uniform with respect to their provided interaction mechanisms. In contrast to other network-based architecture styles, the uniform interface constraint is the main unique characteristic of REST. This constraint applies the software engineering principle of generality to the communication within distributed applications. Elements of architectures provide interfaces that expose uniform means for interaction across all components, independently from their domain functionality. Thereby, the interface is decoupled by design from specific implementation details, enables the independent evolving of implementations, and eases their substitution by alternative implementations. The advantages of this constraint are a simplified overall system architecture and improved visibility, due to the prescribed way of interaction enforced by the uniform interfaces. The disadvantage is a potentially less efficient communication caused by the fact that the uniform interface is not permitting specializations for domain-specific use cases. The constraint can be distinguished in four subordinate interface constraints concerning resources, representations, self-description, and hypermedia.

Resource The notion of a *resource interface constraint* is the most significant interface constraint and a key concept of the architectural style. A resource may be any entity that can be referenced, e.g., a virtual concept, a person, or a measurement, and represents the entity in general, i.e., its semantics, but not specific realizations of the entity, i.e., not any specific values of properties of the entity at a particular point in time. Resources may be non-existing and map to no realization for an indefinite time, i.e., resource may not be realized at all. A particular realization of a resource may change over time, i.e., from once at creation and never again, to continuously, at a high frequency. In contrast, the semantics of a resource must be defined as statically over time, i.e., the values of the realizing entity may change but the meaning of the values must not. For example, in a distributed version control system, the commit identified by the current master branch or a particular release tag can change over time, while the resources, i.e., the master, or a release, stay the same. The advantages of the resource interface constraint are the generalization of concepts independent from their existence, a particular type, or a specific implementation, as well as late binding of representations to the resource through content negotiation. Thereby, the references to resource and their semantics stay stable over time, while their representations may change [64].

Resources are identified by resource identifiers. These identifiers must be unique with respect to the resource they identify, but a resource may be identified by more than one resource identifier. For example, the master branch and a release tag may identify the same commit in a distributed version control system. The sets of all identifiable resources of components form their uniform interfaces, that enable the access to and manipulation of their realizations. In Web-scale multi-stakeholder scenarios, resource identifiers provide the means for referencing between components, and, due to the nature of these scenarios, without relying on centralized identifier management. Therefore, identifiers must change as little as possible, i.e., stay unique and semantically static over time [64]. However, due to no centralized resource identifier management, also failures must be taken into account by design.

Representation The *representation interface constraint* restricts the information exchange between components to the exchange of messages that may contain resource representations. These representations represent the state of resources, i.e., the current state of resources if resources are accessed, or the intended state of resources if resources are manipulated [64]. Representations are accompanied by "representation metadata" that describes the characteristics of the representations, e.g., the type of representation, or the last modified time. Furthermore, responses from servers to clients may contain additional "resource metadata" that is specific to the resource but independent from a particular representation, e.g., information about alternative representations. The data format of representations is defined by media types that enable the use of adequate data formats for different use cases or with different performance characteristics, e.g., streamable, or on-the-fly-processable. Independently from possibly contained representations, "control data" describes the intention of messages. This includes, in requests, the method to be used for access to or manipulation of resources as well as, in responses, means for success and failure handling. In addition, cache control and other parametrization are part of the control data.

Self-Description For the scalability of distributed multi-stakeholder systems at Web-scale, the *self-description interface constraint* is of importance.

> "REST enables intermediate processing by constraining messages to be self-descriptive: interaction is stateless between requests, standard methods and media types are used to indicate semantics and exchange information, and responses explicitly indicate cacheability." [64, pp. 98f]

This constraint implies that messages transferred between components are self-descriptive, i.e., no context or related message is required for its interpretation. Thereby, the constraint enables independent processing of messages at the receiving client or server but, more important, at intermediate components along the route during the request. The self-description interface constraint is a premise of the cache constraint that enables caching of messages at client or server-side.

Hypermedia The *hypermedia interface constraint*, in several cases also called "Hypermedia as the Engine of Application State (HATEOAS)", considers multi-component hypermedia applications from the viewpoint of the uniform interfaces. The state of clients can change only through actions that are dynamically identified within hypermedia by the server, e.g., through links in the text. As a result, REST clients need little to no prior knowledge about how to interact with servers. Beyond entrance resource identifiers for applications, all further interactions the clients may take are discovered within resource representations returned from the servers. The available resource representations and the relations to other resources they may contain are predefined. Therefore, the clients transition through application states by following hypermedia links within representations or by manipulating the representations. In summary, in REST the client-server interaction is driven by hypermedia.

The REST architectural style is, in general, technology-agnostic and can be applied in different application areas. We base our work on the Web-based realization of REST that is supported by public standards and broadly available technologies. In the following, we present the – for this work – most relevant standards URI, HTTP, and LR.

2.2.1.1 Uniform Resource Identifier (URI)

The IETF RFC 3986 on Uniform Resource Identifier (URI) [21] provides a generic syntax and semantics as means for the identification of abstract or physical resources. In addition, the RFC provides means for absolute and relative identifier references, the reference resolution, as well as considerations and implications for the use of URIs on the Web. URIs can be characterized by their three naming elements: uniform, resources, and identifier. They provide a uniform way for describing identifiers and are, thereby, independent from specific access mechanisms. They enable consistent interpretation of their common elements through uniform semantics, allow for the definition of new identifier types without interfering with existing ones, and enable the use of identifiers in a broader context, in particular, if the schema-specific interpretation of identifiers is not required. URIs identify resources, that are defined similarly to REST (c.f., Section 2.2.1), without any particular limitations, i.e., every concept, virtual, or physical thing that is worth to be identified in a given context can be identified as a resource. URIs provide identification by embodying sufficient information, clearly separating resources from each other in a given context, but neither contain the identity of resources nor provide means for accessing the resources.

```
  foo://example.com:8042/over/there?name=ferret#nose
  \_/   \______________/\_________/ \_________/ \__/
   |           |            |            |        |
scheme     authority       path        query   fragment
   |   _____________________|__
  / \ /                        \
  urn:example:animal:ferret:nose
```

Listing 2.1: URI – Syntax Components Examples [21, p. 15]

The syntax of URIs consists of five main components: scheme, authority, path, query, and fragment. Listing 2.1 shows two examples that use some and all of these syntax components. The scheme and path are mandatory for every URI. The scheme component relates URIs to separate, more specialized URI specifications that are not part of RFC 3986, e.g., "http" and "https" defined by the HTTP specification [62]. These scheme-specific specifications may further restrict the URI syntax and semantics, but all adhere to the more generic superset of rules in the URI specification [21]. The optional authority component of URIs defines a namespace that is individually managed by the identified authority and may consist of user information, host, and port. The remaining parts of the URIs are delegated to their particular authorities for further resolution. These remaining parts of URIs start with the path that hierarchically identifies, in addition to query and fragment, the resource within a given scheme and optionally a given authority. The query part adds non-hierarchical data for the identification, i.e., the order of query elements is not important. These are commonly in the form of key-value pairs. URIs optionally end with a fragment that indirectly identifies a resource or sub-resource within a collection of resources or an enclosing main resource located at the given preceding URI. Besides the main syntax components, the URI specification defines fixed characters for their separation, e.g., "?" at the beginning of the query, "#" at the beginning of the fragment, and both for the termination of the path.

The references to URIs may use the complete notation, including all mandatory and, if required, optional syntax components, but may alternatively use relative notations for references within the same scheme and, if existing, the same authority [21]. A reference is relative if the scheme prefix and the following separator are missing. Four different reference types can be distinguished: absolute references, relative references, same-document references, and suffix references. Absolute references are complete URIs without the fragment component and may serve as base URIs for relative references. Relative references utilize the hierarchical structure of URIs and reference relative to the current authority or a given base URI. Thereby, the reference may be a relative path reference, i.e., based on the same hierarchical layer of the URI, or an absolute path reference, i.e., based on the authority of the URI. Same-document references are relative references within the same document that are identified by the preceding URI and use only the fragment as a reference. For the sake of completeness, suffix references describe schema-less references that require human interpretation or a clear application context for complementing the missing parts, e.g., references to websites in human-to-human communications that omit the schema part. Without interpretation, suffix references equal relative references, may lead to misinterpretation, and thus should be avoided.

The resolution of relative references to references with complete URIs requires base URIs that serve as the starting point for the application of the relative references [21]. These base URIs are determined via the first matching of four different but ordered ways: explicitly embedded in the content, from the encapsulating entity, from the retrieval URI, or an application-depended default base URI. While the first three methods determine the base URI for resolution through the location or content of resources, the application-dependent default base URI relies on the context of a particular application. Thereby, the same relative references may be interpreted in different ways by different applications, which may lead to misinterpretations.

The IETF RFC 3986 on Uniform Resource Identifier (URI) [21], published in January 2005, is – at the time of writing – member of the "Standards Track" category, in the "Internet Standard" state, and representing the STD 66. The RFC is based on and derived from several preceding RFCs, in particular, beginning with RFC 1630 on "Universal Resource Identifiers" [19], published in 1994, RFC 1738 on Uniform Resource Locator (URL) [22], published in 1995, the draft standard RFC 2396 on URI [20], published in 1998, and RFC 2732 on Internet Protocol Version 6 (IPv6) addresses in URLs [43], published in 1999. Further RFCs and Best Current Practices (BCPs) are related to RFC 3986 [21, p. 3].

2.2.1.2 Hypertext Transfer Protocol (HTTP)

The Hypertext Transfer Protocol (HTTP) specifies a generic general purpose protocol for stateless request-response communication on the level of applications [62]. The protocol incorporates the REST architectural style (c.f., Section 2.2.1) and represents a major building block of the WWW architecture [90]. To this end, HTTP defines a uniform interface on resources provided by servers and specifies the semantics of request methods as well as messages, that in some cases may contain representations of these resources as payload. HTTP relies, besides the client and server concepts (including user agent and origin server), on further REST concepts for intermediates in the communication, in particular, proxy, gateway, and tunnel, as well as on the concept of caches. In addition, the HTTP specification defines the syntax and semantics of two URI schemes for the identification of resources, in particular, the "http" and the "https" URI schemes.

Interactions that adheres to the HTTP specification are targeting the aforementioned resources. In this context, HTTP defines only the interface in a uniform manner, but not the resources themselves. Resources may be of any nature, similarly to the resource definitions of REST (c.f., Section 2.2.1) and URI (c.f., Section 2.2.1.1). Consequently, resources in HTTP are identified by URIs as defined by RFC 3986 [21]. This identification of resources is separated from the interaction mechanisms in the communication with servers. The abstraction of domain-specific implementation states at request time are the representations of these resources, as defined by REST. These representations can be transferred as the payload in the HTTP interaction to retrieve or modify the state of resources. Thereby, multiple alternative representations can represent the same resource, of which the representation that is most fitting the request preferences is selected as the message payload.

As an alternative to representations, the HTTP messages may contain URIs as payload and, thereby, refer to the locations of further relevant resources. With respect to messages, the HTTP specification defines representation metadata in the form of HTTP message header fields for describing the aforementioned alternative representation, the selection of representations, the resource locations, and the semantics of the representations, e.g., Content-Type, Content-Location, or Content-Length.

Every HTTP request includes a request method as the primary definition of the request semantics, i.e., the request method defines the intention of the client for executing the request. These request methods define resource- and domain-independent means to access and manipulate resources and, thereby, implement the uniform interface restriction of REST (c.f., Section 2.2.1). In addition, further request properties may specialize the requests, e.g., making requests conditional. Table 2.1 presents an overview of the request methods defined by the part of the HTTP specification that is focused on semantics and content [63]. From the set of specified methods, the GET and HEAD methods must be supported, while all other methods are optional. Additional methods have been standardized and may be added to the HTTP method registry of the Internet Assigned Numbers Authority (IANA) after a review by the IETF [63, Section 8]. The HTTP request methods share a set of common properties, in particular, methods may be safe, idempotent, or cacheable, as shown in Table 2.1 and as described in the following.

Method	Description	Properties
GET	Transfer a current representation of the target resource.	Safe Idempotent Cacheable
HEAD	Same as GET, but only transfer the status line and header section.	Safe Idempotent Cacheable
POST	Perform resource-specific processing on the request payload.	Cacheable
PUT	Replace all current representations of the target resource with the request payload.	Idempotent
DELETE	Remove all current representations of the target resource.	Idempotent
CONNECT	Establish a tunnel to the server identified by the target resource.	
OPTIONS	Describe the communication options for the target resource.	Safe Idempotent
TRACE	Perform a message loop-back test along the path to the target resource.	Safe Idempotent

Table 2.1: HTTP – Requests Methods [63, p. 20]

Safe Method Safe methods provide read-only semantics. In particular, their execution leads to no state change on the origin server. However, the origin servers may change states, e.g., increase access counters, or log request details, but these are not requested by the client and are not part of the request semantics. Safe methods are designed to ensure that automatic retrieval processes and performance optimizations do not cause issues on origin servers by accidentally changing their states.

Idempotent Method Idempotent methods provide semantics that require no state change in case of multiple requests, which execute the same idempotent method on the same resource. The origin server may, in a similar manner as for safe methods, implement side effects, but these are not part of the request semantics and must not be expected by the client. Idempotent methods are designed to ensure that requests can be automatically repeated in the case of failures in the interaction with the origin server, without waiting for a response from the origin server, and independently from a possible success or failure of the state change itself.

Cacheable Method Responses to requests that execute cachable methods may be stored and reused to directly answer similar requests in the future, within the boundaries of caching constraints, e.g., the Time to Live (TTL) property of the response.

In addition to the method, requests may contain certain request header fields. As mentioned above, these enable specializations of the request semantics, e.g., conditional requests, by providing the context of requests. In particular, the HTTP specification defines request header fields for the following groups.

Controls The request header includes the fields *Cache-Control*, *Expect*, *Host*, *Max-Forwards*, *Pragma*, *Range*, and *TE*. These fields expand on how requests should be handled by the server and are in detail defined by the HTTP specification on syntax and routing [62], the HTTP specification on range requests [57], and the HTTP specification on caching [59].

Conditionals The request header includes the fields *If-Match*, *If-None-Match*, *If-Modified-Since*, *If-Unmodified-Since*, and *If-Range* for defining conditionals. These fields enable clients to specify preconditions for the execution of the request method based on the state of the resource as defined by the HTTP specification on conditional requests [61].

Content Negotiation The request header includes the fields *Accept*, *Accept-Charset*, *Accept-Encoding*, and *Accept-Language* for realizing content negotiation. These fields enable the client to inform the server about its preferences with respect to the expected payload of the response.

Authentication Credentials The request header includes the fields *Authorization* and *Proxy-Authorization* for communicating authentication credentials. These fields support authentication of clients against servers through basic or digest authentication as defined by the HTTP specification on authentication [60].

Request Context The request header includes the fields *From*, *Referer*, *User-Agent* for setting the request context. These fields enable clients to provide information about the context of a request, in particular, the email address of a human user, the URI of a resource that referred to the target resource, and the product identifier of the implementation that is used to perform the request.

For example, the *Expect* control field informs the server about expected actions that must be supported. The expect value *100-continue* is the only value defined directly by the HTTP specification on semantics and content [63]. This header value indicates that the server should inform the client after validating the request header with an intermediate *100-continue* response code (c.f., Table 2.1) that the validation of the request header fields is not causing already a failure of the request. In case of a failure, the server may instead inform the client with an appropriate response code before the client starts to send a larger request payload.

The counterparts of request methods are response status codes. This three-digit code is classified in code classes, defined by the first digit of the code, that each represents a particular group of response semantics. Table 2.2 presents an overview of the response status codes classes defined by the HTTP specification on semantics and content [63]. Clients must understand the groups but not necessary every status code, in particular, because the status codes are extensible. Unknown status codes must be interpreted as the first code of the class, i.e., the "X00" code. The phrase supplied as a reason for each code (c.f., Table 2.2) may change, depending on the particular use case, from the default to an application-specific and more appropriate phrase. Some status codes are cacheable, e.g., *200 OK*, *203 Non-Authoritative Information*, and *204 No Content* [63].

In addition to the response status code, responses from servers to clients may contain, analog to requests, additional information in certain header fields. These expand on the resource, the response, and included resource representations, e.g., by providing information about the cache characteristics of representations. In particular, the HTTP specification defines the request header fields for the following groups.

Class	Title	Description	Examples
1xx	Informational	The request was received, continuing process	100 Continue 101 Switching Protocols
2xx	Successful	The request was successfully received, understood, and accepted	200 OK 204 No Content
3xx	Redirection	Further action needs to be taken in order to complete the request	300 Multiple Choices 301 Moved Permanently
4xx	Client Error	The request contains bad syntax or cannot be fulfilled	400 Bad Request 404 Not Found
5xx	Server Error	The server failed to fulfill an apparently valid request	500 Internal Server Error 503 Service Unavailable

Table 2.2: HTTP – Response Status Code Classes [63, p. 46]

Control Data The response header fields *Age*, *Cache-Control*, *Expires*, *Date*, *Location*, *Retry-After*, *Vary*, *Warning*. These fields expand on how responses should be handled by the client in addition to the semantics of the status codes. In particular, they may refer to related resources or alternative resource representations and include information about the caching characteristics of the resource representation, as defined by the HTTP specification on caching [59].

Validator Header Fields The response header fields *ETag*, and *Last-Modified*. These fields are provided by the origin servers and identify representations across time and serialization formats. Clients may utilize their values in conditional requests, as defined by the HTTP specification on conditional requests [61], to prevent modification based on outdated information, e.g., to ensure that a resource has not been modified between a response and a dependent follow-up request.

Authentication Challenges The response header fields *WWW-Authenticate*, and *Proxy-Authenticate*. These fields provide clients with challenges after successful authentication that must be used in follow-up requests to the server, as defined by the HTTP specification on authentication [60].

Response Context The response header fields *Accept-Ranges*, *Allow*, and *Server*. These fields provide some additional information about the requested resource that may be of use for follow-up requests.

Understanding the HTTP characteristics in detail is crucial for the work presented in this thesis. To rely on HTTP as a foundation and as the main way of realizing communication guarantees not only interoperability but also scalability and conformity to Web standards. Therefore, instead of defining a new communication protocol or an extension of HTTP, we intentionally chose to stick to the properties that HTTP offers.

In addition to the relevant areas of the HTTP specifications on message syntax and routing [62] as well as semantics and content [63], that have been described above, the HTTP specification includes RFCs for further advanced topics, in particular, conditional requests [61], range requests [57], caching [59], and authentication [60].

In addition to the Hypertext Transfer Protocol Version 1.1 (HTTP/1.1) specification, that is broadly applied and supported, the Hypertext Transfer Protocol Version 2 (HTTP/2) specification [17] has been standardized by the IETF in 2015 as RFC 7540. The development of HTTP/2 has been initiated, in particular, by several downsides of the connection handling and data transport as defined by HTTP/1.1 [62, Section 6], that lead to inefficient use of computing and network resources in current infrastructures and, thereby, have a negative impact on the performance of applications depending on HTTP communication.

> "In particular, HTTP/1.0 allowed only one request to be outstanding at a time on a given TCP connection. HTTP/1.1 added request pipelining, but this only partially addressed request concurrency and still suffers from head-of-line blocking. Therefore, HTTP/1.0 and HTTP/1.1 clients that need to make many requests use mul-

> tiple connections to a server in order to achieve concurrency and thereby reduce latency." [17, p. 3]

Inefficient, verbose, and redundant use of header fields adds to the negative impact on performance. The HTTP/2 specification focuses on more efficient use of the underlying Transmission Control Protocol (TCP) connections and encoding of header fields [126] as an alternative to the HTTP/1.1 connection and transport mechanisms while providing the same semantics as defined by the HTTP/1.1 specifications. Thereby, HTTP/2 provides, from an application point of view, the same capabilities but with changed message syntax and mapping to the transport protocols. [17]

The set of IETF RFCs 7230 to 7235 on HTTP/1.1 [62, 63, 61, 57, 59, 60], published in June 2014, as well as the RFCs 7540 and 7541 on for HTTP/2 [17], published in May 2015, are – at the time of writing – member of the "Standards Track" category and in the "Proposed Standard" state. The RFCs are based on and derived from two preceding RFCs, in particular, largely on RFC 1945 [117] on Hypertext Transfer Protocol Version 1.0 (HTTP/1.0), published in May 1996, and on RFC 2068 [58], an obsolete version of the HTTP/1.1 specification, published in June 1999.

2.2.1.3 Link Relation (LR)

Link Relation (LR) denotes the relation between resources, that is established through Web links [119], i.e., the typed relation between two resources. Web links are closely interlinked with the HTTP specification (c.f., Section 2.2.1.2), i.e., the specification defines the serialization of links in HTTP headers, and other specifications, e.g., Atom [120] or HTML [56].

> "A link can be viewed as a statement of the form 'link context has a link relation type resource at link target, which has target attributes'." [119]

The link context and the link target must be Internationalized Resource Identifiers (IRIs). In many cases, however, URIs or IRIs mapped to URIs are used, in particular, in the context of protocols like HTTP that provide no support for IRIs. The specification imposes no restrictions on the cardinality of links between resources and no means implied by the ordering of links, i.e., the specification enables the definition of many-to-many relations of the same or different types between resources as a set of links in a resource representation. The specification defines the following elements:

Link Context The link context must be an IRI. In the case of the HTTP link header field, this is by default the URI of the associated representation.

Link Relation Type The link relation type defines the semantics of the link. Two different kinds of relationship types exist. The "registered relation types" provide well-defined relation types that are centrally managed by the IANA. In cases, in which the registration of relation types is not feasible or wanted, "extension relation types" serve as an application-specific alternative. Every extension relation type is defined by a URI that identifies the relation type, may provide the definition of semantics, and should be in control of the application owner.

Link Target The link target must be an IRI.

Target Attributes Target attributes are optional key-value pairs that describe the target of the link or the link itself. For example, the media type of the target may be indicated by a target attribute. Except for the HTTP link header field, the specification defines no specific target attributes but leaves their definition to the specification of individual link relation types or link serializations.

In addition, the Web linking specification defines the syntax of links in HTTP header fields but delegates the definition of their syntax in resource representations to specifications that utilize the interlinking of resources. For example, the Atom specification [120], the HTML specification [56], or the specifications of RDF [45] serialization formats include definitions for the serialization of links.

The set of IETF RFCs 8288 on web linking [119], published in October 2017, is – at the time of writing – a member of the "Standards Track" category and in the "Proposed Standard" state. The RFCs is based on and derived from two preceding RFCs, in particular, on RFC 4287 [120] on the Atom syndication format, published in December 2005, and on RFC 5988 [118], an obsolete version of the specification on Web linking, published in October 2010.

2.2.2 Semantic Web Technologies (SWT)

In this section, we introduce the main principles and technologies of the SW, which are of direct relevance for the research contributions of this thesis. In particular, we rely on Semantic Web Technologies (SWT) [49] to enable the explicit representation of knowledge in terms of the data exchanged between the components in distributed architectures, in terms of expressing the roles and functions of the components, and in terms of modeling the communication patterns. As a result, previously heterogeneous data and components can be mapped and combined based on common knowledge representation. In the following, we outline the relevant SWT specifications, in particular, RDF (c.f., Section 2.2.2.1), SPARQL (c.f., Section 2.2.2.2), and N3 (c.f., Section 2.2.2.3).

2.2.2.1 Resource Description Framework (RDF)

The Resource Description Framework (RDF) [45] is a graph-based data model that is described by an abstract syntax and is based on the concept of triples. Every triple is formed by a subject, a predicate, and an object node, where sets of triples form RDF graphs. In RDF graphs, three types of nodes are distinguished – IRI [53], literal, and blank node [45, 141]. By convention, the elements of RDF triples are ordered as listed follows:

- Subject (IRI or blank node),
- Predicate (IRI), and
- Object (IRI, literal, or blank node).

Thereby, subjects and objects are nodes of the corresponding RDF graph and predicates are the directed arcs, which, in addition, may be nodes in the same RDF graph.

In Figure 2.8, for example, the node "BOB", identified by the IRI `http://example.org/bob#me` is the subject of an RDF triple, with the directed arc identified (in prefix form) by the IRI "foaf:topic_interest" as the predicate, and the node "The Mona Lisa", identified by the IRI `http://www.wikidata.org/entity/Q12418` as the object. Several other RDF triples are shown in the figure, each making an RDF statement about the relation between two resources. RDF datasets support the collection of multiple RDF graphs. Thereby, every dataset must include one default graph without a name and may include zero or more named graphs. These named graphs are identified by unique graph names, which may be IRIs or blank nodes. The RDF specification prescribes no semantics for the relation between the identifier and the identified graphs, i.e., the identification is a solely syntactical requirement. [45, 141]

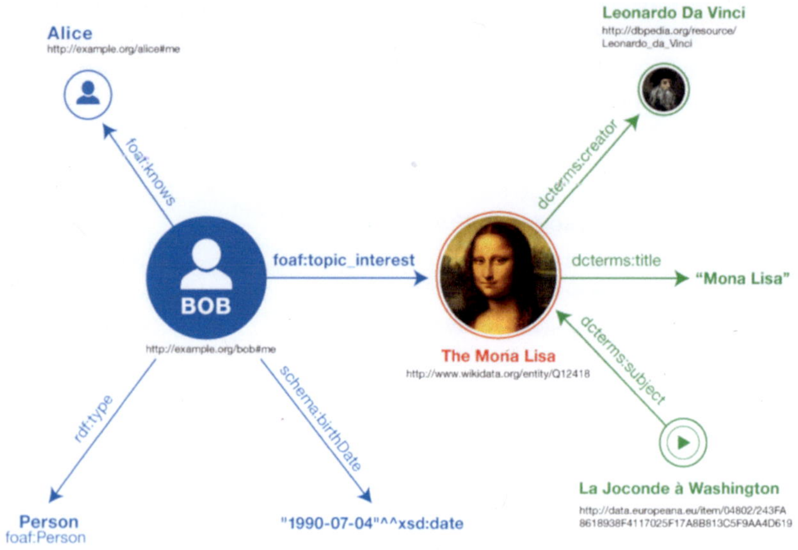

Figure 2.8: RDF – Graph Example [141]

RDF terms subsume the different types of nodes and arcs. As listed above, these can be represented by three different RDF terms, in particular, IRIs, literals, or blank nodes. The specification for IRIs [53] defines a superset of URI (c.f., Section 2.2.1.1) that is less restricting on the character set permitted for the identifiers. While every URI is a valid IRI, not every IRI is a valid URI, but may be mapped to the URI character set by predefined mappings [45, 53]. Literals denote particular values, e.g., number, boolean, date, or time values. Their value is annotated by a datatype and in some cases by a language tag. Blank nodes are local identifiers that depend on specific implementations as well as concrete syntaxes and express relations between resources without explicitly stating their types. While there is no restriction to the design of blank nodes, they must be distinguishable from IRIs and literals. Skolemization may be used to convert blank nodes to IRIs, which should be in the form of well-known URIs [81] and that can be reused beyond the scope of their local implementation.

In addition to the IRIs mentioned above, Figure 2.8 shows, for example, the literal “1990-07-04” with the datatype “xsd:date” that maps the date string, i.e., one of the lexical forms permitted by the specification, to the corresponding date, i.e., the value space. The literal “Mona Lisa” in Figure 2.8 is, for example, a syntax-specific simple literal, i.e., specific for the datatype “xsd:string” [45, 141].

Datatypes enable the typing of RDF literals that denote particular values, e.g., number, boolean, date, or time values. The RDF specification reuses most built-in datatypes of the XML Schema Definition (XSD) [127], prefixed by `http://www.w3.org/2001/XMLSchema#` and excludes a small set of these datatypes, that are specific for the Extensible Markup Language (XML), e.g., “xsd:QName”. The datatypes “rdf:HTML” and “rdf:XMLLiteral” have been added, at the time of writing, non-normative, for the inclusion of HTML and XML as literals in RDF. However, any other non-XSD datatype definition may serve as a datatype in RDF, if the definition adheres to the same abstraction. Literals consist besides the lexical form, i.e., written form, of a datatype IRI, and, in case of the datatype “langString”, of an additional language tag. The datatype IRI, as well as the language tag, enable the mapping of the literal form to the value space of the literal.

Literal Space	**Value Space**
<“true”, xsd:boolean>	true
<“false”, xsd:boolean>	false
<“1”, xsd:boolean>	true
<“0”, xsd:boolean>	false

Table 2.3: XSD – Literal Space to Value Space Mapping Example [45]

Table 2.3 shows, for example, the mapping for boolean values defined by the XSD datatype “xsd:boolean”. While the value space consist of two values, i.e., “true” and “false”, the literal space permits four different lexical forms, i.e., “true” and “false” as well as “1” and “0”. The rows show the complete lexical-to-value-mapping for this datatype.

Construct	**Syntactic Form**	**Description**
Class (a class)	C rdf:type rdfs:Class	C (a resource) is an RDF class
Property (a class)	P rdf:type rdf:Property	P (a resource) is an RDF property
type (a property)	I rdf:type C	I (a resource) is an instance of C (a class)
subClassOf (a property)	C1 rdfs:subClassOf C2	C1 (a class) is a subclass of C2 (a class)
subPropertyOf (a property)	P1 rdfs:subPropertyOf P2	P1 (a property) is a sub-property of P2 (a property)
domain (a property)	P rdfs:domain C	domain of P (a property) is C (a class)
range (a property)	P rdfs:range C	range of P (a property) is C (a class)

Table 2.4: RDFS – Main Constructs [141]

Vocabularies facilitate the modeling of semantics that are used in the annotation of data with RDF. While RDF enables the identification of resources, the inclusion of literal data, and the relation of resources, the semantic meaning of resources, and their relations are identified by IRIs without making further restrictions or assumptions. These restrictions and assumptions, i.e., the semantic modeling, can be provided by conventions, by human-readable descriptions, or formalized by vocabularies that are themselves modeled in

RDF. The Resource Description Framework Schema (RDFS) [37] and the more comprehensive OWL Web Ontology Language (OWL) [164] support the definition of these vocabularies as RDF graphs.

Table 2.4 shows the main constructs provided by RDFS. In particular, RDFS supports the specification of classes and their properties as well as hierarchical structuring of classes and properties with “rdfs:Class”, “rdfs:Property”, “rdfs:subClassOf”, and “rdfs:subPropertyOf”. Properties may have a domain, specified by “rdfs:domain”, as well as a range, specified by “rdfs:range”. Thereby, RDFS enables the restrictions of predicates to their use with subjects and objects of only specific types, i.e., enables the description of class-property assignments and class-class relations. Finally, RDFS defines the typing of resources via “rdf:type”, i.e., the assignment of classes to resource instances. Different vocabularies may be related to each other by standard RDF mechanisms, e.g., by utilizing “owl:sameAs” [125]. Thereby, RDF facilitates not only the relation of information on the data level but also on the vocabulary level.

```
BASE <http://example.org/>
PREFIX foaf: <http://xmlns.com/foaf/0.1/>
PREFIX xsd: <http://www.w3.org/2001/XMLSchema#>
PREFIX schema: <http://schema.org/>
PREFIX dcterms: <http://purl.org/dc/terms/>
PREFIX wd: <http://www.wikidata.org/entity/>

<bob#me>
  a foaf:Person ;
  foaf:knows <alice#me> ;
  schema:birthDate "1990-07-04"^^xsd:date ;
  foaf:topic_interest wd:Q12418 .

wd:Q12418
  dcterms:title "Mona Lisa" ;
  dcterms:creator <http://dbpedia.org/resource/Leonardo_da_Vinci> .

<http://data.europeana.eu/item/04802/243
     FA8618938F4117025F17A8B813C5F9AA4D619>
  dcterms:subject wd:Q12418 .
```

Listing 2.2: RDF – Graph Example in Turtle Serialization [141]

Different formats provide means for serializing RDF graphs and datasets, i.e., representations the logical data model in documents. Thereby, the same RDF graph or dataset can be represented by different documents while being equal on the logical level. A selection of popular RDF serialization formats that have been standardized by the W3C are the XML-based RDF/XML [65], the “Turtle family” of N-Triples [41], N-Quads [40], Turtle [131], and TriG [42], the JavaScript Object Notation (JSON)-based JavaScript Object Notation for Linked Data (JSON-LD) [155], and RDFa [1, 154, 111, 153] as embeddable variant for human-readable websites. All formats support RDF graphs, while only N-Quads, TriG, and JSON-LD support datasets, i.e., multiple RDF graphs in one document. [141]

Listing 2.2 shows, for example, the Turtle serialization of the RDF graph in Figure 2.8. The Turtle format provides a relatively human-readable syntax while being relatively easy processable by machines, i.e., support parsing.

2.2.2.2 SPARQL Protocol and RDF Query Language (SPARQL)

The SPARQL Protocol and RDF Query Language (SPARQL) [6] comprises a set of specifications for querying and manipulating information modeled in RDF. To this end, SPARQL provides a query language, that is extended by query federation capabilities, and defines a set of serialization formats for non-RDF query results. In addition, SPARQL specifies entailment regimes as extensions for handling several standard entailment relations, e.g., provided by native RDF, RDFS, or OWL, to support inferencing in the evaluation of the query. Finally, SPARQL provides an update language for the modification of RDF-modeled information, accompanied by a protocol for interaction with SPARQL query interpreters, and defines a simpler protocol for HTTP-based access and manipulation of graph stores.

In the following, we use the RDF graph example shown in Turtle serialization in Listing 2.3 to show some capabilities of the SPARQL query language in a query example in Listing 2.4 as well as the corresponding query result in Listing 2.5. The RDF graph example includes sub-graphs with information about four people with the names “Alice”, “Bob”, “Charlie”, and “Snoopy”, that are annotated with appropriate ontologies. For every person, the information about people that are known to this person is included as triples, e.g., “Bob” knows “Alice” (“<bob#me> foaf:name "Bob" ; foaf:knows <alice#me> .”). In addition, the information about “Alice” includes a type as well as an email address. The query in Listing 2.4 extracts the information about the name of every person in the RDF graph and about the people known to this person. The result is grouped per person as a set of name and count of friends, i.e., the count of known people. This result is shown in Listing 2.5 in JSON serialization.

```
BASE <http://example.org/>
PREFIX foaf: <http://xmlns.com/foaf/0.1/>
PREFIX rdfs: <http://www.w3.org/2000/01/rdf-schema#>

<alice#me> a foaf:Person ;
  foaf:name "Alice" ;
  foaf:mbox <mailto:alice@example.org> .
  foaf:knows <bob#me> ;
  foaf:knows <charlie#me> ;
  foaf:knows <snoopy> .

<bob#me> foaf:name "Bob" ; foaf:knows <alice#me> .

<charlie#me> foaf:name "Charlie" ; foaf:knows <alice#me> .

<snoopy> foaf:name "Snoopy"@en .
```

Listing 2.3: SPARQL – RDF Graph Example [6]

The SPARQL query language specification [82] defines the syntax and semantics for querying RDF. SPARQL queries are based, in their core, on triple patterns that are similar to RDF triples (c.f., Section 2.2.2.1) of the form subject-predicate-object, but may contain variables at each position. A set of triple patterns comprises as basic graph pattern the most simple form of graph patterns in the SPARQL query language. These graph patterns are matched against the query target, i.e., an RDF graph, and generate a solution for each match of the graph pattern that includes bindings for all variables that are not optional. Matching in SPARQL includes IRIs as well as literals, in particular, with taking their specific datatypes or language tags into account and, for convenience, with short forms for numeric and boolean datatypes. Blank node labels are included in the solutions, but, similarly to RDF (c.f., Section 2.2.2.1), only for local identification of resources to provide means for their differentiation. The set of matched solutions comprise a solution sequence, i.e., zero, one, or multiple solutions, as the base of further query restrictions.

```
PREFIX foaf: <http://xmlns.com/foaf/0.1/>

SELECT ?name ( COUNT( ?friend ) AS ?count )
WHERE {
  ?person foaf:name ?name .
  ?person foaf:knows ?friend .
} GROUP BY ?person ?name
```

Listing 2.4: SPARQL Query Example [6]

The syntax of the SPARQL query language includes, besides SPARQL-specific elements, for the production of "TriplesBlock" [82, Section 19.8] a syntax that is, besides some minor differences [131, Section 4] aligned with the syntax of the RDF serialization format Turtle (c.f., Section 2.2.2.1). Thereby, the SPARQL syntax for RDF terms, in particular, for absolute and relative IRIs, prefixed names, literals, and black nodes, as well as the syntax for triple patterns, including predicate lists, object lists, collections, and "a" for "rdf:type", is almost similar to the Turtle syntax. In addition, the SPARQL query language specification includes a syntax for query variables in the triple patterns syntax, i.e., in the form of variable names prefixed by "?" or "$". The SPARQL query in Listing 2.4, for example, includes a prefix ("PREFIX foaf: <http://xmlns.com/foaf/0.1/>") as well as two triple patterns ("?person foaf:name ?name . ?person foaf:knows ?friend .") with variables ("?person", "?name", and "?friend") in the WHERE clause.

Different graph patterns provide the matching capabilities and means for specifying the expected result of queries. These graph patterns are defined in the WHERE clause of a query, which, by default, consists of a single empty group graph pattern that includes one or multiple additional patterns. The SPARQL query in Listing 2.4 contains, for example, the default group graph pattern, marked by curly braces, that includes a single basic graph pattern, and that again consists of the aforementioned two triple pattern, i.e., the nested graph pattern "{ ?person foaf:name ?name . ?person foaf:knows ?friend . }". The simplest forms of graph patterns are the basic graph pattern, in which all triple patterns must be matched, and the group graph pattern, which includes a set of other patterns that all must be matched. In addition, the optional graph pattern enables the definition of solution parts that may be included, if they can be matched, but do not have to be included and the alternative graph pattern enables the merge of multiple patterns for the same solution match [82]. Finally, also named graphs may be targeted by patterns.

The SPARQL query language specification defines four different forms of queries that are evaluated against the graph pattern solutions and provide each a different kind of result, in particular:

SELECT The SPARQL SELECT query returns variables and their bindings as a projection from all graph pattern solutions to the set of selected variables. This query form supports expressions based on already existing solutions that bind the expression result to a new variable, e.g., "(COUNT(?friend) AS ?count)" in the SELECT query example in Listing 2.4.

CONSTRUCT The SPARQL CONSTRUCT query returns a single RDF graph based on a given graph template. The graph template may consist of both explicit triples and triples patterns variables that include variables. Solutions include all explicit triples as well as required triple patterns with bound variables and are merged in a single RDF graph that is returned as the result. In addition, these queries support through the GRAPH keyword the extraction of complete or partial named graphs. In case of equal template and (basic) graph pattern, the specification defines a short form with omitted WHERE part.

ASK The SPARQL ASK query returns as the result a boolean value that indicates, in the case of "true", that at least one solution for a graph was found, and, in the case of "false", that no solution was found.

DESCRIBE The SPARQL DESCRIBE query returns as the result a single RDF graph that describes resources which have been identified by an IRI or indirectly in the query solutions by a variable. In contrast to all other query forms, the particular extent of the description is determined by the query interpreter and may contain information about the identified resources themselves but also about related resources that are important in the context.

While the results of CONSTRUCT and DESCRIBE queries are valid RDF graphs, that may be serialized in one of the serialization formats for RDF (c.f., Section 2.2.2.1), SELECT and ASK queries return information serialized in one of the specific SPARQL query result formats [82].


```
{
  "head": { "vars": [ "name" , "count" ] } ,
  "results": {
    "bindings": [ {
      "name": { "type": "literal" , "value": "Alice" } ,
      "count": { "datatype": "http://www.w3.org/2001/XMLSchema#integer" , "type
           ": "typed-literal" , "value": "3" }
    } , {
      "name": { "type": "literal" , "value": "Bob" } ,
      "count": { "datatype": "http://www.w3.org/2001/XMLSchema#integer" , "type
           ": "typed-literal" , "value": "1" }
    } , {
      "name": { "type": "literal" , "value": "Charlie" } ,
      "count": { "datatype": "http://www.w3.org/2001/XMLSchema#integer" , "type
           ": "typed-literal" , "value": "1" }
    } ]
  }
}
```


Listing 2.5: SPARQL JSON Query Result Example [6]

A set of SPARQL query result formats provide syntaxes for the serialization of non-RDF query results, that are based on broadly established existing specifications. The specification includes, in particular, the SPARQL query results XML format [15], the SPARQL query results JSON format [145], the SPARQL query results CSV format [144], and the SPARQL query results TSV format [144]. Listing 2.5 shows, for example, the result of the SPARQL query in Listing 2.4 evaluated against the RDF graph in Listing 2.3 serialized in the SPARQL query results JSON format. In particular, a set with the name and the count of friends is encoded per person in the result and typed with datatypes if required. In addition, the data fields for bound variables ("name" and "count") are listed in the beginning. For example, the person with the name "Alice", typed as literal by default with XSD string, has a count of "3" friends, typed with the XSD integer datatype.

We apply the basic principles of SPARQL and the approach of defining patterns to identify information needs in our work. Instead of relying on a specific interface description language, or on providing annotations for the data inputs and outputs of the components, we define the capabilities for data exchange of the components in a distributed architecture by using graph patterns.

2.2.2.3 Notation3 (N3)

Notation3 (N3) [26] is an RDF serialization, which is non-XML but is rather designed to be readable by humans. N3 provides a more compact syntax for RDF than, e.g., Extensible Markup Language for RDF (RDF/XML), and uses the language media type "text/n3". Similarly to Turtle, N3 allows statements that contain full IRIs, e.g., `<http://dbpedia.org/resource/Leonardo_da_Vinci>`, as well as a simple form for string literals, e.g., "Mona Lisa". More specifically, Turtle is the subset of N3 that is restricted to RDF. The fundamentals of N3 are described in N3Logic: A logical framework for the WWW [27], which is a formalization of the logic underlying N3.

In contrast to other RDF serializations, N3 targets to support both data and logic descriptions via the same syntax, which is concise and readable.

> "The aims of the language are to optimize expression of data and logic in the same language, to allow RDF to be expressed, to allow rules to be integrated smoothly with RDF, to allow quoting so that statements about statements can be made, and to be as readable, natural, and symmetrical as possible." [26]

This objective is achieved by a number of options that allow for abbreviations, by omitting repetitions, and by the overall simplicity of the grammar. Some of the key features include:

- Use of prefixes for URI abbreviation (using "@prefix");
- Use of "," for repetition of another object for the same subject and predicate;
- Use of ";" for repetition of another predicate for the same subject;
- Enabling the quoting of N3 graphs within N3 graphs using "{" and "}";

- Use of variables and quantification to allow rules to be expressed.

In terms of grammar and syntax, N3 uses a simple context-free grammar and provides support for syntax elements also introduced by Turtle, e.g., URI prefixes, base URIs, blank nodes, predicate lists, object lists, or collections. It also introduces a number of shorthands for commonly used predicates. Some examples include:

- "a" for "<http://www.w3.org/1999/02/22-rdf-syntax-ns#type>"
- "=" for "<http://www.w3.org/2002/07/owl#sameAs>"
- "=>" for "<http://www.w3.org/2000/10/swap/log#implies>"
- "<=" for "<http://www.w3.org/2000/10/swap/log#implies>" as inverse of "=>"

Benefiting from the aforementioned characteristics, we use N3 as serialization through this thesis for expressing RDF in combination with rules. When it comes to the sole annotation of information, we favor Turtle as the RDF-only subset of N3 but also support other serialization formats.

2.2.3 Linked Data (LD)

Linked Data (LD) [23, 33] as a paradigm paves the way for the evolution from the Web for humans, i.e., the document-focused WWW, towards the WoD for machines, which may subsequently act again on behalf of humans (c.f., Section 2.1). Thus, the WoD focuses on the pragmatic realization of an actual Web that contains interlinked and semantically enriched data. The vision of the SW, in contrast, is broader and more comprehensive than the WoD and includes a wider range of application use cases and technologies (c.f., Section 2.2.2). In this context, LD applies concepts of the Web for human users, e.g., the interlinked hypertext, to data [23], in particular, to structured data. It is targeted towards machines, i.e., is machine-readable, and, therefore, requires explicit semantics of relations, i.e., the type of relations, instead of implicit semantics, i.e., links in HTML, that require human interpretation [33].

LD is built on the architecture introduced by REST (c.f., Section 2.2.1) and the technologies introduced during the evolution of the WWW, in particular,

URI (c.f., Section 2.2.1.1), and HTTP (c.f., Section 2.2.1.2). In addition, LD is built on SWT (c.f., Section 2.2.2), in particular, on machine-readable RDF (c.f., Section 2.2.2.1), to support extensible semantics for the heterogeneous landscape of domains, in which LD is published. The introduced links are restricted in LD to HTTP URIs that are potentially resolvable via HTTP and link resources as defined by REST. In comparison to the REST paradigm, the LD paradigm provides in addition to self-descriptive HTTP messages also self-descriptive data with a graph-based data model, shared vocabularies, and separation of data from presentation and formatting. Application Programming Interfaces (APIs) that are based on HTTP and adhere to the LD paradigm profit from both worlds by providing a uniform interface, if HTTP is used as the application protocol, and a standardized generic and semantically powerful data model. Similarly to the Web, the WoD contains no authoritative instance, and every stakeholder can participate through publication and consumption of LD.

> "The result, which we will refer to as the Web of Data, may more accurately be described as a web of things in the world, described by data on the Web." [33, p. 2]

The idea of LD has been introduced in 2006 by Berners-Lee in an informal W3C design issue [23] and is synthesized to the four LD principles [23, 33]:

1. "Use URIs as names for things"
2. "Use HTTP URIs so that people can look up those names"
3. "When someone looks up a URI, provide useful information, using the standards (RDF, SPARQL)"
4. "Include links to other URIs, so that they can discover more things"

These principles are rules that can be broken without harm but with losing the opportunity of future data reuse [23]. The first principle introduces the use of URIs, which is common in the SW community, e.g., fostered by the use of RDF. The second principle introduces the advantage of HTTP as existing and established Web technology with the Domain Name System (DNS) for handling the delegation of authorities. The third principle introduces the publishing of not only ontologies but also of the datasets that are annotated by these ontologies as well as providing access to these datasets through HTTP. The fourth principle introduces, similarly to the hypertext in the Web for humans, the interlinking of datasets with other related and relevant datasets, to enable link following.

By following these principles, LD enables graph-based information storage, with the triple as the atomic unit, i.e., subject, predicate, object, where the subject and object must be an HTTP URI or a literal and an HTTP URI, and the predicate must be a URI. There are two options for defining identifiers – by using local identifiers, i.e., URI fragments, and by using global identifiers, i.e., full HTTP URIs. The dereferencing of full HTTP URIs, including fragments, is done by retrieving the message that contains the representation (and probably further identifiers) and accessing the information about the referenced resource. As a result, a browsable LD graph [23, 33] enables link following by:

1. "Returning all statements where the node is a subject or object; and"
2. "Describing all blank nodes attached to the node by one arc"

In this way, by employing link following, complete LD graphs can be traversed.

The approach on RWLD is an extension of the initial LD vision, i.e., a read-only graph of interlinked resources, and builds on the idea of combining the architectural paradigms of LD [33] and REST [64]. This combination has been used in several approaches, e.g., Linked Data Fragments (LDF) [162], Linked APIs (LAPIS) [157], Linked Data Services (LIDS) [152], RESTdesc [163], or Linked Open Services (LOS) [108]. As already mentioned, standardization efforts for the integrated use of LD and REST led to the LDP [150] W3C recommendation. Furthermore, LD in combination with REST is used for the foundation of a number of solutions for exposing access to data or creating query interfaces based on SPARQL queries. For instance, grlc [114], evolving on top of tools such as BASIL [46], provides a small server for automatically converting SPARQL queries into LD APIs. In the following, we present the LDP as, at the time of writing, the only standardization of the combined use of REST and LD.

2.2.3.1 Linked Data Platform (LDP)

The Linked Data Platform (LDP) [150] W3C specification defines the coherent use of Web technologies and SWT to enable RWLD [24]. In particular, the

LDP specifies the combined use of HTTP and RDF as well as in some cases the related use of SPARQL. The LDP incorporates and extends the LD paradigm (c.f., Section 2.2.3) for accessing and manipulating resources, in particular, the use of HTTP URIs as resource identifiers (1st LD principle), the use of HTTP as application protocol to create, read, update, and delete resources (2nd LD principle extended by manipulation of resources), as well as RDF as semantically powerful data model (3rd LD principle) with means for interlinking resources (4th LD principle). In addition, the LDP specification defines different types of containers as specialized resources for the management of resources collections, including the HTTP interaction required for accessing and manipulating these collections. The LDP specification intentionally focuses on the definition of resources and resource collections, as well as on the definition of interactions with these. Thereby, the LDP may serve as the base for developing more advanced extensions. For example, an extension of the LDP specification introduces paging support [151] that enables the handling of large resources and resource collections.

The Linked Data Platform Resource (LDPR) is the most basic concept defined by the LDP specification. This concept defines characteristics that are common to all other LDP concepts. In particular, all LDPRs are HTTP resources that are identified by URIs and are accessible as well as modifiable by utilizing the HTTP application protocol.

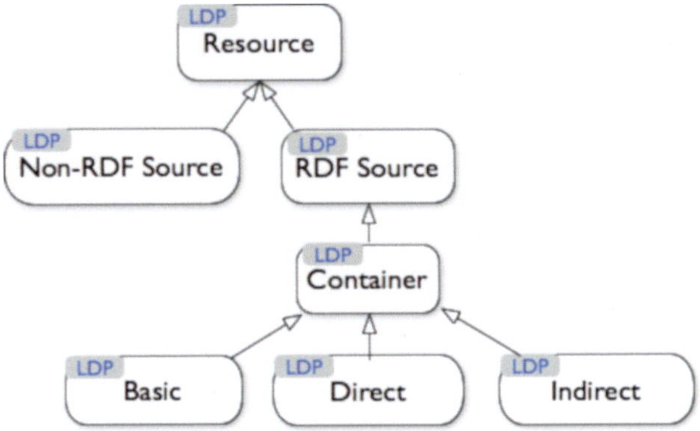

Figure 2.9: LDP – Resource and Container Hierarchy [150]

Figure 2.9 shows two resources types that are subordinate to this generic LDPR – the Linked Data Platform RDF Source (LDP-RS) and the Linked Data Platform Non-RDF Source (LDP-NR). LDP-RSs must adhere to RDF, and LDP servers must provide and accept their state representation in one or more of the available RDF serialization formats, e.g., Turtle, or RDF/XML [150]. LDP-NRs represent all other kinds of resources that are not modeled in accordance with RDF but are of other types, e.g., binary data like images or music, structured data like XML documents, or markup data like HTML. In some cases, LDP-RSs may be associated with LDP-NRs to provide metadata, e.g., the metadata about artist, album, and title of an LDP-NR containing a music song.

The LDPR defines several common characteristics of resources, e.g., mandatory support for HTTP/1.1, or equivalence of request URI and base URI for relative URI resolution. In addition, the LDP makes extensive use of HTTP request and response header fields, e.g., the mandatory *ETag* header in responses, or the publishing of constraints that enable or disable clients to perform certain manipulation of LDPRs. Constraints are encoded as URI references in the HTTP *Link* response header by using the link relation type `http://www.w3.org/ns/ldp#constrainedBy`. Furthermore, every type of resource must be communicated to clients by using the HTTP *Link* response header field, e.g., by using `http://www.w3.org/ns/ldp#Resource` in combination with a link relation of type *type* for LDPRs. With respect to interaction and introduced by the HTTP specification, servers must support the HTTP GET as well as the HTTP HEAD request methods for LDPRs, including a set of request headers. In addition, servers must support the HTTP OPTIONS request method for LDPRs and provide sufficient information about specific, in particular, optional, LDP capabilities. In conformance with the HTTP specification, all other HTTP request methods are optional, but are, in some cases, further detailed by the LDP specification, if servers provide support for them. For subordinate LDP-RSs, the LDP specification defines Turtle as the default RDF serialization format.

With the Linked Data Platform Container (LDPC) the LDP specification defines the semantics and interaction options for the most basic concept of a collection of resources. Collections, as a generic concept, support several use cases, in which membership relations between superordinate and subordinate resources exist. Figure 2.9 shows three different types of containers that are introduced by the LDP specification for supporting different groups of use cases and that are subordinate to the generic LDPR – the Linked Data Platform Basic Container (LDP-BC), the Linked Data Platform Direct Container (LDP-DC), and the Linked Data Platform Indirect Container (LDP-IC).

```
HTTP/1.1 200 OK
Content–Type: text/turtle
Date: Thu, 12 Jun 2014 18:26:59 GMT
ETag: "8caab0784220148bfe98b738d5bb6d13"
Accept–Post: text/turtle, application/ld+json
Allow: POST,GET,OPTIONS,HEAD,PUT
Link: <http://www.w3.org/ns/ldp#BasicContainer> ; rel="type" ,
  <http://www.w3.org/ns/ldp#Resource> ; rel="type"
Transfer–Encoding: chunked

@prefix dcterms: <http://purl.org/dc/terms/> .
@prefix ldp: <http://www.w3.org/ns/ldp#> .

<http://example.org/c1/> a ldp:BasicContainer ;
  dcterms:title "A very simple container" ;
  ldp:contains <r1> , <r2> , <r3> .
```

Listing 2.6: LDP – LDP-BC Example in Turtle Serialization [150]

Listing 2.6 shows a simple example of an LDP-BC in response to an HTTP GET request. The representation contains information about the container, i.e., “dcterms:title "A very simple container"”, as well as about the contained members, i.e., “ldp:contains <r1>, <r2>, <r3>”. In addition, several HTTP response header fields provide metadata about the resource, e.g., the link relations that provide information about the container types LDP-BC and LDPR, i.e., “Link: [...]”.

The LDP defines two types of relationships between superordinate resources, i.e., collections, and subordinated resources, i.e., resources contained in collections: containment and membership. Containment defines the relation of a container to the resources that are managed by the container. Therefore, containment triples define the content of LDPCs, i.e., still existing members that have been created in interaction with LDPCs. The form of containment is fixed to the triple pattern with the LDPC URI as subject, followed by the predicate “ldp:contains”, and the URI of the member resource as object. In contrast, membership defines the actual superordinate-subordinate relationship, with respect to the current domain. Membership triples enable the use of domain-specific vocabularies for defining membership relations between the LDPC and the subordinate resources or between a domain-specific superordinate resource and the subordinate resources. In the simplest case, the LDP-BC, this relation equals the containment relation, and no domain-specific membership triples are used. In the case of LDP-DC and LDP-IC, this relationship is managed separately with a set of membership triples. For example, Figure 2.10 shows a direct container that contains (“ldp:contain”) photo resources in superordinate-subordinate relation (“foaf:depiction”) to a person resource.

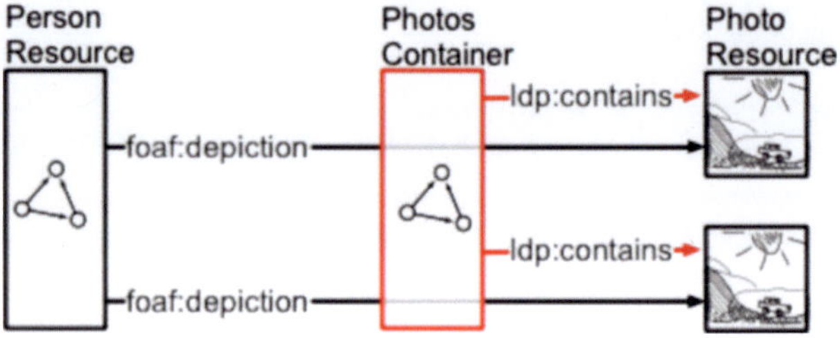

Figure 2.10: LDP – LDP-DC Example [115]

2.3 Concepts and Terminology

With respect to our viewpoint on distributed applications, we define different core concepts that provide a certain level of abstraction for generalization but at the same time keep important characteristics with respect to the challenges of integration.

2.3.1 Component

With the term *component*, we denote the atomic building blocks of integration that provide a function to the network. In Figure 2.11, we mark components with *C* and provide an enlarged visualization on the right that details the inner elements of components. A component encapsulates certain domain-specific function (c.f., Section 2.3.1.1) as a black box and provides access to this function through different interaction mechanisms (c.f., Section 2.3.3), in particular interfaces (c.f., Section 2.3.3.1), requests (c.f., Section 2.3.3.2), and optional responses (c.f., Section 2.3.3.3). We denote in the detailed component in Figure 2.11 the domain-specific function with *F*, the interface with a square, an incoming request of another component with an inbound dashed arrow, and an outgoing request to the interface of another component with an outbound dashed arrow. In this case, we do not show the other component that executes requests to or receives requests from the detailed component. By enabling data flows (c.f., Section 2.3.2.1) through these interaction mechanisms, we enable the integration of components into distributed applications (c.f., Section 2.3.2). In the following, we use a simple running example with two components, the first representing a heating system and the seconds representing a temperature sensor.

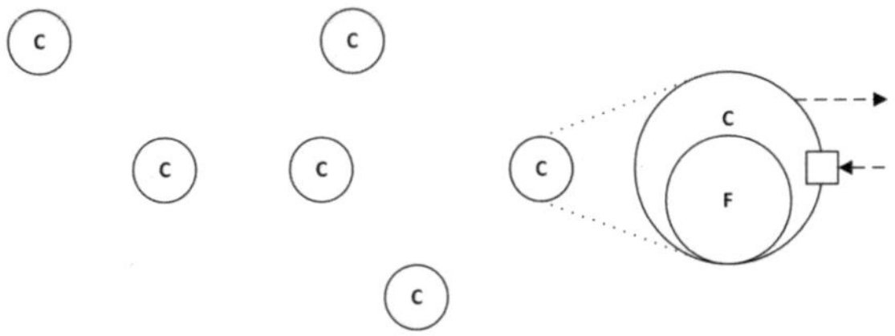

Figure 2.11: Concepts and Terminology – Component

2.3.1.1 Function

With the term *function*, we denote domain-specific functions and data that we keep as black boxes. In Figure 2.11, we mark the function of the enlarged component with *F*. Functions provide information or require information to work, or both. Thereby, we abstract away from specialized domain-specific issues and focus on general integration challenges. For example, the component that represents the heating system may have access to information about the current temperature or the target temperature of the system, and to the function of switching the heating system on and off or of heating up and cooling down the heating system, by setting a target temperature. Overall, this component encapsulates the domain-specific heating function as a black box that enables certain provisioning and consumption of information.

2.3.2 Application

With the term *application*, we denote distributed applications that are a composition of components, combine the distinct function of these participating components, and, thereby, provide a value-added function that exceeds the function of the individual components. In Figure 2.12, we mark the distributed application with *A*. This distributed application includes a selection of the components in its composition, that we showed in Figure 2.11. To provide the value-added function, the components in the composition of distributed applications must collaborate and, therefore, the components establish data flows (c.f., Section 2.3.2.1) between each other to exchange information required for this collaboration. These data flows are established through interaction mechanisms (c.f., Section 2.3.3). However, in order to run a distributed application, at least one component per distributed application is needed to process actively (c.f., Section 2.3.5) and execute requests, while other components may passively react. In addition, we indicate in Figure 2.12 with person icons that different stakeholders may be responsible for the components and the application. Different stakeholders may design, develop, and provide the components and integrate these components into distributed applications. These stakeholders do not have to be of the same organization but may be independent of each other.

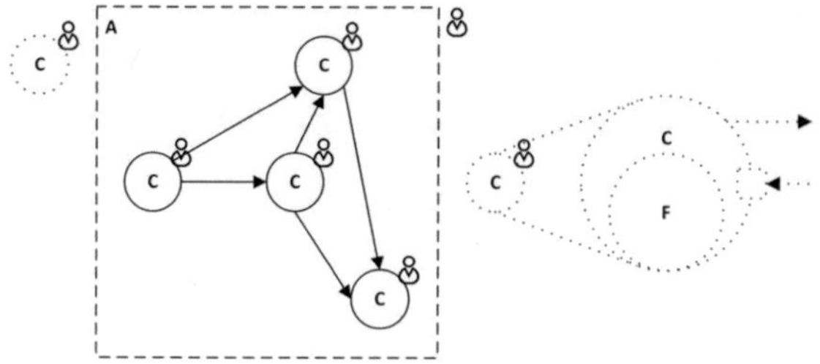

Figure 2.12: Concepts and Terminology – Application

2.3.2.1 Data Flow

With the term *data flow*, we denote the aforementioned flow of data between different components in the compositions of distributed applications. In Figure 2.12, we mark data flows with solid arrows between the components. These components establish data flows with the help of interaction mechanisms (c.f., Section 2.3.3). Thereby, the direction of interaction is, in general, independent from the data flow, i.e., the required information may be transferred as payload in requests (push interaction) or responses (pull interaction). In addition, the cardinality of data flows between components is not restricted and may be one-to-one, one-to-many, or many-to-many. In the case of bidirectional data flows, these data flows are realized as two separated data flows or one data flow that contains information as payload in the requests and responses. However, the data flows of distributed applications are, in general, specific to particular integration scenarios, depending on the set of components, and on their required collaboration.

2.3.2.2 Application Logic

With the term *application logic*, we denote the coordination and collaboration of components in the compositions of distributed applications. For example, this includes the data flows to be established, the data transformations that are required, the decisions to be made about the execution of requests, or the active and passive triggering of processing. In summary, the application logic comprises the means, which are required on top of the domain-specific function of components, to realize their collaboration and, thereby, to provide the value-added function of the distributed application. For example, the temperature sensor provides measurements in Celsius, and the heating system requires measurements in Fahrenheit to be able to adjust the heating. In addition, the temperature sensor can provide the measurements at an interface, and the heating system can request this information, or the other way round. In our case, the way in which the transformation between Celsius and Fahrenheit is realized, the way in which the transfer of this temperature information is realized, and the decision in what way the heating must be adjusted, are denoted as application logic that is specific to the integration scenario of these two components.

However, for example, complex data transformations or calculations may be encapsulated as the domain-specific function of separate components.

2.3.3 Interaction

With the term *interaction*, we denote the mechanisms mentioned above to establish data flows between components and, thereby, enable their collaboration in the composition of distributed applications. In Figure 2.13, we mark the requests between components with dashed arrows, the interfaces with squares, and the established data flows with solid arrows. The interaction between two components requires that one of these components provides an interface (c.f., Section 2.3.3.1) and that the other component executes a request (c.f., Section 2.3.3.2) on this interface. Optionally, the component that provides the interface may respond with a response (c.f., Section 2.3.3.3). Thereby, we can establish the same data flow with a pull or a push interaction. In the case of a pull, the responses include the payload (c.f., Section 2.3.3.4) representing the data flow and, in the case of a push, the requests include the payload.

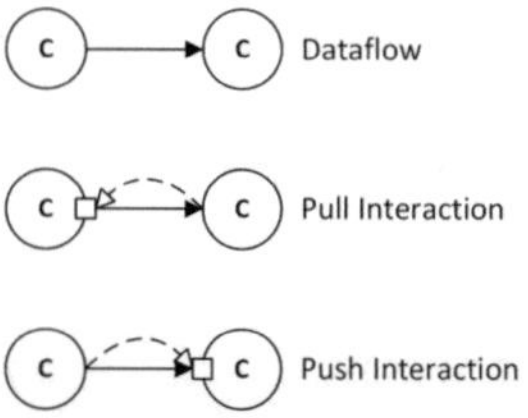

Figure 2.13: Concepts and Terminology – Interaction

2.3.3.1 Interface

With the term *interface*, we denote the means that components provide to expose relevant parts of their states to the network, to receive requests of other components with respect to this state, and to respond to these requests. In addition, components may react to state changes through requests to their interfaces. In Figure 2.13, we mark the interfaces with squares on the components.

2.3.3.2 Request

With the term *request*, we denote the means that components provide to use the interfaces of other components and to receive responses. In addition, components may react to the responses of their requests at the interfaces of other components. In Figure 2.13, we mark the requests between components with dashed arrows.

2.3.3.3 Response

With the term *response*, we denote the response of a component to the request of another component at its interface. In Figure 2.13, we mark the responses implicitly with dashed arrows, i.e., the response has the opposite direction of the request.

2.3.3.4 Payload

With the term *payload*, we denote the data that is contained in a request or a response. In Figure 2.13, we mark the payload implicitly with the solid arrows for data flows, i.e., the flow of data in a specific direction requires a payload in the request or response that realizes the data flow. Thereby, the payload is optional and may be contained only in the request, in the response, or in both, depending on the requirements of the integration scenario.

2.3.4 Meta-interaction

With the term *meta-interaction*, we denote the interaction in the deployment phase of the lifecycle (c.f., Section 2.3.6) of a distributed application, that prepares the interaction during the runtime phase of the distributed application. Thereby, we distinguish between publish-subscribe (c.f., Section 2.3.4.1) and collect-subscribe (c.f., Section 2.3.4.2) meta-interaction.

2.3.4.1 Publish-subscribe Meta-interaction

With the term *publish-subscribe meta-interaction*, we denote meta-interaction, in which components provide interfaces that enable other components to register their interfaces for receiving certain data as the payload of request to these interfaces, i.e., push interaction, in later phases. For example, the temperature sensor component may provide a publish-subscribe interface that enables other components, e.g., the heater system component, to register their interfaces. In later phases, the temperature sensor component will transfer, e.g., temperature measurements, as the payload of requests at the registered interface of the heater system component.

2.3.4.2 Collect-subscribe Meta-interaction

With the term *collect-subscribe meta-interaction*, we denote meta-interaction, in which components provide interfaces that enable other components to register their interfaces for the collection of payload through requests at these interfaces, i.e., pull interaction, in later phases. For example, the heater system component provides a collect-subscribe interface that enables other components, e.g., the temperature sensor component, to register their interfaces. In later phases, the heater system component requests temperature measurements at the registered interface of the temperature sensor, that transfers the temperature measurement as payload in the response.

2.3.5 Processing

With the term *processing*, we denote the active or passive processing of components with respect to the provisioning of updated state representation at their interfaces and the execution of requests to other components. In Figure 2.14, we mark the active processing with a clock symbol and the passive processing with a letter symbol. In addition, we provide a scenario-derived example of active and passive processing in Section 3.1.2.1.

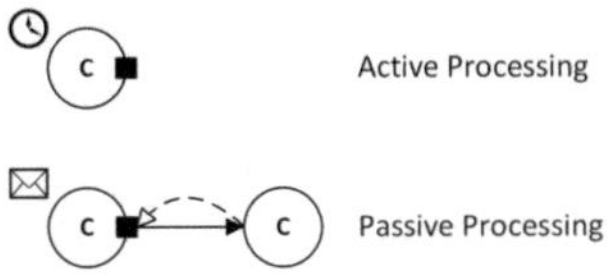

Figure 2.14: Concepts and Terminology – Processing

2.3.5.1 Active Processing

With the term *active processing*, we denote the processing that is triggered by events that are external to the applications, i.e., not introduced by other components of the application. For example, the processing of the temperature sensor component may be triggered at a fixed frequency that is determined by a clock, by measurements of a sensor that is part of the component, when the difference between measures exceeds a given threshold, or the processing may be executed by the manual intervention of a human user.

2.3.5.2 Passive Processing

With the term *passive processing*, we denote the processing that is triggered by events that are internal to the application, i.e., introduced by other components of the application. For example, the temperature sensor component may measure the temperature with its included sensor, once a request of the heater system component is executed at the interface.

2.3.6 Lifecycle

With the term *lifecycle*, we denote the separate but interwoven lifecycles of components and distributed applications. In Figure 2.15, we provide a simple visualization of the phases, in which we separate the lifecycle. In addition, we provide in Section 3.2.3.2 a comparison of lifecycles with respect to our architecture for designing adaptable components.

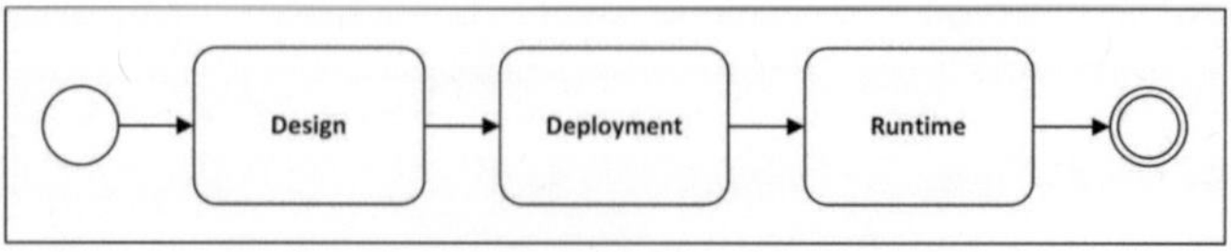

Figure 2.15: Concepts and Terminology – Lifecycle

2.3.6.1 Component Lifecycle

With the term *component lifecycle*, we denote the lifecycle of components, which are independently designed, deployed, and ran. During runtime, they participate in distributed applications as described in the sections above.

2.3.6.2 Application Lifecycle

With the term *application lifecycle*, we denote the lifecycle of applications, which are, similarly to components, designed, deployed, and ran. In this case, design denotes the selection and composition of components, deployment denotes the composition-specific adaptation of components, i.e., the adaptation of interfaces, interactions, and processing, and runtime denotes the established data flows between participating components, i.e., provisioning of the value-added function through the collaboration of the components.

3 Component Adaptation and Decentralized Application Control

In this chapter, we detail our work on providing a solution for the adaptation of components and the decentralized control of distributed applications. We focus on three main areas: 1) addressing the challenges of having one application based on a set of heterogeneous components, different devices, and multifold data; 2) dealing with the coordination of components as part of providing the function of an overall application, without having a central management authority; and 3) providing a solution for adapting and updating a running application, without having to redeploy or re-instantiate the application, i.e., adaptation at runtime.

In the following, we first introduce the context of our work on realizing decentralized control and present a motivation scenario. Next we describe the specific challenges that we aim to address and provide a detailed problem analysis. We derive design requirements for our architectural solution and provide an architecture for distributed applications with decentralized control. Based on the application use case, we demonstrate the practical applicability of our approach by giving the details on an exemplary implementation. Finally, we conclude by presenting an evaluation of the functional capabilities of our approach, including the conformance to our design requirements, and the performance aspects of our implementation.

The content of this chapter is partially based on the publications by Keppmann et al. [103, 102, 99, 105].

3.1 Introduction

Driven by current technology developments, we are witnessing the increasing popularity and adoption of the IoT [66, 9], the WoT [167, 72, 70, 68], and the

SWoT [143, 128] (c.f., Section 2.1), as well as of related visions such as the I4.0 [109, 86]. At the same time, the evolution of the Web [18, 25, 28] continues with technology developments that are driven by the SW [30, 29, 146] and the WoD [33, 32]. These trends are, on the one hand, accompanied by an increasingly heterogeneous landscape of small, embedded, and highly modularized devices and applications, by multitudes of manufactures and developers, and the pervasion of network-accessible "things" within all areas of life. On the other hand, they are also characterized by an increasing publication of all kinds of machine-readable data on the Web that can be seamlessly consumed through Web technologies and subsequently reused and combined in applications.

The aforementioned technology developments are tightly associated with the growing complexity of handling the integration of heterogeneous components as part of distributed applications, which fulfill certain needs by providing value-added function based on the combination of the involved components. Thereby, these applications may be composed of components that are available on the local network or that are accessed remotely. In addition, these components may be specific to the application use case or provide generic function for several independent application use cases. We notice these technological integration challenges not only at the data and protocol level, but also at the application level. Furthermore, multiple stakeholders may be involved in the development, provisioning, and integration of components, adding another layer of complexity to the technological challenges.

Coping with such diverse multi-stakeholder data integration scenarios is a known challenge, which is already addressed by several approaches that are tackling the related problems. For example, the LODC [112] is one solution for multi-stakeholder data integration that enables publishing and consuming of semantically annotated data by following the LD principles [23, 33]. Thereby, adhering to the underlying LD principles enables integration at semantic level, data model level, as well as protocol level (c.f., Section 2.2.3). In this context, the LDP recommendation [150] of the W3C combines the LD principles with the REST paradigm [64] and specifies RWLD resources and containers (c.f., Section 2.2.3.1). By enabling RWLD, the LDP may serve as integration technology for applications in a heterogeneous landscape of components.

However, establishing a consensus on the level of protocol, data model, and semantics is not enough. The actual design and granularity of interfaces, interaction, and semantic annotations as well as the deployment of application-specific dataflows and logic with respect to the requirements of specific integration scenarios introduces several new problems. In particular, these problems are aggravated as more stakeholders get involved in the development, provisioning, and integration of components to distributed applications. By extending and interweaving the RWLD integration architecture with further SWT, e.g., SPARQL, or N3, we approach these challenges and propose an architectural solution for several related problems without breaking the compatibility with the established consensus on the level of protocol, data model, and semantics.

3.1.1 Scenario

We motivate the problems that we address with a specific use case scenario, which we use as a running example throughout the chapter. Current technology developments influence not only our day-to-day activities but also businesses and the way products and services are developed and produced. In this context, we look at a typical situation in the manufacturing floors of factories, in which the safety of humans is an ongoing effort.

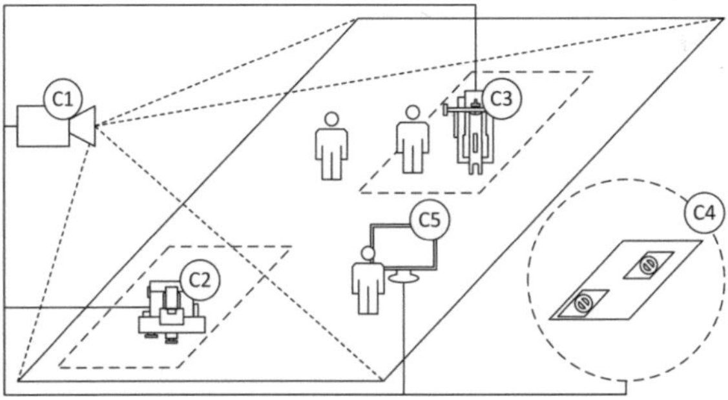

Figure 3.1: Scenario – Monitoring a Factory Floor

In particular, the unintentional intrusion of humans into the operational areas of machines or robots increases the risk of injury. One way to tackle this problem is the tracking of human bodies and movements and the matching of the coordinates of their body parts against floor layouts with included safety areas, to automatically trigger warning alarms or emergency stops of machines and robots.

Figure 3.1 shows a simple overview of the monitoring setup in our scenario, which involves the following infrastructure and components, i.e., devices, services, and resources.

Tracker (C1) The tracking (C1) component consists of depth video cameras with integrated body tracking algorithms, that provide body tracking to identify the joints and the skeleton structure of people who are in range as well as their coordinates with respect to the location of the depth camera.

Machine (C2, C3) The setup comprises production machines, alarms, mobile devices, and sensors that provide data about their current state and support appropriate reactions, e.g., emergency stops, or alarms. In our scenario, we explicitly model two machines as components (C2, C3).

Layout (C4) The layout (C4) component is a virtual resource that provides data about the layout of the factory floor, including the position of the tracker, the different machines, and their safety zones. This data is rather static but may be updated if machines are newly installed or moved to different locations.

Screen (C5) The screen (C5) component provides information about the current state of the monitored factory floor and visualizes the floor plan, machines, safety zones, and alarms in an integrated manner.

Network The network itself is not a component but represents the underlying infrastructure that connects all components and enables interaction between these components in a generic and domain-independent manner.

The monitoring application in our scenario, visualized in Figure 3.1, is implemented as a distributed application. With respect to the function of every single component, the application provides the value-added function of saving humans from injuries by utilizing warnings or emergency shutdowns. To reach this goal, the involved components, i.e., tracking, machines, robots, alarms, or mobile devices, need to exchange data to provide information about the current safety state of humans on the factory floor and, if required, to react on this safety state, e.g., execute an emergency stop if a human joint is within a safety zone. Furthermore, determining when human joints intrude into safety zones is realized by matching the joint coordinates, calculated by the tracking algorithms, against the layout of the factory floor with the included safety zone coordinates. Both, the matching of coordinates as well as informing devices about required actions are controlling elements, i.e., application logic, that is part of the distributed application but not, in the first place, of a single component.

The specific challenges that we want to highlight with our distributed application scenario are threefold.

1. Different types of devices, with diverse interfaces, that produce and consume a variety of data with different semantics, formats, and structure, must be integrated. These components are not necessarily manufactured, provided, or integrated by the same but by different stakeholders.
2. While the components must be coordinated as part of providing the value-added function of the overall application, we want to avoid a centralized coordinating component, but advocate a distributed solution.
3. The positions of the machines or the safety areas may change over time. However, having to redesign and redeploy all components of the application every time the setup changes is time-consuming and inefficient.

Therefore, a flexible solution is required, where the tracking service and devices can be developed during their design time and additional adaptations to specific requirements of the integration scenario can be integrated later, i.e., during deployment, or runtime. In the following, we use this scenario to support the detailed problem analysis, to motivate design requirements for our architecture, to exemplify the proposed architecture, to provide an exemplary implementation, and to derive an evaluation scenario.

3.1.2 Challenges

Some important aspects of dealing with integration in the context of distributed applications still remain unaddressed, especially in the context of existing approaches that focus on the integration of components from a data-centric point of view. Still, the challenges on the level of protocols, interactions, data formats, data models, and semantics are pressing problems that need to be addressed (c.f., Communication Heterogeneity in Section 3.1.2.1; Information Heterogeneity in Section 3.1.2.2). Furthermore, we face challenges with respect to the requirements of integration scenarios, in which multiple stakeholders are independently involved in the development, provisioning, and integration of distinct components (c.f., Requirements Unawareness in Section 3.1.2.3; Development Inefficiency in Section 3.1.2.4). In addition, we witness challenges that result from creating and controlling composite applications from a set of components that have different functions but that collaborate to provide the value-added function of the application, by transferring data between each other through interactions over a network (c.f., Decentralized Control in Section 3.1.2.5; Control Deployment in Section 3.1.2.6). In the following, we discuss these challenges in more detail.

3.1.2.1 Communication Heterogeneity

During the integration of a number of distinct components, that are developed, provided, and integrated by different stakeholders, we face *Communication Heterogeneity* in terms of different interaction, meta-interaction, and processing patterns used for communication (c.f., Figure 2.12). The communication between components is required to establish data flows and, thereby, exchange messages that embody the information required for providing the overall functionality of the composite application. The technical details and conventions of interactions, meta-interactions, and processing may be subject to the specification of protocols.

In the first place, data flows between components can be established through complimentary interaction patterns (c.f., Section 2.3.3). On the one hand, components may provide interfaces to expose their function on the network, thereby enabling other components to issue requests against these interfaces, and, by exchanging data in these request, to use the function of the components. On the other hand, components themselves may issue requests to the interfaces of other components to use their function by transferring data to or from these components. Thereby, both interaction patterns are capable of transferring data from components to other components, i.e., pushing data, or to transfer data from other components to the components, i.e., pulling data. For example, the machine components (C2, C3) in our scenario provide interfaces that are used by the tracker component (C1) to issue requests that trigger emergency shutdown, if security breaches appear. In contrast, the layout component (C4) provides an interface that enables the tracker component (C1) and the screen component (C5) to pull information about the layout of the factory floor on demand.

In addition, components may provide capabilities at their interfaces to enable in advance the registration of intented data flows by other components through meta-interaction (c.f., Section 2.3.4). On the one hand, components may subscribe themselves for receiving certain data that is published at the other component, i.e., publish-subscribe meta-interaction. On the other hand, components may subscribe themselves for the collection of data through requests by the other component that is provided at their interfaces, i.e., collect-subscribe meta-interaction. For example, the tracker component (C1) provides an interface that enables other components, e.g., mobile devices, to register themselves for security breaches at all or at a selection of machines, in order to be able to take respective actions, e.g., informing the human users via alarms.

Furthermore, requests that transfer data to or from other components and the provisioning of data at interfaces can be initiated by different processing patterns (c.f., Section 2.3.5). On the one hand, components may be actively processing and have the data available at their interface or transfer it through requests to other components. On the other hand, components may be passively processing and provide data on demand. For example, the tracker component (C1), that is actively processing, records the factory floor at the fixed frequency of the depth video camera. After every interval, the component processes the data, i.e., calculates the coordinates of joints for the body tracking and provides this information at an interface or transfers the data to other components through requests. In contrast, in a different application scenario, the tracker component (C1) could be passively processing and records the factory floor only if other components request the body tracking information at the interface, then processes the data, and responds with the information. Optionally the component may cache this information for subsequent request for a predefined TTL. The same processing patterns can be applied for requests of components to other components. In the end, per distributed application, at least one component must provide active processing to directly or indirectly trigger the processing of all other components that provide passive processing.

Integrating several components with diverting requirements on interaction, meta-interaction, and processing patterns into one distributed application is a challenge, in particular, if different stakeholders design these means for communication a priori and not aligned with each other.

3.1.2.2 Information Heterogeneity

The *Information Heterogeneity* of data that components communicate through interactions between each other is another integration issue. On the one hand, this heterogeneity appears regarding different data formats and data models, i.e., the way, in which information is conceptually structured and represented as data structures. On the other hand, this heterogeneity appears regarding the non-existing or diverging semantics of the data, i.e., the meaning of data across a heterogeneous landscape of components.

Components may use different formats to encode the information that is transferred via interactions to or from interfaces. With respect to the REST architectural style (c.f., Section 2.2.1), this encoded information is the representation of the resources, i.e., of the underlying entities that are described by this information. Components having to support different and diverging data formats, that must be integrated into one application, increases the integration effort even more. For example, the tracker component (C1) may provide information about security breaches serialized in JSON-LD, while the machine components (C2, C3) partially support only XML as serialization data format.

Besides different data formats for representing the same information, the conceptual structure of the information may adhere to the same or different data models. In the first place, different data formats for the same data model allow conversion between these data formats and, thereby, utilization of the optimal format depending on the use case. However, if the data models for representing information diverge between components, the integration is, in general, more challenging. For example, the RDF data model enables the description of information about entities and their relations in a graph-based manner without enforcing a particular data format (e.g., RDF/XML, Turtle, or JSON-LD).

Furthermore, even if components provide overlapping support for a set of data formats and the data, that is transferred between components, adheres to the same data model, the semantics of the data may remain unclear, i.e., the same data is interpreted in different ways by different components. For example, the screen component (C5) in our scenario receives coordinates about the layout of the factory floor from the layout component (C4) in centimeters. At the same time, the screen component (C5) receives coordinates of human joints from the tracker component (C1) in millimeters. This different interpretation of the coordinates must be considered by the screen component in order to be able to display a correct overview of the current safety situation.

Integrating several components with diverting data formats, data models, and data semantics into one distributed application is a challenge, in particular and similar to the heterogeneity of communication, if different stakeholders design these the representation of information a priori and not aligned with each other.

3.1.2.3 Requirements Unawareness

In integration scenarios, in which components are built by several manufacturers or developers and in which these components are provided and integrated by others, the manufacturers of components hardly know the requirements of all possible integration scenarios at design time and, thereby, face *Requirements Unawareness*. Therefore, they can only provide default interaction mechanisms but are unable to adapt components to provide the optimal solutions for specific use cases.

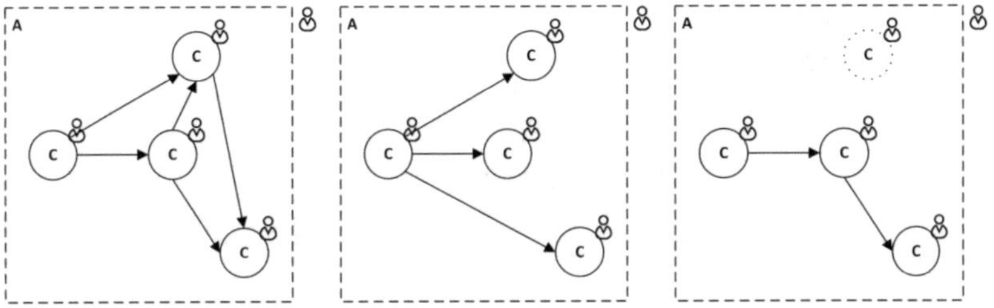

Figure 3.2: Problems – Requirements Unawareness

In Figure 3.2, we abstractly visualize three different applications composed from the same set of components but with different data flows, which are specific to the respective integration scenarios. The integrating stakeholders, indicated by the person icons, are aware of the requirements of their integration scenarios but use already existing components that different stakeholders may provide. These stakeholders manufactured their components before the integrating stakeholders knew their specific requirements. In addition, the problems *Communication Heterogeneity* and *Information Heterogeneity* apply. Two drivers of this problem are the increasing modularization and the multi-stakeholder situations.

In contrast to monolithic software architectures, current technology developments that accompany visions such as the IoT, WoT, and WoD, propagate small, modular components and, subsequently, foster the composition of applications with value-added function. On the one hand, this modularization leads to the specialization of components that tend to be smaller and focused on a specific function. On the other hand, this modularization leads to generalization, i.e., while being more specialized, the function itself becomes more generic in terms of the potential use in multiple application cases. To foresee the requirements of all these application cases and, subsequently, to provide the optimal communication mechanisms (c.f., Section 3.1.2.1) as well as the optimal information (c.f., Section 3.1.2.2), is no-longer feasible at design time of the component. For example, the tracker component (C1) in our scenario is specialized on the function of body tracking in the area that is covered by the depth camera. This function, in contrast, is not specific to our application scenario, but is generalized enough to provide a potential use in several application cases, e.g., in areas like art, games, sport, and several others.

The problem is aggravated the more stakeholders are involved in the development, provisioning, and integration of the components that are included in the composition of applications. In such multi-stakeholder integration scenarios, reaching an agreement on a common set of communication mechanisms and representation of information is challenging. The more heterogeneous and non-overlapping this set is, the more customized solutions must be developed during the process of integration. In contrast, multiple components developed by one stakeholder tend to be more compatible in terms of integration-relevant technologies.

3.1.2.4 Development Inefficiency

Even if the requirements of all integration scenarios would be known beforehand, we face a *Development Inefficiency* issue. This problem finds its expression in the dimensions complexity of components and development as well as unprofitability of development.

While the components get more modularized and, thereby, more specialized with generic use for more application cases, the adaptation of their communication capabilities and information representation may lead again to more complexity. In other words, implementing all requirements in one component or several variants of a component, each with the requirements of a different integration scenarios, leads to complex architectures or complex developments respectively.

As a result, this development of complex components or several variants of components may also be inefficient in terms of time and, subsequently, in terms of business requirements. In other words, the time-consuming implementation of all potential requirements may be, more often than not, unprofitable.

3.1.2.5 Decentralized Control

With respect to the individual components, which collaboratively form a distributed application, and, therefore, must provide appropriate means for communication and representation of information, the distributed applications itself requires controlling logic that coordinates the functions of the participating components. In our scenario, this controlling application logic is, for example, the matching of body tracking coordinates with the coordinates of the safety areas, deriving the decisions about security breaches, and, subsequently, triggering the execution of emergency stops. This controlling logic is not part of the original function of individual components. In particular, enabling this controlling logic as *Decentralized Control*, that is distributed on several distinct and independently developed components, is challenging. Depending on the integration scenarios, centralized control, decentralized control, and mixed, i.e., hybrid control, are valid integration patterns.

The default pattern for the integration of a composition of components into an application is a custom component, which controls the application in a centralized manner, by pulling data from source components and pushing it to sink components, with optional calculation and decision making in between. We visualize this situation with the application on the left in Figure 3.3. In this scenario, the integrating stakeholder developed the component in the middle with the sole function of coordinating the collaboration of the three other preexisting components. In the scenario in the middle, these components take over the use case-specific application logic of coordinating the collaboration in addition to their domain-specific function. The application in the scenario on the right combines both integration patterns. The custom component as well as the preexisting components handle parts of the use case-specific application logic and establish the data flows. For example, we do not include a custom controller component in our scenario but require that all controlling application logic, such as matching of coordinates, or sending appropriate requests, in the case of security breaches, is performed by the participating components on behalf of the overall application.

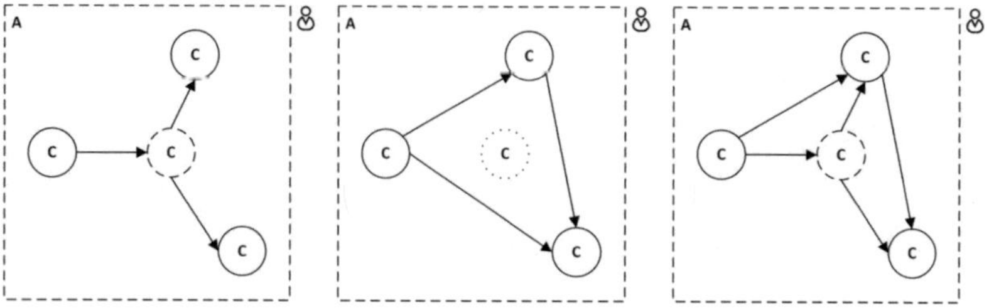

Figure 3.3: Problems – Centralized, Decentralized, and Hybrid Control Patterns

The challenging control pattern is the decentralized control one. While centralized control is a valid integration pattern, integration scenarios may require partial or complete decentralized control, i.e., the controlling logic that is specific to the distributed application must be handled by the participating components themselves. We visualize this scenario with the application in the middle in Figure 3.3. The reasons for such a solution are manifold and include, e.g., omission of custom controlling components, separation of concerns, prevention of performance bottlenecks, satisfaction of latency requirements, or enabling redundancy of functions. For example, the tracker component (C1) in our scenario, that provides body tracking of humans, should react with requests to the machine components (C2, C3), if certain coordinates are not within the safety areas, after matching the body tracking with the coordinates of the safety areas, provided by the layout component (C4). The first machine component (C2) should react to a valid request with an emergency stop and, in addition, propagate the emergency stop to the second machine component (C3), that is, for example, within the same production line.

Consequently, hybrid integration scenarios are also valid and challenging, in which custom controller components partially handle the application logic, while other parts of the application logic are handled by the other components. We visualize this scenario with the application on the right in Figure 3.3.

3.1.2.6 Control Deployment

Closely related to the controlling application logic, we need to be capable to actually instruct the participating components to adapt their behavior according to this logic and, thereby, face a *Control Deployment* problem. In particular, if multiple stakeholder are involved and we face *Requirements Unawareness* and *Development Inefficiency*, the instruction of components to enable *Decentralized Control* is required after their design and development, i.e., during the integration in specific integration scenarios.

If both the component lifecycles and the application lifecycle (c.f., Section 2.3.6) are within the control of the integrating stakeholder, the controlling application logic can be integrated in the components by adaptation through redesign. However, in multi-stakeholder situations, these lifecycles take place at different points in time, i.e., components are designed and provided before the design and deployment of the application starts. For example, the tracker component (C1) in our scenario has been designed with its domain function, i.e., body tracking, and is provided as a component before the integration scenario is even known. No controlling application logic, e.g., requesting the layout, or matching the coordinates, has been implemented in the component in advance. In a similar fashion, this applies to all other components in our scenario.

In these cases, we face the problem of instructing individual components during their deployment or runtime with the controlling application logic. The challenge here is that there are no means to represent this application logic in a domain-independent manner. Furthermore, components provide no means for deploying and interpreting this application logic. In addition, the representation and deployment of application logic is related to *Communication Heterogeneity* and *Information Heterogeneity*, i.e., may add another layer of complexity to these problems. The representation of controlling application logic adds to the heterogeneity of information and the deployment of application logic adds to the heterogeneity of communication, if this deployment is executed through interactions at runtime.

3.1.3 Related Work

Semantic approaches have already been developed and applied in the context of adaptation for distributed solutions for both data and applications. In this context, related work can be split into three main areas: 1) distributed Read-Write Linked Data (RWLD), 2) creating composite applications based on Web of Things (WoT) technologies, and 3) applications based on the Semantic Web of Things (SWoT).

Read-Write Linked Data builds on the idea of combining the architectural paradigms of Linked Data [33] and REST [64]. This combination has been used in several approaches, e.g., LDF [162], LAPIS [157], LIDS [152], RESTdesc [163], or LOS [108]. As already mentioned, standardization efforts for the integrated use of Linked Data and REST led to the LDP [150] W3C recommendation. Furthermore, Linked Data in combination with REST is used for the foundation of a number of solutions for exposing access to data or creating query interfaces based on SPARQL queries. For instance, grlc [114], evolving on top of tools such as BASIL [46], provides a small server for automatically converting SPARQL queries into Linked Data APIs.

The IoT [9] paradigm is about connecting every device, application, object, i.e., thing, to the network, in particular the Internet and thus to ensure connectivity. The Web of Things (WoT) [70] in order to provide integration of devices, applications, objects, i.e., "things", not only on the network layer, i.e., the internet, but also on the application layer, i.e., the web. This can be achieved by making things part of the web by providing their capabilities as REST services, based on URIs for identification and HTTP as application protocol for transport and interaction. Integrating these technologies has been, for example, addressed for embedded devices in [54].

The extension of IoT to WoT is primarily focused on the interoperability between things on the application layer. In order to foster horizontal integration and interoperability the Semantic Web of Things (SWoT) [91] focuses a common understanding of multiple capabilities and resources towards a larger ecosystem by introducing Semantic Web technologies to the IoT. Challenges related to SWoT have been, for example, addressed by the SPITFIRE [128] project, or the MOCAP [139], both in the area of sensors. We build upon several synergies introduced by a common resource-oriented viewpoint of the LD and REST paradigms. These paradigms also play a key role in WoT and in particular SWoT to cope with heterogeneous data models and interaction mechanisms. However, integrating decentralized components into applications without central control, even with a clear interaction model and semantically powerful data model, requires to distribute the controlling intelligence, at least to some extent, to the components. Our approach aims to enable the adaptation of components to specific application scenarios at runtime, while still being compatible with other approaches based on read-write LD REST resources.

3.1.4 Contributions

With respect to the challenges presented in Section 3.1.2 and advancing the current state of the art, we make the following contributions:

- In Section 3.2.1, we conduct a *Requirements Analysis* with respect to the identified challenges and derive high-level requirements for SWoT applications in general as well as detailed requirements for components that must be supported as part of our approach.
- We present in Section 3.2.2 our *Smart Component-based Integration Architecture* that enables the composition of distributed applications from components, by utilizing a subset of these components that follow our approach for making adaptations.
- An essential element of the integration is the *Smart Component (SC)* concept and architecture, which we present in Section 3.2.3 – first, by presenting the high-level architecture, and, second, by elaborating on the architectural details that enable us to fulfill the requirements.
- The SC approach is implemented in a domain-independent manner by the *Smart Component Adaptation Layer (SCAL)*, which we describe in Section 3.3.1 and where we give an overview of the elements participating in the software architecture.

- We describe the *Smart Component Adaptation Ontology (SCAO)* as part of the implementation in Section 3.3.2, which enables us to describe the adaptations of SCs.
- In Section 3.3.3, we describe the *NIREST Smart Component* as an exemplary domain-specific SC for body tracking, which supports our approach for adaptations at runtime.
- We evaluate our approach and its implementation by conducting an *Evaluation of Function* in Section 3.4.1, in which we show the SC-based integration of two application compositions by adapting and re-adapting SCs to provide the required interaction and processing. By evaluating these adaptations step-by-step, we emphasize the fulfillment of the requirements and, thereby, the solution provided with respect to the challenges.
- In addition to the evaluation of function, we present the results of the *Evaluation of Performance* by measuring the overhead of our implementation on top of the domain-specific function.

3.2 Approach for Smart Component-based Integration

With increasing modularization, various integration burdens become more visible. This can be observed, for example, during the integration of smart home sensors, classical web services, household appliances, and mobile devices into a single home automation application, or, during the integration of industrial machines with monitoring and alarm systems, as described in our integration scenario in Section 3.1.1. This situation is aggravated in multi-stakeholder situations, in which components originate from different domains and manufactures. In these cases, we are challenged with the creation of a common integration architecture, that enables the collaboration of all components, including mappings for compatibility between data models and protocols.

We described a selection of problems, that are relevant in the context of this approach, in Section 3.1.2. The first two integration challenges, which we selected, are: 1) the different interaction and processing mechanisms, which we described as Communication Heterogeneity (c.f., Section 3.1.2.1), and 2) the incompatible data models, data formats, as well as missing or ambiguous data semantics that hamper the integration, which we described as Information Heterogeneity (c.f., Section 3.1.2.2). In particular, in multi-stakeholder situations the creation of a common integration architecture requires broadly accepted paradigms and standardized technologies. Aligned with the visions (c.f., Section 2.1) on the IoT, WoT, and SWoT as well as on the Web, SW, and WoD, we, therefore, build as preliminaries on established architectural paradigms and principles for addressing the aforementioned two problem areas. In particular, we build on the REST and LD paradigms, with their related technologies and specifications. In addition, we incorporate technologies from the SWT in our approach.

As the first foundational part of our approach, we build on the REST [64] to overcome Communication Heterogeneity. The REST paradigm introduces a set of architectural constraints that restrict the degrees of freedom for interfaces as well as the interaction with these interfaces and, thereby, ease the integration. We described the REST paradigm in detail in Section 2.2.1. In a nutshell, the support for REST can be described by the Richardson maturity model [165] in four subsequent levels:

0. No support, request are tunneled through HTTP.
1. Resources are distinguished and identified by URIs.
2. HTTP verbs enable resource access and manipulation.
3. Embedded hypermedia controls relate interface parts.

While REST is architecture-agnostic in general, we use the variant that is built on Web technologies such as URIs and HTTP as implied by the Richardson maturity model.

As the second foundational part of our approach, we build on the LD [23, 33] principles to overcome Information Heterogeneity. We described LD in detail in Section 2.2.3. LD provides means for capturing and accessing information and its semantics by combining the REST paradigms in its Web-based variant with SWT technologies. Thereby, LD does not limit the heterogeneity of information in terms of domains.

Several technologies accompany the REST and LD paradigms, in particular, LDP, LR, HTTP, URI, and RDF. The LDP (c.f., Section 2.2.3.1) incorporates these technologies and their specifications in one single specification that defines the basics of RWLD with respect to the REST and LD paradigms. Therefore, the LDP specification is our choice as a foundation for addressing Communication Heterogeneity and Information Heterogeneity. However, components that adhere to the LD paradigm subsequently adhere, in general, to our integration architecture (c.f., Section 3.4). Therefore, these should expose relevant parts of their state as resources identified by URIs (c.f., Section 2.2.1.1), that are accessible through HTTP (c.f., Section 2.2.1.2) as application protocol, provide representations that adhere to the RDF (c.f., Section 2.2.2.1) data model, and use Link Relations (c.f., Section 2.2.1.3) in their resource representations to connect to relevant resources.

We are aware, that the enforcement of the one, common integration architecture on every component may not always be the best solution and probably in specific cases can even negatively affect the overall function. For instance, certain protocols and data formats might suit local conditions considerably better than the integration architecture, e.g., in the case of wireless transmission protocols with low energy and computing power consumption. In these cases, dedicated components may be required as proxies or gateways between domain-specific architectures and the common integration architecture. The appearance of proxies and gateways, i.e., reverse proxies, is already foreseen by the REST architectural style (c.f., Section 2.2.1). In addition, we present an approach on the mapping of domain-specific architectures and our integration architecture in Chapter 4.

3.2.1 Requirements

Requirements Engineering (RE) [89] aims to determine, model, and specify the required and desired properties of software systems. However, what we are currently witnessing in the context of developing WoT and SWoT systems is the diversity of domain-specific and use case-specific systems, that are not so much concerned with thorough requirements analysis but are rather focused on quickly providing the function that is needed. We argue that the reasons for this are twofold. First, RE is only now starting to develop the means to support WoT and SWoT system development, beginning with first steps, for example, in the representation of context. Second, traditional RE builds on the assumption that the knowledge, which is used to formulate the requirements exists a priori and can be captured and specified. However, for WoT systems this assumption quite frequently does not hold.

CPS–RQ1 Compositionality
Defining components and composing them
CPS–RQ2 Distributed Sensing, Computation and Control
No centralised sensing, computation or control
CPS–RQ3 Physical Interfaces and Integration
Realising contact with the physical world
CPS–RQ4 Human Interfaces and Integration
Need to interface the CPS with human influence and perception
CPS–RQ5 Information
From Data to Knowledge: capturing raw–data–to–trusted–knowledge dependency
CPS–RQ6 Privacy, Trust, Security
Privacy, trust and security requirements for systems based on the physical layer
CPS–RQ7 Modelling and Analysis – Heterogeneity, Scales, Views
Dealing with heterogeneity in terms of creating scales and views over data
CPS–RQ8 Software
Traditional programming languages and structures are not really suitable
CPS–RQ9 Robustness, Adaptation, Reconfiguration
Dealing with dynamic environments
CPS–RQ10 Societal Impact
Need for social acceptance of the new systems
CPS–RQ11 Verification, Testing and Certification
Approaches for ensuring correctness

Listing 3.1: Cyber-physical System Requirements [116]

The IoT, the WoT and, subsequently, the SWoT share many characteristics with Wireless Sensor and Actuator Networks and Cyber-physical Systems (CPSs), which involve the connection of real world objects into networked information systems including the Web [48]. Therefore, we approach the requirements analysis by exploring how the requirements for CPSs propagate to also define the WoT systems. In particular, the top requirements for building CPSs [116], i.e., Cyber-physical System Requirements (CPS-RQs), are summarized in Listing 3.1.

WoT and SWoT frameworks for CPS systems can be developed to augment the IoT and thus deal with issues such as information-centric protocols, deterministic Quality of Service (QoS), context-awareness, etc. In this way, some of the requirements listed above can already be addressed. Still, quite a few of the listed points remain relevant on the WoT and SWoT level or translate to new ones. In the following we have used the CPS-RQs and the motivation scenario in order to define requirements for realizing WoT and, in consequence, SWoT applications, i.e., Semantic Web of Things Requirements (SWoT-RQs). These requirements are summarized in Listing 3.2.

SWoT−RQ1 Provide Device Abstraction in Terms of Components
Overcoming devices heterogeneity by defining a converging abstraction over devices in terms of components (CPS−RQ1)
SWoT−RQ2 Support Uniform Interfaces and Integration
Defining compatible uniform interfaces for devices, which support the creation of composite applications (CPS−RQ3)
SWoT−RQ3 Knowledge Representation
Overcoming data heterogeneity via semantic representation (CPS−RQ5, CPS−RQ7)
SWoT−RQ4 Support Distributed Computation and Control
No centralised computation or control, application logic is distributed among participating components, without having a centralised controller (CPS−RQ2)
SWoT−RQ5 Enable Robustness, Adaptation, Reconfiguration
Supporting adaptability and reconfiguration not only at design time but also at deployment and runtime (CPS−RQ9)
SWoT−RQ6 Provide Human Interfaces and Interaction
Need to interface with human influence (CPS−RQ4)
SWoT−RQ7 Ensure Privacy, Trust, Security
Privacy, trust and security specific for WoT systems (CPS−RQ6)
SWoT−RQ8 Provide Adequate Software
Programming languages and structures suitable for WoT (CPS−RQ8)
SWoT−RQ9 Consider Societal Impact
Need for social acceptance of the new systems (CPS−RQ10)
SWoT−RQ10 Support Verification, Testing and Certification:
Approaches for ensuring correctness (CPS−RQ11)

Listing 3.2: Semantic Web of Things Requirements

In our work, we focus on the first five requirements SWoT-RQ1 to SWoT-RQ5. These selection of SWoT-RQs relates to our challenges in Section 3.1.2. In the following, we derive detailed requirements for our approach with respect to these challenges and, thereby, for the selected SWoT-RQs. We use existing Web and SW paradigms and technologies to address these requirements.

3.2.1.1 Compliance with Integration Paradigms

Our first requirement, with respect to the challenges related to the problems of Communication Heterogeneity (c.f., Section 3.1.2.1) and Information Heterogeneity (c.f., Section 3.1.2.2) is the *Compliance with Integration Paradigms*. In Section 3.2, we introduced broadly accepted paradigms and technologies, on which we rely on as foundation to address basic integration challenges. In particular, we build on the REST and LD paradigms and their related technologies. Consequently, we require that our approach must incorporate both paradigms, while extending the related technology to address the more advanced problem areas. On the one hand, we thereby foster the acceptance and lower the technological barriers of our approach. On the other hand, we ensure the compatibility with existing components that already adhere to these paradigms. We denote this requirement with R1.1 for later reference.

Implementing the LDP recommendation In particular, we require that interfaces and interactions of components following our approach implement the W3C LDP recommendation (c.f., Section 2.2.3.1), that specifies for the first time the integrated use of both paradigms LD and REST. The specification handles provisioning of resources adhering to RDF, of non-RDF resources, and of container resources, a sub-concept of RDF resources for resource collections. The LDP specifies also how clients must interact with these resources. In particular, the REST paradigm enforces HTTP as a true application protocol by enabling resource-oriented interfaces for applications that support the semantics of HTTP methods and status codes. As a consequence of the LD principles, we require the use of RDF as the primary data model for the semantic annotation of data that is provided by or sent to interfaces. However, we do not prohibit the use of specialized data models and formats, described and linked from RDF resources, since theses are supported by the LDP recommendation in the form of non-RDF resources.

Example The layout component (C4) in our scenario (c.f., Section 3.1.1) is part of the composition and adheres to the integration paradigms, but is not implemented by following our approach, i.e., the component provides read-only access through HTTP to resources that provide representations modeled in RDF. In contrast, the tracker component (C1) is implemented by following our approach and, therefore, must provide interfaces and requests that adhere to the LDP specification.

3.2.1.2 Adaptability of Interaction and Processing

Our second requirement, with respect to the challenges related to the problems Communication Heterogeneity (c.f., Section 3.1.2.1) and Information Heterogeneity (c.f., Section 3.1.2.2) in combination with the problem Decentralized Control (c.f., Section 3.1.2.5), is the *Adaptability of Interaction and Processing*. While we require compliance with the integration paradigms, we are challenged by the support for application logic in a decentralized manner, i.e., components take over the application logic in collaboration. With respect to other components in the composition of an application, this application logic is expressed by the interaction of a component, i.e., provided interfaces and executed requests, and the processing of a component, i.e., actively or passively executing requests or updating interfaces. In addition, certain calculations, transformations, or decision processes are part of this application logic. Consequently, we require that our approach enables the adaptability of interaction and processing.

Adaptation of the interfaces First, we must enable the adaptation of the interfaces that components provide as part of the composition of an application. This includes, on the one hand, the number, structure, and identifiers of resources, i.e., the granularity of the interface. On the other hand, this includes the relevant data to be provided per resource and the semantic annotations of the data. In addition, this also includes the handling of incoming data with respect to the domain-specific function of the components.

Adaptation of the requests Second, we must enable the adaptation of the requests that components execute and, thereby, establish data flows with interfaces of other components in the composition. In the case of push communication, this includes the selection of relevant data as payload of requests, the semantic annotations of the data, the identifiers of remote interfaces, and the methods to be used for requests at these interfaces. In the case of pull communication, this includes the identifiers of remote interfaces, the methods to be used for requests, and the handling of incoming data with respect to the function of components.

Processing of the data Third, we must be able to influence how components are processing the data, in accordance with their interfaces and requests. This includes the definition of triggers for active processing based on time or external events, and the definition of triggers for passive processing based on events caused by other components. We do not require, but also do not prohibit, the processing within the function of components to be adjustable in the same way. Thus, the processing of data for interface updates or execution of interactions may be coupled to or decoupled from the processing pattern of the function.

Example We modeled the tracker component (C1) in our scenario (c.f., Section 3.1.1) as an actively processing component that must be adapted to tie the requests to other components and the update of interfaces to the recording frequency of the depth camera, i.e., to the processing of the function. As a consequence, the component can be adapted to tie requests for emergency stops to machine components (C2, C3) with this frequency, i.e., the tracker component (C1) informs the machine components (C2, C3) as soon as possible through push communication. In addition, the tracker component (C1) should be adapted to provide information about tracked bodies and emergency stops at the interface. The provisioning of this information must be adapted to fit the requirements of the screen component (C5) that is not implemented by following our approach but is instead actively processing and capable of pulling the information from the respective resources of the tracker component (C1). Furthermore, the first machine component (C2), that is designed by following our approach, is passively processing, and should be adapted to inform its domain-specific function and the second machine (C3) as soon as requests for emergency stops occur.

3.2.1.3 Separation of Design, Adaptation, and Runtime

Our third requirement, with respect to the challenges related to Requirements Unawareness (c.f., Section 3.1.2.3) and Development Inefficiency (c.f., Section 3.1.2.4) in combination with the problem of Control Deployment (c.f., Section 3.1.2.6), is the *Separation of Design, Adaptation, and Runtime*. While we require the adaptability of interaction and processing, we are challenged by the support for this adaptability in multi-stakeholder situations, in which the design, provisioning, and integration are not completely in hands of the integrating stakeholder, who is aware of all requirements of the integration scenario, but rather in hands of different stakeholders. Consequently, we require that our approach enables the adaptability of interaction and processing in late stages, e.g., during the deployment or the runtime of components. Thereby, we require that our approach enables the design of components, which is decoupled from the adaptations that are deployed later in time.

Realizing domain-specific function during design time First, we require that the domain-specific function of components can be developed and implemented during design time. In particular, integration requirements should not force the design to be tailored and restricted to individual scenarios but be focused on the domain-specific function with broader applicability. Since every single requirement for the integration with other components is, in general, not known at design time, the architecture should provide the means necessary for enabling adaptations to these after development.

Declaring adaptations during deployment and runtime Second, we require that adaptations can be declared during deployment or, as advanced requirement, be declared during the runtime of components. In the latter case, means for adaptation should adhere to the same integration paradigms that we have chosen as preliminaries. The adaptations must be separated from the design to support the adaptation of components during the integration with other components in specific integration scenarios, which might be unknown at design time. Thereby, no modifications of the implementation of the domain-specific function should be required to support multi-stakeholder scenarios, in which the implementation of a component is not within the reach of the integrating stakeholder.

Separating processing from adaptation Third, we require that processing, passive or active, is separated from the actual adaptations. Adaptations may contain information about processing details but should not initiate processing via their deployment. Thereby, we enable a priori planning, creation, and deployment of adaptations and explicit transition to the participation of components in distributed applications, i.e., the runtime of the distributed applications. In addition, separate sets of adaptations for participation in different distributed applications may be supported, for which the adaptation can be individually deployed and the processing can be individually started or stopped. Hereby, we introduce separation of concerns with respect to the integration requirements of different applications.

Example All components in our integration scenario (c.f., Section 3.1.1) are designed independently from each other. In other words, the components have been developed before the integration scenario was known. While other components are not designed by following our approach but adhere to the integration paradigms, the tracker component (C1) and the first machine component (C2) support the adaptation of their interaction and processing at runtime. In our first integration step, we deploy all components at the factory floor, connect them to the network, and start the components, i.e., the components are at runtime. In our second integration step, we deploy the application logic (described in examples above) partially to the tracker component (C1), e.g., calculating security breaches and executing requests to the machine components (C2, C3), and to the first machine component (C2), e.g., informing the second machine component (C3) in case of issues.

3.2.2 Smart Component-based Integration Architecture

The fulfillment of the IoT vision and, in particular, the WoT vision requires the extension of the current Web with support that enables real-world objects, i.e., things, to seamlessly become part of the Web. In this context, we are challenged to take the next logical step beyond having only data semantics or only interconnected things in order to achieve a Web where real world objects can be seamlessly integrated. To achieve this evolution, we need to be able to harvest the combined value of several smaller things, by composing them into larger and distributed applications, which provide value-added function.

In Figure 3.4, we exemplify our integration architecture on the basis of our integration scenario (c.f., Section 3.1.1). This integration architecture includes, in general, components and, in detail, components that adhere to the integration paradigms (C3, C4, C5) as well as adaptable components that follow our Smart Component (SC) approach (C1, C2). In Section 3.2.3, we introduce the SC architecture in more detail. With the architecture of SCs, our goal is not to impose the one architecture for adaptable components. Instead we aim to provide a set of constraints and principles backed up by specific building blocks, that address the requirements, which we described in Section 3.2.1, and that are aligned with our integration architecture, that we describe in the following.

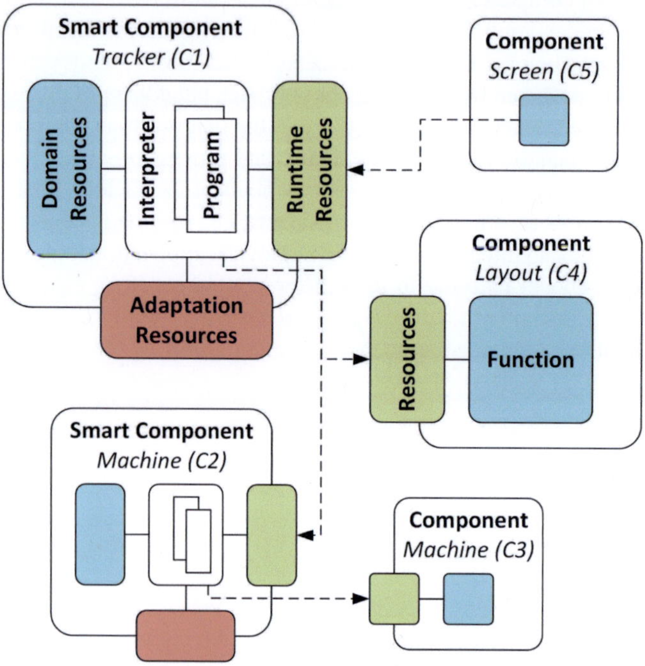

Figure 3.4: Smart Component-based Integration Architecture

Our approach for enabling distributed applications is based on introducing an abstraction for the convergence of all participating devices, data sources, algorithms, implemented capabilities, etc., in terms of components that provide resources and are accessible via uniform interfaces. These components can be composed into applications. In general, the components provide the same interaction capabilities, independently whether they following our SC approach or not. In particular, they provide interfaces and execute requests in the same way, i.e., they adhere to the same integration paradigms. Thereby, we enable the integration of several components by utilizing only a subset of SCs.

For example, in Figure 3.4, we utilize the tracker and machine SCs (C1, C2) and three other components (C3, C4, C5), that adhere to the integration paradigms, but are not following our approach. However, both SCs enable us to integrate all components into one application in this specific integration scenario. To provide support for a decentralized solution, without centralized computation or control, we introduce an interpretation layer between the domain-specific function of SCs, and the APIs, which they expose to the network. This layer enables, on the one hand, the adaptability of their interfaces and requests to the requirements of the specific integration scenarios and, on the other hand, the deployment of application logic, that is formalized as rules. The application logic can range from simple calculations to custom behavior or decisions, which can be reconfigured at both design time and runtime. We elaborate on the details of the SC architecture in Section 3.2.3. As a result, our component-based approach enables a flexible way to compose larger distributed applications.

3.2.2.1 Component

We introduce the abstraction of a *Component* (c.f., Section 2.3.1), which encapsulates certain domain-specific function. By integrating these domain-specific functions, we can compose distributed applications to achieve added-value. These domain-specific functions can range from pure data sets, e.g., the layout component (C4) of the factory floor with safety zones, to devices that dynamically produce data, e.g., the tracker component (C1), to systems that react to state changes, e.g., the machine components (C2, C3), which stop if their safety zones are violated.

The only common capability that we introduce for all types of components is their adherence to the integration paradigms that we introduced as foundations of our approach in Section 3.2. In particular, they must adhere to the REST and LD paradigms. Thereby, in the context of the IoT, WoT, and SWoT visions, the classical client and server roles are becoming inapplicable. We can build components that provide an API, with which other components interact, or we can build components, which interact with the APIs of other components, or we can build components, which include both. For example, a mobile device can have a client role by displaying information, e.g., a map or the current temperature, and at the same time act as a server, e.g., by providing the current geolocation, all in one scenario. Therefore, we do not distinguish between clients and servers, but whether components provide interfaces, execute requests, or show both capabilities. For example, in Figure 3.4, the layout component (C4) provides an interface, the screen component (C5) executes requests to the tracker component (C1), and the tracker component (C1) executes requests and provides an interface.

In addition, we differentiate between actively processing components, which independently update the resources at their interfaces or execute requests to other components, and passively processing components, which require preceding requests from other components of the same application before they can update the resources at their interfaces or execute requests (c.f., Section 2.3.5). For example, the screen component (C5) must be actively processing, as the component is not providing an interface but only executing requests. This execution of requests may be triggered by time, the frequency of the screen hardware, or by external events, but is not triggered through requests from other components. In contrast, the tracker component (C1) may update the resources at its interface actively with every new image of the included depth camera, i.e., independently from other components, or only on demand, e.g., if requested by the screen component (C5).

3.2.3 Smart Component

We introduce the notion of a *Smart Component (SC)*, when a component is following our architectural approach for building adaptable components. In Figure 3.5, we give an overview of the high-level architecture of SCs. The use of "smart" as a way to characterize certain features is currently very common and a bit overused. However, it captures very well the properties of SCs that we want to highlight, namely the encapsulation of autonomous application logic and the adaptability of interfaces, requests, and processing.

We take advantage of the resource-oriented viewpoint within the REST architectural paradigm. Resources expose relevant parts of the state of SCs to the network, identified by URIs and accessible as well as modifiable through HTTP. Remote components may interact with the resources of SCs, to react to the local states of the SCs or to transition the SCs into new states. The HTTP communication with resources is stateless and the resources may be grouped as sub-resources of container resources. Thereby, container resources conceptually contain a set of sub-resources and follow a defined behavior for accessing and modifying this set, as, for example, specified by the LDP specification.

We do not make the assumption that all components of applications need to be SCs or that all devices must offer REST interfaces directly. For certain use cases, it makes more sense to take custom implementations, including highly specialized protocols, as they are, and to encapsulate them to expose their resources through a RWLD API. In this way we enable the overall integration, while the interactions behind the encapsulating interface remain invisible.

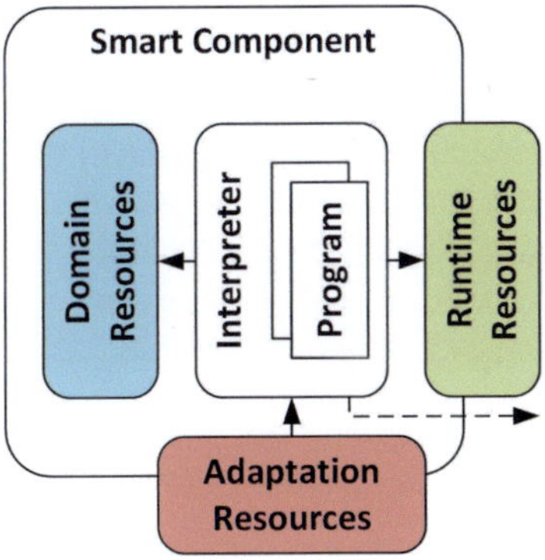

Figure 3.5: Smart Component – High-level Architecture

3.2.3.1 High-level Architecture of Smart Components

The high-level architecture of SCs includes a set of *Resources*, which provide state representations adhering to the RDF model and can be available only internally or be exposed as part of the interface. Therefore, we distinguish between *Domain Resources*, *Runtime Resources*, and *Adaptation Resources*.

Domain Resource (DR) DRs encapsulate domain-specific data and function that is custom to SCs and represent parts of their states. By accessing or modifying DRs, we can get the states of SCs or can cause the systems to react by changing their states through resource modifications. However, these resources are only accessible internally and are, following our black box approach, not identifiable or accessible in a way that is prescribed by our integration architecture.

Runtime Resource (RR) RRs are part of the public API of SCs and are exposed to the network. RRs adhere to both architectural paradigms, LD and REST, i.e., they are identified by URIs, accessible by HTTP with interaction restricted to HTTP verbs, and, by default, represented according to RDF. We declare these resources as graph patterns that define which part of the DRs should be exposed over the public interface. With respect to the LDP specification, RRs may also provide non-RDF representations that are linked by associated RDF RRs. As part of the public API, the RRs can be accessed or modified by other components.

Adaptation Resource (AR) ARs are part of the public API of SCs and are exposed to the network. ARs provide the means for adaptation of the SCs. By interacting with these resources, we are able to access and modify both the definition of RRs as well as the rules defining the decentralized application logic of the SCs.

Every SC encapsulates an *Interpreter* that provides the capabilities to 1) access and manipulate the state of DRs, 2) access and manipulate the state of resources of other components, 3) evaluate graph patterns of RRs, and 4) interpret decentralized application logic written in a declarative rule language. In other words, the purpose of the interpreter is to negotiate between the private API of a component, represented by DRs, the public API of a component, represented by RRs, and the interaction with resources provided by other components.

We specify the decentralized application logic within a component as a set of rules that we refer to as *Program*. The declarative rule language, in which these programs are defined, provides adequate means to express RDF graph transformations, inferencing, and interactions with resources of other components. Optionally, the language may support, in coordination with the interpreter, further capabilities to ease the declaration of programs, e.g., built-in mathematical functions for calculations, which exceed pure rule-based logic.

We call the actual interpretation of a program and evaluation of triple patterns by the interpreter a *Run*. During a run, the interpreter maintains an internal RDF graph with all states of known resources. This RDF graph is enriched 1) by the states of DRs, 2) by requested states of RRs, and 3) by inferred knowledge.

The integration of the interpreter and the DRs, i.e., the encapsulated domain-specific data and function, is seen as part of the black box within the component.

3.2.3.2 Detailed Architecture of Smart Components

In the following, we introduce the detailed architecture of our SC approach in Figure 3.6 that enables SCs with adaptable interfaces, interactions, and processing, provides sufficient technical soundness, and satisfies our requirements.

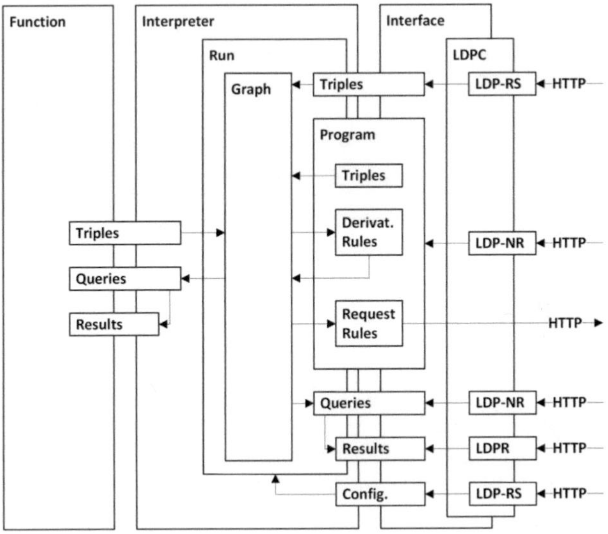

Figure 3.6: Smart Component – Architecture

Separation of Concerns In the architecture diagram in Figure 3.7, we distinguish between function, interpreter, and interface as the three major layers of the SC architecture. These layers provide *Separation of Concerns* with respect to the domain-specific function of SCs and the interface of SCs, which these provide to other components. The negotiation between these layers, e.g., calculations, decisions, adaptations of resources provided at the interface, or adaptations of requests, that SCs execute as part of the different compositions of applications, is taken over by the interpreter layer.

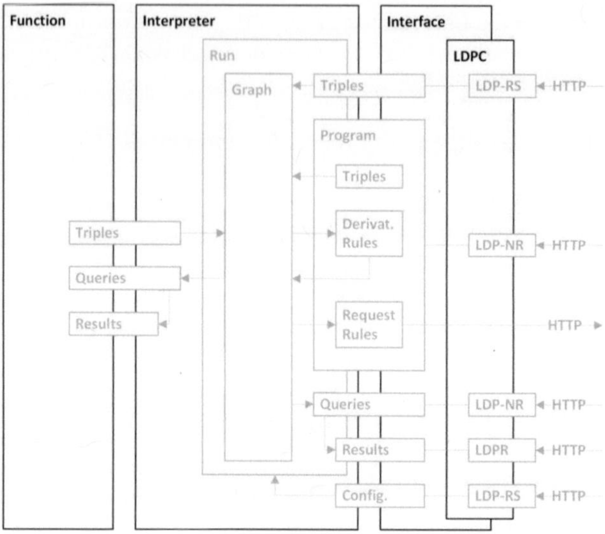

Figure 3.7: Smart Component – Architecture: Separation of Concerns

Function With the function layer, we denote all local domain-specific function of the SCs. Thereby, SCs may provide relatively simple, e.g., in the case of temperature sensors, or advanced function, e.g., in the case of data storage. In addition, SCs may integrate other domain-specific interaction and processing mechanisms, but, with respect to our chosen integration architecture, we show only the relevant details. The only requirement, which the domain-specific function must adhere to, is the lifting and lowering of data – provisioning of relevant information in RDF to the interpreter layer, in case of lifting and, in case of lowering, the provisioning of queries declared in SPARQL and the processing of their results.

Interpreter With the interpreter layer, we denote an evaluation engine that supports the evaluation of N3 [26] rule programs and SPARQL queries. During every evaluation run, the interpreter maintains an internal RDF graph that is enriched with information provided by the domain-specific function, by resources exposed at the interface, and by calculations of the rule programs. The rules contained in the N3 rule programs are iteratively evaluated against this internal RDF graph until a fix point is reached, i.e., until an enrichment of the graph leads to no additional execution of rules. Finally, the SPARQL queries are evaluated against the state of the RDF graph at this fix point and their results are propagated to the local domain-specific function or are exposed as resources to the interface.

Interface With the interface layer, we denote an API that is compliant with the LDP specification and is exposed by SCs to the network. At the root, i.e., the entry URI of the interface, an LDPC, e.g., an LDP-BC, forms the base container for the creation, manipulation, and deletion of resources via HTTP interactions over the network. Thereby, we enable, on the one hand, the creation and manipulation of triples and the access to query results. On the other hand, we enable adaptation of the SCs by creating and manipulating programs, queries, and configurations. These are each represented by LDPRs, depending on their data model as LDP-RS, e.g., in the case of triples and configurations, or as LDP-NR, e.g., in the case of N3 rule programs and SPARQL queries. These resources are members of the base container or optional subordinated containers. With respect to the provisioning of resources in general, our architecture does not prohibit but also does not require to have additional LDPRs, which provide direct access to domain-specific functions, i.e., additional static interfaces.

As defined in our SC-based integration architecture, components adhering to this architecture provide interfaces to the network that adhere, by default, to the LD and REST paradigms, and, if they follow our approach, are compliant with the LDP recommendation. Thereby, we satisfy the requirement Compliance with Integration Paradigms (c.f., Section 3.2.1.1). Since we have chosen the Linked Data and REST, incorporated by the LDP recommendation, as common integration paradigms and architecture, we, thereby, provide a solution for challenges of the problems Communication Heterogeneity (c.f., Section 3.1.2.1) and Information Heterogeneity (c.f., Section 3.1.2.2).

Declaration of Adaptations In our architecture diagram in Figure 3.8, we utilize triples and queries for integrating the domain-specific function and the interpreter of SCs. Thereby, we enable, on the one hand, internal data flows of information from the function to the interpreter. In addition, we enable internal data flows of information, which is provided as a result of the interpretation of queries, from the interpreter to the function. On the other hand, we utilize programs, queries, and configurations for the adaptation of the interpreter and the integration with other components. These adaptations are exposed as resources at the LDP interface, i.e., the ARs (c.f., Section 3.2.3), and enable the application-specific adaptation of SCs through the network and based on the function, but independently in terms of time.

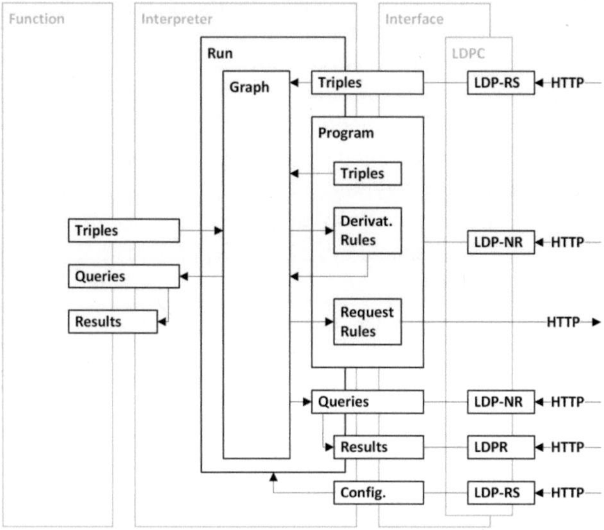

Figure 3.8: Smart Component – Architecture: Declarations of Adaptations

Triples To prevent confusion with the internal RDF graph, which is maintained by the interpreter for every evaluation of programs and queries, we denote all further RDF graphs as triples (c.f., Section 2.2.2.1). Relevant information about the current state of SCs is provided as triples by the domain-specific function. Furthermore, additional information adhering to the RDF data model can be created as LDP-RS at the LDP interface by using RDF serialization formats.

Queries With SPARQL queries (c.f., Section 2.2.2.2), we provide the means for selecting subsets of information stored in the internal RDF graph of the interpreter at the end of every evaluation, i.e., at the fix points. On the one hand, we enable the selection of information, which is relevant for the functioning of the component. Developers predefine these queries during the design of SCs, provide these to the interpreter, and, thereby, encode relevant information needs that influence the internal state of their SCs at runtime. On the other hand, we enable the creation of queries as LDP-NR at the LDP interface, i.e., as ARs (c.f., Section 3.2.3). In this case, the query results are exposed as LDPR, more precisely as LDP-NR for table-based content types of results or as LDP-RS for RDF results.

```
@prefix rdf: <http://www.w3.org/1999/02/22-rdf-syntax-ns#> .
@prefix http: <http://www.w3.org/2011/http#> .
@prefix http-m: <http://www.w3.org/2011/http-methods#> .
@prefix ex: <http://example.local/vocab#> .

# Derivation rule
{ ex:foo ex:bar ?object . } => { ex:foooo ex:barrr ?object . } .

# Request rule
{
  ex:foooo ex:barrr ?object .
} => {
  [] http:mthd
    http-m:PUT ;
    http:requestURI <http://example.local/resource> ;
    http:body {
      <> ex:foobar ?object .
    } .
} .
```

Listing 3.3: Derivation and Request Rule Example

Programs By supporting the interpretation of N3 rule programs (c.f., Section 2.2.2.3), created as LDP-NR at the LDP interface, i.e., as ARs (c.f., Section 3.2.3), we add important adaptation capabilities. First, as a superset of RDF, N3 programs may contain static triples, e.g., configuration settings, which are added during each evaluation of the interpreter to the internal RDF graph. Second, with the help of derivation rules we enable the enrichment of the internal RDF graph. Thereby, we support, for example, transformation of annotations, reasoning, or complete entailment rule sets, e.g., for the RDFS or for the OWL-LD subset of the OWL. Third, with request rules, we treat rules differently from other rules, if their heads contain information about HTTP requests. This information about HTTP requests is annotated with the W3C HTTP Vocabulary [106]. Instead of enriching the internal RDF graph, the interpreter executes the described HTTP requests on the network and adds the payloads of their responses to the internal RDF graph. Thereby, we enable the declaration of HTTP requests as part of N3 rule programs. In Listing 3.3, we show simple examples for a derivation as well as a request rule. Optionally, we support built-in functions in N3 rule programs to ease certain tasks, e.g., the calculation of mathematical formulas without using external services.

Configuration With run configurations (in Figure 3.6 annotated with "Config.") we relate the aforementioned concepts in one LDP-RS, i.e., as ARs (c.f., Section 3.2.3). Every run configuration declares interpreter settings, programs and queries to be evaluated, resources for query results, and triggers. With the concept of triggers, we provide the means for specifying when the interpreter should evaluate programs and queries. We distinguish between active triggers, e.g., frequency, or delay, and passive triggers, e.g., on resource requested, on resource expired, or on resource changed. Aligned with our implementation of an adaptation layer (c.f., Section 3.3.1), we develop an adaptation ontology (c.f., Section 3.3.2) for the specification of these run configurations. In short, all aforementioned concepts can be annotated to declare run instances in RDF. Run configurations adhere to the RDF data model and can be created as LDP-RS at the LDP interface of the component with the aforementioned content types.

With the here described adaptation capabilities, we satisfy the requirement Adaptability of Interaction and Processing (c.f., Section 3.2.1.2). As we enable the adaptation of interfaces with queries, the adaptation of requests with request rules, and the adaptation of processing patterns with triggers, we, thereby, provide a solution for the challenges of the problems Communication Heterogeneity (c.f., Section 3.1.2.1) and Information Heterogeneity (c.f., Section 3.1.2.2) in combination with the problem Decentralized Control (c.f., Section 3.1.2.5).

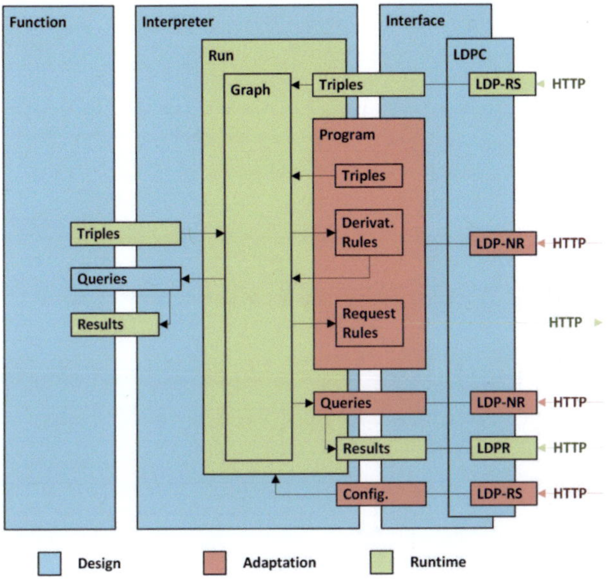

Figure 3.9: Smart Component – Architecture: Separation of Lifecycles

Separation of Lifecycles In the architecture diagram in Figure 3.9, we mark the elements of the SC architecture in different colors that indicate their assignment to corresponding distinct steps in the lifecycle of SCs. In particular, blue elements of the architecture are assigned to the design phase, red elements are assigned to the adaptation phase, and green elements are assigned to the runtime phase. By explicitly considering these distinct phases in our architecture, we enable the separation of the lifecycle of SCs from the lifecycle of applications, in whose compositions the SCs participate, i.e., the design and deployment of SCs is decoupled from the design, deployment, and runtime of a distributed application (c.f., Section 2.3).

In a simplified manner, we visualize both lifecycles in Figure 3.10. Thereby, vertically connected phases are, in general, time-wise aligned. In particular, the deployment phase of an application aligns with the adaptation of SCs, which is realized by deploying triples, programs, and queries as resources at their LDP interfaces, i.e., as ARs (c.f., Section 3.2.3). Subsequently, when the runs of the SCs are started, i.e., the interpretation of programs and queries, the SCs enter their runtime phase and also the related distributed application transits to the runtime phase.

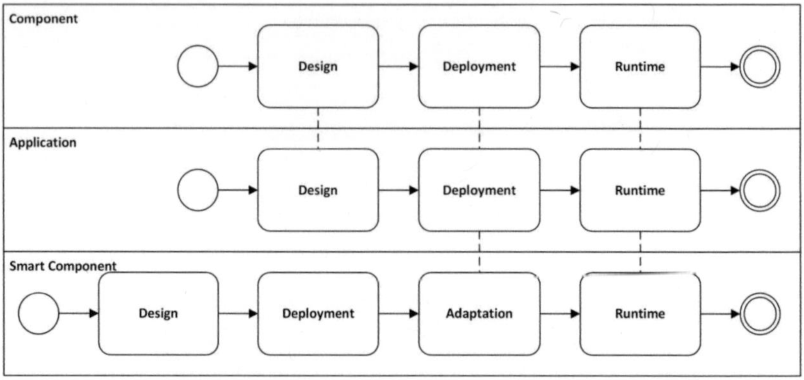

Figure 3.10: Smart Component – Lifecycles of Applications, Components, and Smart Components

Design We mark the elements, which are designed and implemented by the original developer of a SC, in blue. These are, in particular, the domain-specific function of the SC, the integration of the interpreter with the domain-specific function, which is realized by providing RDF and SPARQL queries to the interpreter, and the access to the adaptation capabilities of the interpreter by providing an LDP interface. In Figure 3.10, this phase is the first phase in the lifecycle of SCs.

Adaptation We mark the elements of the adaptation phase in red. These are deployed by integrating stakeholders with respect to distributed applications, based on the requirements of their specific integration scenarios. On the one hand, for the adaptation through their LDP interfaces, the SCs must be deployed and running to provide these interfaces. In this state, the SCs themselves are started, but not yet part of any composition of a distributed application. Once the interpreter runs are started, the SCs are, passively or actively, part of the runtime of the respective distributed applications.

For greater usability, adaptations may be stored in a persistent manner, i.e., adaptations survive the stops and restarts of the components. This will, on the other hand, enable the deployment of adaptations as part of the deployment of SCs, i.e., adaptations are added a priori to the SCs and are already available when the SCs are started. However, our architecture does not specify or prohibit the persistence of adaptations. In Figure 3.10, this phase is the third phase of the lifecycle of SCs. The SCs can be adapted during or after their deployment, i.e., the second phase in Figure 3.10, thus while the SCs are already running but only provide the LDP interface for deploying ARs (c.f., Section 3.2.3).

Runtime We mark the elements of the runtime phase, which are available during the interpreter runs, in green. The runtime is the phase when components participate in distributed applications via requests to other components, which are declared as request rules during adaptation, or by providing interfaces to other components, declared as queries during adaptation. However, we did not specify the transition from these adaptations to the actual interpreter runs, i.e., participation in distributed applications. In order to be compliant with the LDP recommendation, we enable transitions from declared run configurations to run instances by executing the HTTP POST method on the resources of run configurations at the LDP interface. In particular, the LDP recommendation states for LDPRs with respect to support for the HTTP POST method:

> "Per [RFC7231], this HTTP method is optional and this specification does not require LDP servers to support it. When a LDP server supports this method, this specification imposes no new requirements for LDPRs." [150]

As stated by the LDP recommendation, HTTP POST is explicitly not restricted for LDPRs, and, thereby, not for LDP-NRs and LDP-RSs, but only for LDPCs and its variants. For LDPCs, the recommendation specifies manipulation of resource collections through HTTP POST. An interpreter run is instantiated based on a run configuration, if the HTTP POST method was executed at an LDP-RS, the LDP-RS contains a run configuration, and the contained run configuration is valid. An interpreter run is terminated, if the LDP-RS representing the run instance is deleted by executing the HTTP DELETE method. The location of this resource, i.e., its identifier, is part of the run configuration. For increased usability, the run state of the interpreters may be part of optional persistence and, thereby, enable recovery of states, e.g., automatic restarts of runs after stops and restarts of components.

With support for and distinction of the aforementioned three phases, starting with the design of components, moving on to the adaptation of components, and up to the runtime of components, we satisfy the requirement Separation of Design, Adaptation, and Runtime (c.f., Section 3.2.1.3). Since every step can be individually handled with respect to time, though still building upon each other, we also provide a solution for the challenges Requirements Unawareness (c.f., Section 3.1.2.3) and Development Inefficiency (c.f., Section 3.1.2.4) in combination with the problem Control Deployment (c.f., Section 3.1.2.6).

3.3 Implementation of the Smart Component Adaptation Framework

In the following, we provide an overview of relevant implementations with respect to our SC approach. In particular, we present in Section 3.3.1 the implementation of an adaptation layer, which provides a complete prototypical realization of our approach. In Section 3.3.2, we present an ontology to describe adaptations. In particular, the run configurations are annotated with this ontology and, thereby, declare the relationship between different programs, queries, and further resources. Finally, we present in Section 3.3.3 the integration of the adaptation layer with domain-specific functions. In particular, we present the implementation of a SC that provides body tracking capabilities as a domain-specific function and, thereby, serves as the basis for our functional evaluation in Section 3.4.1, aligned to our initial integration scenario.

3.3.1 Smart Component Adaptation Layer

With the *Smart Component Adaptation Layer (SCAL)*[1], we provide a prototypical implementation of our approach. SCAL is, on the one hand, a file system-based LDP server and, on the other hand, supports adaptation by inte-

[1] `https://rslv.link/ZSvE`

grating an interpreter for N3 rule programs and SPARQL queries that provides RWLD capabilities. In particular, the interpreter enables rule-triggered HTTP requests and querying of RDF payload in HTTP responses; thereby, it supports link following as well as decision making based on retrieved information.

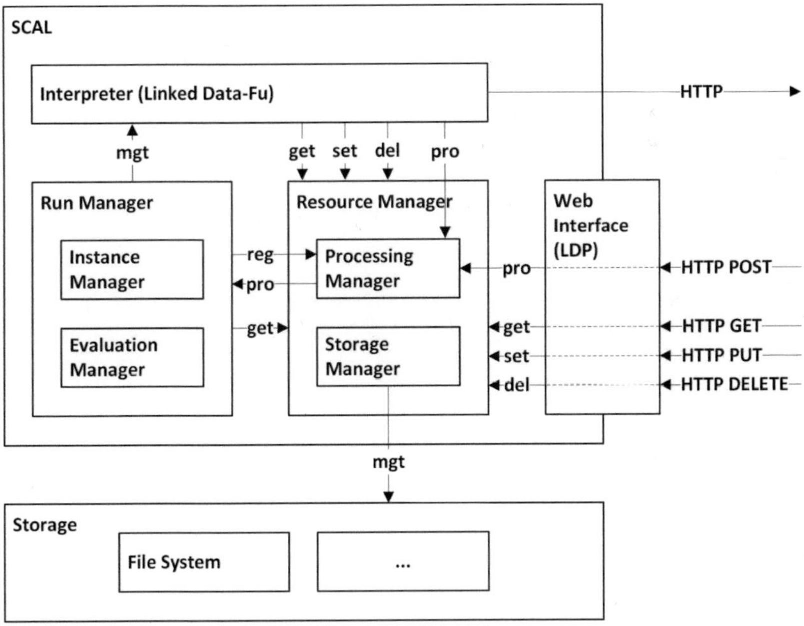

Figure 3.11: Smart Component Adaptation Layer

In Figure 3.11, we give an overview of the internal software architecture of this adaptation layer. The software architecture of SCAL consists, on the one hand, of the LDP server, which includes the LDP-compliant web interface, the resource manager that manages resources provided by the interface, and the storage that is utilized by the resource manager for persistence. On the other hand, the software architecture of SCAL consists of the Linked Data-Fu (LD-Fu) server, which extends the LDP server and includes the LD-Fu interpreter, the run manager that manages the interpreter in collaboration with the resource manager, and listeners registered at the LDP server for specific requests at the web interface.

3.3.1.1 Linked Data Platform Server

Our implementation of the SCAL is in its core based on an LDP server. The implementation supports different storage backends, the creation and modification of different LDPRs, and the nesting of LDPCs. Internally, the resources are managed independently from the LDP interface by a resources manager that, in addition, supports programmatic integration with other software libraries. A processing manager handles the registration of event listeners and, thereby, provides capabilities that are required by the run manager of the interpreter, e.g., the processing of HTTP POST requests by listeners, or the registration of on-request triggers. A storage manager provides persistent storage of resource representations and abstracts from the actual storage medium, e.g., the file system or a database.

Web Interface With the web interface, we provide an LDP-BC at the base of the exposed LDP interface of the adaptation layer. This LDP interface supports the creation and modification of LDP-RS, LDP-NR, and LDP-BC as well as nesting of containers. The web interface is designed in a light-weight manner and manages only the correct handling of HTTP requests and responses, including HTTP headers and response codes. Further handling of the payload, that is part of requests, or the provisioning of payload for answering requests is delegated to the resource manager, which we describe below. Furthermore, the decision about the support for specific HTTP methods with respect to requested resources is delegated.

Data Models and Formats Driven by the clear distinction between the RDF data model and RDF serialization formats, e.g., RDF/XML, Turtle, or JSON-LD, we support an extensible set of different data models and formats. On the one hand, this includes the parsing of different data formats to an appropriate object representation. Thereby, we parse data formats of the same data model to the same object representation. On the other hand, we support the serialization of information, which adheres to a specific data model, into one of its related data formats. We support, for example, different RDF serialization formats for reading and writing of resources at the LDP interface, or different table-based formats such as Comma Separated Values (CSV), or Tab Separated Values (TSV) for the serialization of SPARQL query results.

Data Model and Format Converters In addition to the support for parsing and serialization of data models and formats, we support on-the-fly conversion between different data models and formats. On the one hand, we support the, in most cases, lossless on-the-fly conversion between data formats of the same data model. On the other hand, the same technique can be utilized to convert between different data models and their respective data formats. However, this conversion may not be lossless. Thereby, we enable, for example, read and write access to LDP-RS, independently of the RDF serialization format of the stored representations, i.e., the same resource can be read and written with different RDF serialization formats.

Resource Manager At the core of the LDP server, we provide the resource manager, which serves as an abstraction for the handling of resources, i.e., the LDP interface as well as further integrated elements of the software architecture may interact with the stored resources. Hereby, these elements may create or manipulate resources that are accessible through the LDP interface at the network. For example, we utilize this abstraction to let the run manager of the interpreter get required resources, e.g., run configurations, programs, or queries, and, subsequently, setup a run of the interpreter.

Storage Manager As part of the resource manager, we provide the storage manager, which serves as an abstraction for the persistence of resources and thereby, enables separations of concerns. In particular, the resource manager must not be aware of any storage medium or access mechanisms. The access to or manipulation of persistently stored resources is delegated by the resource manager to the storage manager. By default, we support persistence based on a file system, i.e., LDP-BC form a directory structure and LDP-RS as well as LDP-NR are the files in this directory structure. However, several other storage media may be implemented, e.g., persistent storage based on databases.

Processing Manager As part of the resource manager, we provide, with the help of the processing manager, support for the explicit handling of data processing requests, e.g., handling HTTP POST requests at the LDP interface. Furthermore, the processing handler may redirect any other request targeted at the resource manager. In both cases, elements of the software architecture register listeners at the process manager, that provide a set of constraints to narrow the type of requests that are of interest, e.g., by specifying the HTTP method, or data model of the payload. For example, the run manager registers listeners for specific resource paths, if the run configuration includes on-request triggers for processing. Thereby, we enable passive processing.

3.3.1.2 Linked Data-Fu Server

On top of the LDP server, our SCAL implementation integrates an interpreter for N3 and SPARQL evaluation as well as HTTP request execution. The interpreter is managed by a separate run manager, which handles the setup of runs, the triggering of evaluation steps, and the integration with the resource manager.

Interpreter As interpreter, we build on Linked Data-Fu (LD-Fu)[2] [156, 158], an interpreter for N3 rule programs with SPARQL query capabilities. LD-Fu supports our requirements with respect to the evaluation of N3 rule programs and SPARQL queries, provides means for executing request rules, and supports mathematical operations with built-in functions.

Run Manager While the LD-Fu interpreter handles the program and query evaluation as well as HTTP requests, a run manager internally handles the interpreter runs and, partially, the triggering of evaluation steps. Therefore, the run manager registers listeners at the process manager for the handling of incoming HTTP POST requests on resources that contain run configurations. On HTTP POST requests, the run manager validates the run configuration and, if the configuration is valid, setups, starts, and stops interpreter runs as well as triggers evaluation steps during runs, with time-based or event-based triggers.

Web Interface Our SCAL implementation exposes a web interface to the network and is capable to execute HTTP request at the interfaces of other components. Thereby, the interface is the LDP interface of the LDP server, enhanced with SC capabilities. For adaptations that are

[2] `https://rslv.link/ZSvS`

deployed at the LDP interface and declare interactions, i.e., N3 programs that include request rules, the LD-Fu interpreter handles the requests to interfaces of other components.

3.3.1.3 Integration

We support different means for the integration of SCAL with the domain-specific function of components. In detail, we support running SCAL standalone, i.e., integrating solely through HTTP requests, integration with the domain-specific function through the storage subsystem, or, as the most efficient option, programmatic integration as a software library. In the latter case, we support the direct programmatic registration of RDF sources and SPARQL queries by the domain functionality.

Standalone The SCAL implementation does not dependent on any domain-specific function. Therefore, SCAL may run in standalone mode and provide the LDP interface and adaptation capabilities. A standalone deployment supports cases, in which the SCAL implementation is used as centralized, coordinating component. In these cases, RDF data is only provided by other components and is retrieved and manipulated through HTTP requests.

Wrapper For the integration with existing domain-specific functions, SCAL can be integrated as a wrapper on top of existing LD or RWLD interfaces. In this case, SCAL runs alongside the component and redirects HTTP between the native interface of the component and other components, adapted to the requirements of the specific integration scenario. However, this form of integration may not perform as well as the direct programmatic integration as a library.

Library As the most interleaved and, in general, best performing integration, we support the integration of the SCAL implementation as a software library. In this case, the component must lift the domain-specific function to the RDF data model and provide relevant data to the adaptation layer. In addition, the component may provide SPARQL queries and integrate the processing and lowering of query results.

3.3.2 Smart Component Adaptation Ontology

In our SCAL implementation of the SC approach in Section 3.3.1, the run manager is responsible for handling HTTP POST requests, containing run configurations, to the LDP interfaces of resources. The run manager relies on the validity and semantics of the run configurations to setup in a correct manner the interpreter, triggers, and other related components, needed during the runtime of the SC. Therefore, we develop the *Smart Component Adaptation Ontology (SCAO)*[3] for the description of run configurations and tie the validity of run configurations to the ontology. This ontology describes, on the one hand, run configurations and, on the other hand, adheres to our integration paradigms by enabling the description of runs in RDF, i.e., run configurations are LDP-RSs at the LDPs interfaces of SCs that, optionally, link further LDP-NRs, e.g., N3 programs, or SPARQL queries. In Figure 3.12, we show and group relevant concepts of the SC approach, their relations, and indicate their data models or formats, but without showing all properties in detail. The RDF subset of concepts and relations is described by SCAO, while N3 and SPARQL resources are linked from run configurations that are annotated with SCAO.

In the following, we describe in short the different groups of concepts and relations, which are described by SCAO or linked in documents annotated with SCAO. These are in most cases, derived from the SC architecture that we described in Section 3.2.3.2.

> **Run** The run group of concepts and relations contains the core elements of the SC approach in RDF, including, runs, programs, queries, triggers, and resources, which are described by SCAO. Thereby, a run defines the uppermost element in a run configuration and may link to an arbitrary number of programs and queries. Neither of both is required, but at least one program or one query is included in non-trivial run configurations. In addition, at least one and up to several triggers are linked by a run, and these define the processing of the SC, i.e., the points in time, at which interpreters execute distinct steps of runs that evaluate programs and queries. Programs and queries in a run configuration link their declarations. In particular, programs link resources that contain N3 rule programs and queries link resources that contain SPARQL queries.

[3] `https://rslv.link/ZSvf`

Triggers in a run configuration may directly include their declaration described in RDF with SCAO. In addition to their declaration, specified queries link one or several resource descriptions, that specify the location and means for access, which are the sinks for query results. In the same way, the run itself links to locations that should be updated with a description of its state during an actual running interpretation of the run. The descriptions of resources in a run configuration may directly include their declaration described in RDF with SCAO.

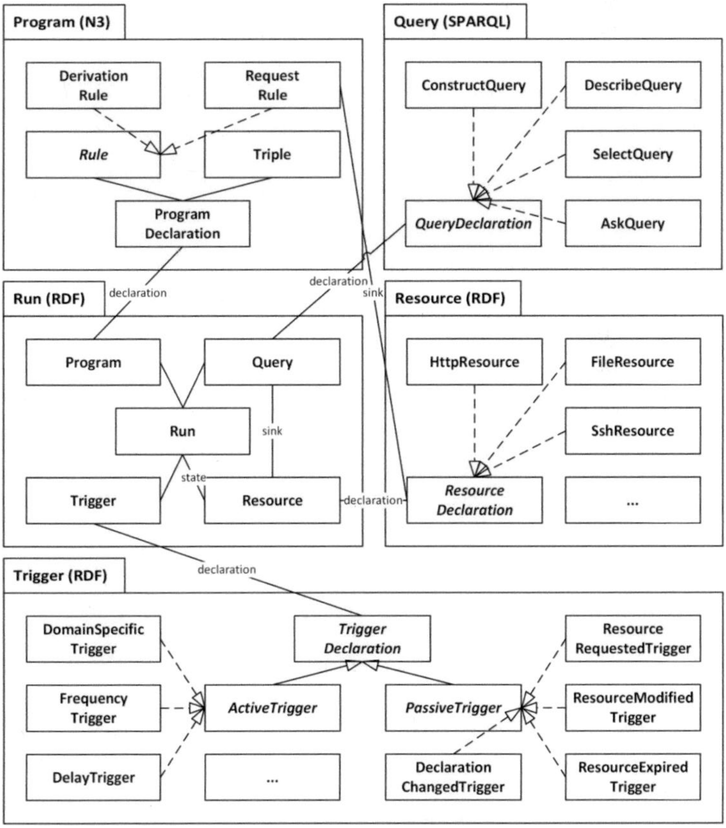

Figure 3.12: Smart Component Adaptation Ontology

Program The program group of concepts and relations contains the elements of program declarations in N3, including, triples, deduction rules, and request rules. These programs are specified by the W3C [26] (c.f., Section 2.2.2.3) and, with respect to the interpretation of vocabularies that describe HTTP requests and mathematical operations, by the work on LD-Fu [156, 158]. As a superset of N-Triples and Turtle, N3 program declarations may contain an arbitrary number of RDF triples. In addition, programs may contain an arbitrary number of derivation and request rules. In the latter case, the request rules specify the sink of their request that, implicitly, equals our specification of resources in SCAO.

Query The query group of concepts and relations contains the declaration of queries in SPARQL, which are referenced by the query concept in a run group. These queries are specified by the W3C [6] (c.f., Section 2.2.2.2). The query declaration may have one of the supported types, i.e., construct, describe, select, or ask query. However, only in the cases of construct and describe queries, the result is guaranteed to adhere to the RDF data model.

Trigger The trigger group of concepts and relations contains the declaration of triggers in RDF, which are described by SCAO and are referenced by the trigger concept in the run group. We distinguish between active and passive triggers that lead to the active and passive processing of SCAL with respect to other components of a distributed application. In the set of active triggers, the domain-specific trigger enables the domain-specific function, if properly integrated with SCAL, to trigger the processing. In addition, the time-based frequency and delay triggers setup active processing by keeping a defined time between the starts of subsequent steps of a run for a frequency, and between the last stop and next start of steps of a run for a delay. In the set of passive triggers, we feature different event-based triggers that are related to the interaction with or the state of resources. However, the set of supported triggers is neither complete nor completely implemented by the prototypical implementation of SCAL and thus is extensible in the future.

Resource The resource group of concepts and relations contains the declaration of resources in RDF, which are described by SCAO and are referenced by different concepts in the run group. In the prototypical implementation of SCAL, we support the definition of resources at the local LDP interface as the sink for query results or the state of the executed run. In our adaptation ontology, we generalize the concept of resources beyond local resources, which are accessible through HTTP. While this is still the default, the resources may not be part of the local interface and require additional description of HTTP methods. In addition, other protocols may be supported to describe more advanced integration capabilities of the SCAL implementation. However, the set of supported resources is neither complete nor completely implemented by the prototypical implementation of SCAL and thus is extensible in the future.

With the prototypical SCAL implementation in combination with SCAO as ontology to describe runs, trigger declarations, and resource declarations, with N3 to describe the declaration of programs, and with SPARQL to describe the declaration of queries, we provide a set of technologies that implements the SC approach.

3.3.3 NIREST Smart Component

In the following, we present the implementation of *Natural Interaction via REST (NIREST)*[4], a SC implementation that encapsulates body tracking capabilities as a domain-specific function. In Figure 3.13 we show the integrated visualization of Point of Interests (POIs) data and a representation of a tracked body, which has been deployed and integrated as a demonstration use case. The image on the right is a visualization of the depth video image that the depth video camera provides. The recognized shape of a person is highlighted in green by the body tracking algorithms. In addition, the tracked skeleton is visualized with lines, spanned between the coordinates of the tracked joint points. In the image on the left, the NIREST SC has been integrated with a second component that provides a use case in a Virtual Reality (VR). In particular, the body tracking information is utilized to visualize the skeleton of tracked people on a virtual map that contains POIs. In this way people can walk around and explore the map. In addition, different gestures are recognized and trigger certain behavior, e.g., to reset the map, or to display additional information

[4] `https://rslv.link/ZSv6`

about the visited POIs, which is requested on demand and subsequently visualized. In this demonstration use case, the SC capabilities enable this integration scenario, by adapting the interaction between the components, and by adapting the application logic for matching coordinates. In the functional evaluation in Section 3.4.1, we provide a detailed example and different types of adaptations, based on NIREST and aligned with our scenario.

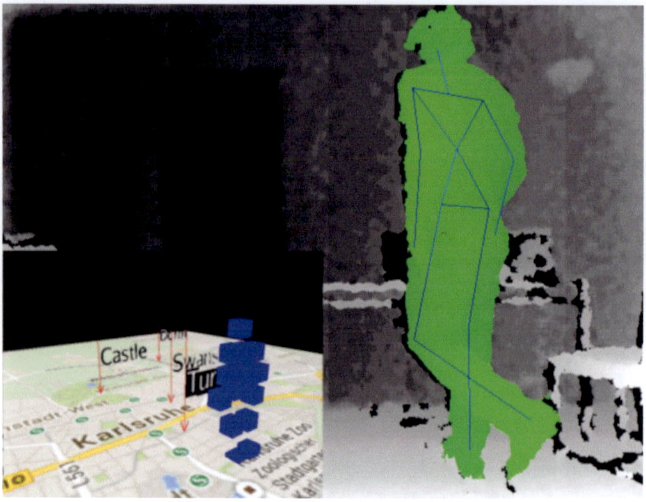

Figure 3.13: Domain-specific Smart Component

The implementation of NIREST combines different technologies to provide access to sensor details, recognized persons, and skeleton coordinates, which are extracted on-the-fly from a depth video sensor. With respect to hardware, NIREST requires a depth video camera connected to the system that provides the NIREST software. We utilize specialized frameworks as a hardware abstraction layer between the sensor hardware and the middleware libraries or applications, which enable the unified access to the sensor hardware, e.g., to color video, depth video, sensor metadata, or device events. Building on top, we integrate a middleware that accesses the depth video provided by the hardware abstraction layer and implements different tracking algorithms. Thereby, we gain access to the tracking algorithms that support the recognition of objects in front of the sensors. In addition, the algorithms provide the coordinates of the derived skeleton joints as well as basic support for gestures. Finally, the acquired information is annotated, lifted to the RDF data model, and provided to the interpreter.

In order to enable SC capabilities on top of the body tracking capabilities of NIREST, we integrate SCAL as adaption layer with the body tracking as the domain-specific function. Thereby, SCAL handles all interaction of NIREST with respect to other components on the network. The information about tracked bodies, e.g., coordinates of joints, center of masses, or confidence values for coordinates, that have been lifted to RDF, are provided to the interpreter of SCAL. In addition, we couple the processing of SCAL to the frequency of the depth video camera as an additional domain-specific trigger for active processing. After deployment, the NIREST SC is running, tracks persons in range of the depth camera, and provides an LDP interface to the network, that enables the deployment of adaptations and, thereby, the integration with other components.

3.4 Evaluation

We provide a thorough evaluation of our approach and implementation based on our evaluation scenario in Figure 3.14, which is a simplified version our motivation scenario in Figure 3.1 and, subsequently, in Figure 3.4. In this scenario, we consider the tracker SC (C1), the first machine SC (C2), and the second machine component (C3). On the left side we visualize the distributed application, which we compose first, where the first machine SC (C2) informs itself trough pull interaction and reacts to distance alarms provided by the tracker SC (C1). On the right side, in a second step, we re-adapt the application by switching from pull to push communication and by moving decisions partially to the first machine SC (C2), which, in addition, informs the second machine component (C3) through push interaction.

We evaluate the functional capabilities of our approach in Section 3.4.1, including the conformance to our design requirements, and the performance aspects of our implementation in Section 3.4.2. In particular, we show the adaptability of SCs with respect to: 1) their processing by declaring application logic; 2) their interfaces by declaring information to be exposed as runtime resources; 3) their requests by declaring a pull-based data flow; and 4) their interpreter runs by declaring the composition. Subsequently, we show the separation of the adaptation and runtime phases, and the re-adaptation of SCs. In addition, we evaluate the conformity of our SC architecture with respect to the design requirements in Section 3.2.1. Finally, we provide performance measurements with respect to the overhead of the adaptation layer and reference a large-scale evaluation scenario related to our distributed benchmarking environment (presented in Chapter 5), which is implemented by utilizing our SC approach.

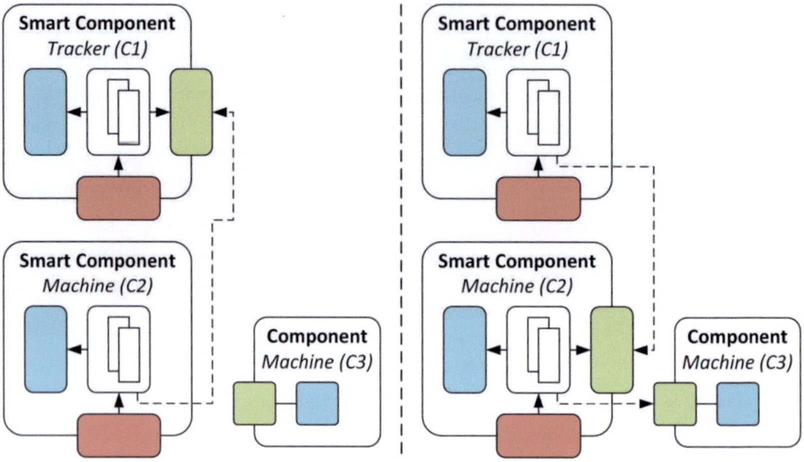

Figure 3.14: Evaluation Scenario

3.4.1 Evaluation of Function

We assume that the components are already deployed and started, but neither provide the data nor the communication that is required by our evaluation scenario, i.e., the components are not aware of any application logic, interfaces, or requests, that are specific to our evaluation scenario. The tracker and the first machine SCs provide their adaptation interfaces as entry points for adaptation at "https://c1.local/" (C1) and "http://c2.local/" (C2). In addition, the second machine component (C3), which is a regular component that supports the integration paradigms, provides a RWLD interface at "http://c3.local/". The SCs provide at their entry point an LDPC, in particular, an LDP-BC. Thereby, SCs enable the creation of sub-resources and sub-containers, that may contain AR and RR (c.f., Section 3.2.3.1). Every resource that contains triples, programs, or queries, and that is created as sub-resource of these containers, can be included by a run configuration in the evaluation during interpreter runs.

In the following section, we provide tables that include all HTTP requests needed to deploy an AR at the interfaces, in order to deploy the required adaptation. We specify for each command the identifier, i.e., the target URI, the method, i.e., HTTP verb, the content type, and, optionally, the payload, that is sent to the target URI as part of the request. These commands may be executed by any HTTP-conform client.

3.4.1.1 Domain Resources

```
@prefix rdf: <http://www.w3.org/1999/02/22-rdf-syntax-ns#> .
@prefix xsd: <http://www.w3.org/2001/XMLSchema#> .
@prefix nirest: <https://vocab.local/nirest#> .

</skeleton/0>
  nirest:skeleton [
    nirest:jointPoint [
      nirest:coordinate [
      nirest:x "459.8463"^^xsd:float ;
      nirest:y "404.0497"^^xsd:float ;
      nirest:z "2037.2391"^^xsd:float ;
      a nirest:Coordinate ] ;
    a nirest:RightHandJointPoint ] ;
  # ...
```

Listing 3.4: Domain Resources of the Tracker Smart Component (C1)

In Listing 3.4, we show a snippet of the RDF, which the domain-specific function of the tracker SC (C1) provides as DR to the adaptation layer. The integrated tracking algorithms recognize people in the depth video images, who are in range of the depth video camera. Once recognized, the algorithms calculate the coordinates of the center of mass, of the different joint points, and, in addition, also determine the confidence values for each of these coordinates.

In the listing, we show in Turtle serialization the coordinates of the right hand joint in the tracked skeleton of a person. The right hand joint is only one out of several supported joints, the remainder of which we omit in our listing due to space constraints. The skeleton is identified by an internal URI that is not exposed to the network. This information of the skeleton, joined with the information of all other tracked skeletons, is provided as DR to the adaptation layer. Subsequently, this information is included in the internal knowledge graph that is maintained during every interpreter run of the tracker SC. In the following, due to space constraints, we omit prefixes in listings and tables, which contain RDF or SPARQL.

3.4.1.2 Processing Adaptation

<table>
<tr><td rowspan="2">#</td><td>Identifier</td><td>Method</td><td>Content Type</td></tr>
<tr><td colspan="3">Payload</td></tr>
<tr><td rowspan="2">01</td><td>https://c1.local/program-distance</td><td>PUT</td><td>text/n3</td></tr>
<tr><td colspan="3"><pre>{ ?point nirest:coordinate ?coordinate .
  ?coordinate nirest:x ?x ; nirest:y ?y ; nirest:z ?z .
  (?x "2") math:exponentiation ?x_ex .
  (?y "2") math:exponentiation ?y_ex .
  (?z "2") math:exponentiation ?z_ex .
  (?x_ex ?y_ex ?z_ex) math:sum ?sum .
  ?sum math:sqrt ?square_root .
  ?square_root math:lessThan "1000.0" .
} => {
  ?point scenario:distance ?square_root .
  ?point scenario:alarm "true" . } .</pre></td></tr>
</table>

Table 3.1: Processing Adaptation of the Tracker Smart Component (C1)

In order to adapt the application logic of the tracker SC (C1) to our evaluation scenario, we interact with the LDPC of the SC and create a sub-resource with a rule program, identified by "`https://c1.local/program-distance`", as shown in Command #01 in Table 3.1. The N3 rule program, included in the payload, contains a single rule, which calculates the Euclidean distance from the sensor to each coordinate that has been included from the DR into the internal RDF knowledge graph of the interpreter. Therefore, in the body of the rule, the coordinates of every joint are matched with their three dimensions and their values are bound to variables, independently from the type of joint. Next, we use built-in mathematical functions interpreted by the LD-Fu engine, which calculate the results and bind them to additional variables. Once the condition that the distance is less than 1000 millimeters is true, the internal RDF graph is enriched with a triple, adding the distance as well as a custom alarm triple to the sub-graph of the respective point. As a consequence to this rule, we mark all joint points that are within the given distance of the tracker SC (C1) with a custom alarm during every evaluation of the interpreter. In the following, we are now able to use this information in further rules and queries.

3.4.1.3 Interface Adaptation

<table>
<tr><td rowspan="2">#</td><td>Identifier</td><td>Method</td><td>Content Type</td></tr>
<tr><td colspan="3">Payload</td></tr>
<tr><td rowspan="2">02</td><td>https://c1.local/query-alarm</td><td>PUT</td><td>application/sparql-query</td></tr>
<tr><td colspan="3">CONSTRUCT {
?point scenario:stop "true" .
} WHERE {
?point scenario:alarm "true" . }</td></tr>
</table>

Table 3.2: Interface Adaptation of the Tracker Smart Component (C1)

With respect to the first step of our evaluation scenario, we need to establish communication between the SCs. In particular, the first machine SC (C2) should request information about emergency stops, which the tracker SC (C1) provides. Therefore, we adapt the tracker SC (C1) to provide RR for passive provisioning of information about alarms. The RR is based on a AR, in particular, a SPARQL query, which is created as a sub-resource of the LDP-BC by Command #02 in Table 3.2 and is identified by the URI "`http:`

`//c1.local/query-alarm`". The SPARQL CONSTRUCT query, that we include as payload, constructs a custom stop triple if the internal RDF graph has been enriched by the N3 rule program, i.e., the N3 rule program in Table 3.1 has marked sub-graphs of joints with an alarm triple.

During every evaluation of the interpreter, the SPARQL CONSTRUCT query is evaluated. The RR, where we provide the query result for external HTTP requests, is declared by the run configuration described in Section 3.4.1.5. Once the interpreter run is started, the result is provided for any valid content type of a supported RDF serialization format, which is determined by the accept header of the HTTP GET request at the RR.

3.4.1.4 Request Adaptation

In addition to the interface of the tracker SC (C1), which we adapted in Section 3.4.1.3, we also need to establish the data flow to the first machine SC (C2). Therefore, we adapt the application logic of the first machine SC (C2) by adding a request rule deployed within a N3 rule program, which requests the information from the RR at the interface of the tracker SC (C1) that provides the information about emergency stops.

#	Identifier	Method	Content Type
	Payload		
03	https://c2.local/program-request	PUT	text/n3
	{ [] http:mthd httpm:GET ; http:requestURI <http://c1.local/result–alarm> . } .		

Table 3.3: Request Adaptation of the Machine Smart Component (C2)

The Command #03 in Table 3.3 includes this program as payload, which is identified by the URI "`https://c2.local/program-request`". The single rule included in the program is a head-only rule, i.e., no condition in the rule body has to be met and the head is executed during every evaluation of the program. We use specific ontologies to annotate the HTTP requests, in particular, marked by the prefixes "http" and "httpm". HTTP requests described in this way, are interpreted by the LD-Fu engine as HTTP commands and are executed as HTTP requests, instead of adding the rule head to the internal RDF graph. However, if the answers to requests include valid RDF, the payload is added to the internal RDF graph of the current interpreter run and may be subject to further rules.

In our case, we instruct the interpreter of the first machine SC (C2) to issue a HTTP GET request to the content of the RR of the tracker SC (C1), identified by the URI "`https://c1.local/result-alarm`", during every run and add it to the internal RDF graph. Thereby, the data flow between the tracker SC (C1) and the first machine SC (C2) is established in a pull-based manner, as required by the first version of the evaluation scenario.

We do not explicitly show how information about an emergency stop is internally handled by the first machine SC (C2). This may be, for example, analogously solved by a query added during design time and registered by the domain-specific function at the interpreter, that causes the machine to react appropriately if the information about an emergency stop is available.

3.4.1.5 Run Adaptation

With the adaptations of application logic, of interfaces, and of requests in Sections 3.4.1.2, 3.4.1.3, and 3.4.1.4, we declared different adaptations of the SCs, but did not declare their interplay with respect to the distributed application in our evaluation scenario. We declare this interplay with run configurations, that define which adaptations of the SCs should be evaluated by interpreters and which triggers lead to these evaluations. Hereby, a run represents the run of an interpreter that may include triples of different resources, and evaluate a set of programs and queries in one or several evaluation steps, that are again triggered by the domain-specific function, time, or events caused by other components. By supporting function-based, time-based as well as event-based evaluation steps, we enable both the active and passive processing for SCs. With the distinction of separately configured interpreter runs, we support the separately evaluated sets of triples, programs, and queries. Thereby, we enable the participation of SCs in multiple compositions of independently distributed applications at the same time.

<table>
<tr><th rowspan="2">#</th><th>Identifier</th><th>Method</th><th>Content Type</th></tr>
<tr><th colspan="3">Payload</th></tr>
<tr><td rowspan="2">04</td><td>https://c1.local/run</td><td>PUT</td><td>text/turtle</td></tr>
<tr><td colspan="3"><> a sc:Run ;
  sc:state <run–state> ;
  sc:program [a sc:Program ;
    sc:declaration <program–distance>] ;
  sc:query [a sc:Query ;
    sc:declaration <query–alarm> ;
    sc:sink <result–alarm>] ;
  sc:trigger a sc:Trigger, sc:DomainSpecificTrigger .</td></tr>
<tr><td rowspan="2">05</td><td>https://c2.local/run</td><td>PUT</td><td>text/turtle</td></tr>
<tr><td colspan="3"><> a sc:Run ;
  sc:state <run–state> ;
  sc:program [a sc:Program ;
    sc:declaration <program–request>] ;
  sc:trigger [a sc:Trigger, sc:DelayTrigger ;
    sc:delay "100"] .</td></tr>
</table>

Table 3.4: Run Adaptation of the Smart Components (C1, C2)

The Commands #04 and #05 in Table 3.4 show these run adaptations for the tracker SC (C1) and for the first machine SC (C2). Both commands create resources that contain run configurations, identified by `http://c1.local/run` for the tracker SC (C1) and by `http://c2.local/run` for the first machine SC (C2). The processing of the tracker SC (C1) is actively triggered by the domain-specific function, i.e., is bound to the frequency of the depth camera. Therefore, we declare no additional triggers but only the inclusion of the program `<program-distance>`, that calculates the distance of joints as well as the query `<query-alarm>`, with the query results to be provided at `<result-alarm>`. The processing of the first machine SC (C2) is declared to be triggered with a fixed frequency of 100 milliseconds. For the evaluation, during every interpreter step, the program `<program-request>` is declared and it executes the requests to retrieve information from the query result resources at the tracker SC (C1). In both programs, the URIs of resources are relative to the base URI of the SCs.

3.4.1.6 Runtime Switch

In Section 3.2.3.2, we described the separation of the different lifecycles in our architecture. In addition to the separation of the design time and the adaptation time of SCs, also the time of adaptation is separated from the runtime of SCs, with respect to the compositions of distributed applications, in which they participate. In particular, the switch from adaptations of SCs to their active or passive participation in distributed applications is supported by HTTP POST requests on resources that contain their run configuration, which is compliant with the overall LDP conformity of the interface.

#	Identifier	Method	Content Type
	Payload		
06	https://c1.local/run	POST	
07	https://c2.local/run	POST	

Table 3.5: Switch of the Smart Components (C1, C2) to Runtime

In Section 3.4.1.5, we described the run configurations of the tracker SC (C1) and of the first machine SC (C2), which declare the interplay of different adaptations as well as processing triggers, i.e., the declarative configuration of the adaptation layer. In Table 3.5, we show the Commands #06 and #07 that instruct both SCs to evaluate their run configurations and, if these are valid, to start with the declared interpretation of programs and queries. Thereby, both SCs switch to active processing – the tracker SC (C1) triggered by the domain-specific function, i.e., the depth camera, and the first machine SC (C2) triggered by time.

3.4.1.7 Re-adaptation

To show the flexibility of our approach, we re-adapt the distributed application at runtime to new requirements. Instead of pulling information about emergency stops from the tracker SC (C1), the first machine SC (C2) should get informed as soon as a distance alarm is recognized. Furthermore, the first machine SC (C2) should decide by itself to inform a subcomponent – the second machine SC (C2), if the distance is less than half of the original threshold. We show the commands used for the adaptation in Tables 3.6 and 3.7.

#	Identifier	Method	Content Type
	Payload		
08	https://c1.local/program-request	PUT	text/n3

	{ ?point scenario:alarm "true" ; scenario:distance ?distance .
	} => {
	[] http:mthd http−m:PUT ;
	http:requestURI <http://c2.local/alarm> ;
	http:body {
	<> scenario:alarm "true" ;
	scenario:threshold "1000.0" ;
	scenario:distance ?distance . } . } .		

09	https://c1.local/run	PUT	text/turtle
	<> a sc:Run ; sc:state <run−state> ; sc:program [a sc:Program ; sc:declaration <program−distance>] , [a sc:Program ; sc:declaration <program−request>] ; sc:trigger a sc:Trigger, sc:DomainSpecificTrigger .		
10	https://c1.local/query-alarm	DELETE	
11	https://c1.local/run-state	DELETE	
12	https://c1.local/run	POST	

Table 3.6: Re-adaptation of the Tracker Smart Component (C1)

First, we re-adapt the tracker SC (C1) as shown in Command #08 to #12 in Table 3.6. Therefore, we deploy in Command #08 a separate program with a single interaction rule, that is identified by the URI `https://c1.local/`

`program-request`. With this request rule, we replace the pull-based interaction of the first machine SC (C2) by a push-based interaction of the tracker SC (C1). The body of the rule is valid if a distance alarm is available in the internal RDF graph, which is calculated by the derivation rule in Section 3.4.1.2. In this case, the head of the rule is evaluated, which instructs the interpreter to execute a HTTP PUT request to the interface of the first machine SC (C2). In the payload, we include, in addition to the alarm, the current distance of the related joint as well as the threshold information, which has been used to calculate the alarm. The HTTP PUT request causes the interpreter of the first machine SC (C2), due to an on-request trigger, to add the given RDF payload to the internal RDF graph and include it in the next evaluation step of all programs and queries. Optionally, we can delete the obsolete query resource, which we created for the first version of our evaluation scenario, as shown in Command #10. Finally, in Command #11 and #12, we stop the current run of the tracker SC (C1) and start it based on the new run configuration.

Second, we re-adapt the first machine SC (C2) as shown in Command #13 to #16 in Table 3.7. Therefore, we update in Command #13 the program at the URI `https://c2.local/program-request`, which contained the pull request to the tracker SC (C1) in the first version of our evaluation scenario. The new program contains again a request rule, but this time with a constraining body that is valid if information about an alarm, the related threshold, and the related distance is available. In addition, the threshold is divided by two and the distance must be less than this new threshold to validate the body. Therefore, we reuse the distance that has been configured for the tracker SC (C1), has been transferred alongside the distance alarms to the first machine SC (C2), and, in consequence, is available in the internal RDF graph of the first machine SC (C2). In the head of the rule, we declare a HTTP PUT request to the static interface of the second machine component (C3) at `https://c3.local/static` that is compliant with our integration paradigms. Once the condition is true, the rule head is evaluated by the interpreter, which then executes the HTTP request and informs the second machine component (C3). Finally, in Command #15 and #16, we stop the current run of the first machine SC (C2) and start it, based on the new run configuration.

In comparison to the first version of our evaluation scenario, in the second version we switched from pull-based to push-based communication, split the decision logic, and distributed this logic to two SCs.

#	Identifier	Method	Content Type
	Payload		
13	https://c2.local/program-request	PUT	text/n3

	{ ?point scenario:alarm "true" ;
	scenario:threshold ?threshold ;
	scenario:distance ?distance .
	(?threshold "2") math:quotient ?quotient .
	?distance math:lessThan ?quotient .
	} => {
	[] http:mthd http−m:PUT ;
	http:requestURI <https://c3.local/static> ;
	http:body {
	<> scenario:stop "true" . } . } .		

14	https://c2.local/run	PUT	text/turtle
	<> a sc:Run ; sc:state <run−state> ; sc:program [a sc:Program ; sc:declaration <program−request>] ; sc:trigger [a sc:Trigger, sc:ResourceRequestedTrigger ; sc:uri <alarm> ; sc:method "PUT"] .		
15	https://c2.local/run-state	DELETE	
16	https://c2.local/run	POST	

Table 3.7: Re-adaptation of the Machine Smart Component (C2)

3.4.1.8 Requirements Conformity

Our approach and implementation are based on components, which are an abstraction that we introduce to overcome device heterogeneity (SWoT-RQ1). Furthermore, we support uniform interfaces and integration by relying on the REST and LD paradigms (SWoT-RQ2). Similarly, we use semantic representations for the interfaces and data exchange in order to overcome data heterogeneity (SWoT-RQ3). The approach of having distributed logic, within each component, supports distributed computation and control (SWoT-RQ4). Finally, we enable the key features of robustness, adaptation, and reconfiguration by providing interfaces and internal logic that can be reconfigured both at design and runtime (SWoT-RQ5). In addition, we also provide prototypical software implementation in order to evaluate the feasibility of our approach, e.g., SCAL as implementation of the SC approach based on the LD-Fu interpreter and declarative rule language (SWoT-RQ8).

3.4.2 Evaluation of Performance

In this section we describe the results of the performance evaluation tests. In particular, we show that the overhead, required for the implementation of our approach, does not result in significant processing delays. Thus the use of SCs does not hinder the implementation of distributed applications in terms of effecting the performance negatively.

3.4.2.1 Interpreter Overhead

We focus on measuring the processing overhead caused by the interpreter instance and program runs. In Figure 3.15 we visualize the measurements for the interpreter runtimes for our scenario example. We performed the experiments on an, at the time of measurements, average computer, in particular, an Intel Core i7-3520M CPU 2.90GHz 16GB RAM. During interpreter runs with 100 consecutive steps, i.e., consecutive evaluations by the interpreter, with 100ms delay between the steps, we measured the duration of running an instance without programs or declared resources (ins), and sequentially added the calculation program (ins/cal), the declared resource (ins/cal/res), and the interaction program (ins/cal/res/int). The diagram on the left shows the measured durations, without the actual execution of the HTTP interaction. In the diagram on the right, we include the HTTP interaction to a host on the same machine (ins/cal/res/int (http)). Despite some outliers, the duration for an instance without programs or declared resources (ins) is about 0.4ms (median: 0.42ms), and the duration for an instance with programs and resources is about 0.9ms (median: 0.86ms, 0.83ms, and 0.89ms). Finally the measured duration with executed local HTTP interaction is about 6.6ms (median: 6.63ms). Therefore, the overall overhead of using smart components results in minimal delays.

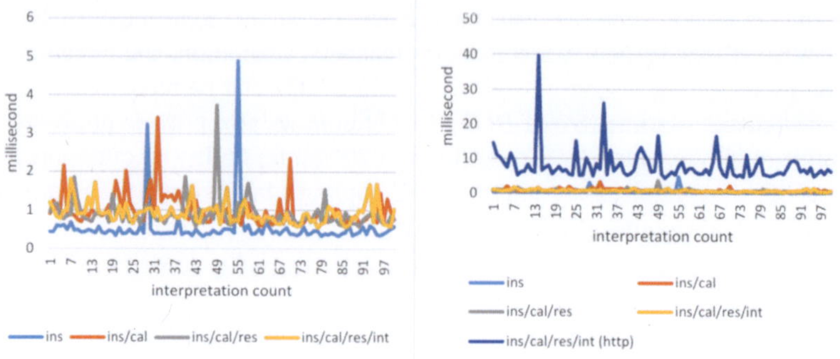

Figure 3.15: Runtimes of Interpretations: HTTP Interaction Excluded/Included

3.4.2.2 Distributed Benchmark

In addition to the overhead of the interpreter, which is focused on a single SC, we utilized our approach and prototypical SCAL implementation for the setup of larger experiments in Chapter 5. The results of these experiments are presented during the evaluation of distributed benchmarking in Section 5.4.2. In particular, we use the Distributed LUBM (DLUBM), our distributed benchmark environment for LD query engines, in combination with our SCAL implementation to deploy DLUBM setups based on SCs. Thereby, we enable the deployment of query evaluation in a centralized as well as two decentralized ways and, based on the setup, compare the query evaluation performance in these settings.

3.5 Summary

Technology trends lead to an increase in the complexity of handling the integration of heterogeneous components as part of distributed applications. We witness these integration difficulties not only at data and protocol level, but also at application level. Therefore, supporting integration in multi-stakeholder scenarios requires new architectural approaches for adapting components, while building on existing technologies and thus ensuring broader acceptance. We focus on two main aspects: overcoming not only data but also device and interface heterogeneity, and enabling adaptable and scalable decentralized applications. To this end, we use semantics to capture the domain-specific capabilities and rules to enable the embedding of controlling logic within the interfaces of components for supporting decentralized solutions. We introduce the concept of a SC that provides an abstraction level, which supports the unified handling of devices, data sources, functions, etc., all participating in integrated distributed applications. We support the reconfiguration of the controlling logic at runtime to provide options for customizing and adapting the applications. Furthermore, we show how our approach can be applied by introducing a reference architecture that we back up by a specific framework implementation. We believe that providing support for interoperability but also offering simple mechanisms for adapting the interfaces and controlling logic of components are key for contributing towards the evolution of the Web.

4 Interaction Optimization and Mapping

In this chapter, we present our work on the optimization of data flows and on mapping interactions between architectures in distributed applications. We use our contributions on decentralized control in Chapter 3 as a foundation for developing the here presented solutions. In particular, we focus on three main areas: 1) we elaborate on the challenges that arise from non-optimal interaction patterns between components that are characterized by different frequencies for providing and consuming data; 2) we explore the architecture of an established and broadly available distributed system – Robot Operating System (ROS), and focus on the challenges that arise from including non-compliant system components into our integration architecture; and 3) we provide solutions for both of these areas supported by the SC approach as well as exemplary implementations.

In the following, we first introduce the context of our work on interaction optimization and mapping, and present a motivation scenario. Next, we describe the specific challenges that we aim to address and provide a detailed problem analysis. For both problem areas, we derive requirements for our solutions. Based on these requirements, we provide: 1) a frequency-based algorithm for optimizing pull and push interaction patterns, and 2) a mapping of concepts and interactions between ROS and our integration architecture. Based on our application scenario, we demonstrate the practical applicability of our approach by presenting an exemplary implementation. Finally, we conclude with a short evaluation and show the applicability of the algorithm on our application scenario.

The content of this chapter is partially based on the publications by Keppmann et al. [103, 101, 100].

4.1 Introduction

Recent years are marked by the widespread use and adoption of mobile devices and smart sensors, as well as by the increasing modularization and distribution of formerly monolithic systems. These technology developments accompany visions such as the IoT [66, 9], the WoT [167, 72, 70, 68], and the SWoT [143, 128], as well as related visions such as the I4.0 [109, 86]. At the same time, new application use cases based on Web technologies emerge, which no longer involve mainly central servers and various clients but, instead, include several heterogeneous devices. Thereby, these developments influence the evolution of the Web [18, 25, 28], the SW [30, 29, 146], and the WoD [33, 32]. While the devices become smaller and smarter, they reveal at the same time new and changed characteristics and trade-offs, e.g., in terms of energy consumption, computing power, network connection, bandwidth availability, or dynamic and static data provisioning. For example, the modularization and distribution of applications based on Web and SW technologies in the area of video sensors, tracking, augmented reality, and virtual reality is only one of the recent developments in industry and research [16]. The integration of local and remote, mobile and stationary devices into one distributed application has become achievable and at the same time raises new challenges.

In particular, the characteristics of new mobile and sensor-based application areas, but also the modularization of formerly monolithic systems through Web and SW technologies, differ from traditional Web scenarios, since they rely to a greater extent on the communication and the data integration between several components in a network. These applications are more complex in terms of distribution, modularization, and integration. In addition, the classical server and client roles become obsolete. For instance, it is common that the components, which are part of compositions in distributed applications play multiple roles. For example, components may have the role of data source, data sink, controller, processor, or multiple of the aforementioned roles. In addition, components are complemented by diverse characteristics. For example, components may represent standalone and embedded devices, energy-efficient low-cost single-board computers and high performance servers, or mobile and network attached devices. Distributed applications are composed out of these components in order to provide value-added function, while individual components may be part of multiple distributed applications. In addition to establishing the data flows and data integration within a composition of components, also the efficient realization of the required interactions between components is challenging.

Furthermore, the visions of a pervasive IoT, WoT, and SWoT require the integration of heterogeneous software and hardware. Whenever it comes to making architectural decisions, there is a trade off between the general applicability of the architecture for increased independence of specific domains and the development of specialized architectures that may be more efficient for domain-specific use cases. In this context, we advocate an approach that supports the development of specialized solutions by enabling their subsequent integration in a broader context that is facilitated by rather domain-independent integration architectures. However, this integration of architectures is challenging, particular to domain-specific architectures, and may bring trade-offs in terms of efficiency and function.

In Chapter 3, we based the composition of components into distributed applications, their means for interaction, their representation of information, and subsequently our SC approach on an integration architecture based on the REST [64] and LD [23, 33] paradigms. The REST paradigm unifies the view on components and restricts their interaction mechanisms to a fixed set of common methods. As a consequences of restricting the interaction of components, the paradigm eases their integration. The LD paradigm introduces SWT for cross-domain semantic interoperability and enables, in combination with the REST paradigm as RWLD, the integration of components into distributed applications in a heterogeneous software landscape. The increasing popularity of these paradigms and broad availability of their utilized technologies led to the development of the LDP [150] specification. In the following, these paradigms and their technologies represent the common integration architecture that we utilize to illustrate the identified challenges as well as our approaches and solutions.

Based on our integration architecture and with respect to the efficient realization of the interaction within compositions of components, we focus on the problems that result from having different interaction patterns for establishing the data flows. The current shift away from the classical server and client roles has implications on this interaction between components. The traditional Web architecture assumes a request/response model, where clients establish the connection to servers. However, currently more and more integration scenarios assume multiple roles per component. This leads to situations, in which the role for establishing the communication is no longer mainly assigned to clients. In particular, we can select between different interaction patterns, e.g., pull and push interaction patterns, to establish the same data flows between components. While both push and pull interactions can enable the data flow between two components, one may be less efficient in terms of optimal data transmission, latency times, or bandwidth use.

With respect to investigating the integration of domain-specific architectures with our integration architecture, we focus on the problems that arise from the integration of the domain-specific ROS [132] architecture. In the field of robotics, the ROS architecture is a key player for the efficient integration of modularized robotic systems. While specialized robotic components would require custom implementations and solutions for their efficient integration, ROS enables an overall unified communication and handling of the systems in this domain. The result is an isolated group of interconnected domain-specific components that can communicate in a unified way, since they conform to the ROS architecture. However, these robotic systems are increasingly used in a broader context, for instance for developing flight and cockpit simulators, that benefit from the use of specialized hardware and software components. In these cases, the advantages of a domain-independent integration architecture may outweigh the advantages of a domain-specific architecture. While the implementation of the integration architecture at every specialized component is an option, a more generic approach can be realized by creating mappings between both architectures via proxy components that provide the capability of participating in applications of both worlds and enable cross-architecture data flows. However, the mapping of the architectural elements as well as of the exchanged information is effort and time-consuming. Thus pervasive integration scenarios, as promoted by the IoT, WoT, and SWoT, can benefit from specialized architectures (e.g., ROS) for specific use cases in combination with Web-scale architectures (e.g., adhering to the REST and LD paradigms), which are capable of overcoming the heterogeneity.

4.1.1 Scenario

We exemplify the challenges with a sample scenario, which we derive from our scenario on monitoring factory floors in Section 3.1.1. Here, we change some of the components and focus on specific, more relevant characteristics. In Figure 4.1, we provide an overview of the monitoring application, which includes the components in its composition and the data flows between these components. In contrast to the initial scenario, enabling the value-added function of the application is not the primary aim. Instead, we focus on supporting the data flows as well as the rates, at which components can consume and produce data.

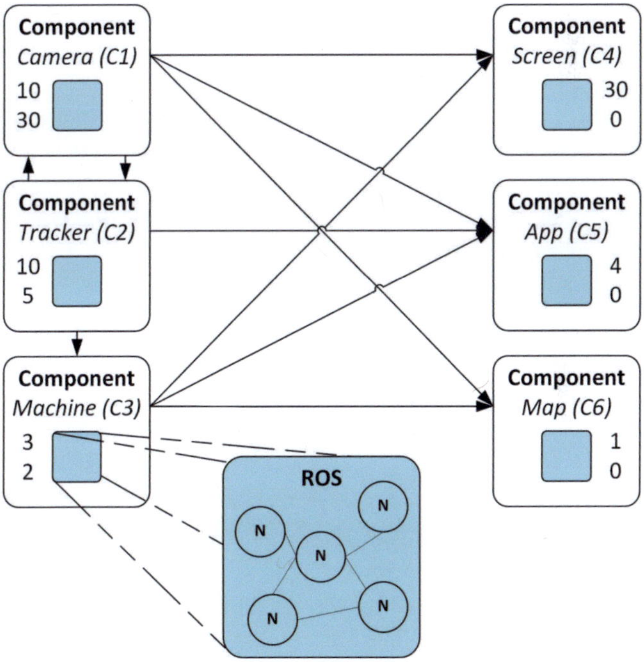

Figure 4.1: Scenario

In Figure 4.1, we indicate these rates by annotating the in- and out-frequencies of every component. In particular, the number at the top represents the in-frequency and the number at the bottom represents the out-frequency. Thereby, the in-frequencies stand for the rates, at which components are able to consume information from other components to execute their domain-specific functions. The out-frequencies stand for the rates, at which components provide updated information, based on their domain-specific functions, to other components. In order to simplify the scenario, all components actively process based on time, i.e., they provide stable in- and out-frequencies. In addition to the data flows and frequencies, the machine component (C3) represents a distributed ROS application that we indicate by zooming in on its domain-specific function, which is in turn, again a distributed ROS application.

In the following, we describe the components of the composition, including their domain-specific functions and the frequencies, at which they can provide or consume information.

Camera (C1) The *camera* component (C1) is a depth video camera that provides thirty times per second new color and depth images, i.e., at a frequency of 30 hertz (Hz). At the same time, the depth video camera processes tracking information and follows the position of tracked people in the room. To follow a person, the camera reacts every 100 milliseconds (ms), i.e., at a frequency of 10 Hz, to new position coordinates by adjusting the angle of its electric motor.

Tracker (C2) The *tracker* component (C2) is a low-cost single-board computer that is connected to the network, and provides body tracking and position coordinates of recognized people. It is can analyze ten times per second the depth video images provided by the camera component, i.e., at a frequency of 10 Hz. Furthermore, the applied algorithm processes these images and provides every 200 ms, i.e., at a frequency of 5 Hz, tracking information about recognized people.

Machine (C3) The *machine* component (C3) represents a factory machine and provides two times per second, i.e., at a frequency of 2 Hz, the current state of the machine, including, e.g., its current operating state, the power consumption of an engine, or the speed of a conveyor. In addition, the machine component supports three times per seconds the emergency stop of its moving parts, i.e., at a rate of 3 Hz. In contrast to the black-box approach towards describing the domain-specific functions of the other components, we provide details on the function of the machine component. The different parts of the machine are managed by utilizing the ROS architecture. In particular, the different parts appear as ROS nodes that are connected through a network and collaborate via different elements that are provided by the ROS architecture.

Screen (C4) The *screen* component (C4) visualizes to human users the color images of the camera component as well as the state of the machine component and updates this visualization thirty times per second, i.e., at a rate of 30 Hz. The screen component provides no information to other components.

App (C5) The *app* component (C5) is a mobile app on a smartphone or a tablet that shows the color video provided by the camera component as well as the state of the machine component and updates four times per second, i.e., at a frequency of 4 Hz, as a trade-off between energy consumption and update rate. In addition, the app alarms human users whenever the tracker component recognizes that there is a breach of the security zone of the machine component. No information is provided by the app component to other components.

Map (C6) The map component (C6) is a Web-based map that provides an overview of the factory floor to human users, including the state of the machine component and the current video provided by the camera component. Due to a low user-driven access rate, the overview updates once every second, i.e., at a rate of 1 Hz. No information is provided by the map component to other components.

4.1.2 Challenges

The allocation of multiple roles to components in distributed applications as well as the inclusion of domain-specific, specialized architectures pose new challenges on the realization of data flows between components as well as across architectural borders. With respect to the realization of data flows between components, we face challenges that relate to the selection and implementation of interaction patterns (c.f., Interaction Inefficiency in Section 4.1.2.1; Meta-interaction Patterns in Section 4.1.2.2). Furthermore, in the context of realizing the data flows between a common integration architecture and domain-specific, specialized architectures, we face typical data integration challenges but on the level of architectures (c.f., Non-compliant Communication in Section 4.1.2.3; Non-compliant Representation in Section 4.1.2.4). In the following, we discuss these challenges in more detail.

4.1.2.1 Interaction Inefficiency

With respect to the realization of data flows between components, we are challenged with the problem of *Interaction Inefficiency*. The components participating in the composition of distributed applications collaborate by exchanging information between each other and, thereby, provide the value-added function of the application. To realize these data flows based on our integration architecture, the components interact by executing requests and receiving responses. However, this interaction is not guaranteed to be efficient in every case. Several factors may hamper the optimal interaction, e.g., bandwidth limitations, insufficient computing power, unstable network connectivity, or bad design that leads to denial of service situation. One basic factor that we focus on, is the interaction pattern that components use to realize their data flows. Thereby, we differentiate between the *pull* interaction pattern and the *push* interaction pattern. Both interaction patterns are capable of enabling the same data flows. In the case of a pull, the information is requested by the sink components from the source components, which send the information as the payload of the responses. In the case of a push, the information is sent as the payload of the requests from the source components to the sink components, which confirm the receipt via responses. In some cases, the combination of both patterns in one request-response pair may be beneficial. In addition, the selection of interaction patterns is again influenced by different factors. For example, some of these factors include: latency requirements, payload size, bandwidth limitations, or the frequencies, at which components can consume or provide data. In the following, we focus on the data consumption/provisioning frequencies. For example, the camera component (C1) can consume information about tracked people at a rate of 10 Hz and provides depth and color video images at a rate of 30 Hz. In summary, choosing the right interaction pattern during the design and, in particular, in dynamic situations – at runtime, is challenging.

4.1.2.2 Meta-interaction Patterns

Related to the aforementioned problem of Interaction Inefficiency and, especially, in the context of dynamically changing situations, we are facing the problem of *Meta-interaction Patterns*. In application use cases, in which the situation of components and data flows, as well as the factors that influence the selection of interaction patterns are rather static, we can optimize the interaction with respect to these factors during the design of applications. However, in non-static application use cases, we are challenged with the optimization of interactions at runtime. On the one hand, if the final data flows are not completely determined a priori but at runtime, e.g., if components are added and removed on-the-fly, the optimal interaction patterns must be determined at runtime. On the other hand, even if all data flows are predetermined and the initial selection of interaction patterns is optimal for the initial situation, the factors that influence the choice of interaction patterns may change over time and subsequently lead to non-optimal interaction. In this case, the choice of interaction patterns must be re-evaluated at runtime to adjust the non-optimal interaction patterns. For example, the app component (C5) in our scenario in Section 4.1.1 could appear multiple times, as part of a larger variant of the scenario. The app components track people, who enter the monitored area, and expose their individually configured update rates for the visualization. In this case, the optimization of the data flows from the camera component (C1), the tracker component (C2), and the machine component (C3) must be realized during the runtime of the distributed application.

Therefore, we are challenged to provide support of appropriate meta-interaction patterns that enable components to influence not only their actively executed requests but also the behavior of other components with respect to their interaction. Our integration architecture, which is based on the REST and LD paradigms and, subsequently, on the LDP implementation, does not include explicit and standardized concepts that provide support for meta-interaction. As a consequence, the handling of meta-interaction remains a challenge and needs to be addressed separately.

4.1.2.3 Non-compliant Communication

With respect to realizing data flows that cross the border between domain-specific, specialized architectures and our common integration architecture, we are challenged to address the *Non-compliant Communication* of information. In particular, we face problems that are similar to the communication integration challenges in a heterogeneous landscape of components (Section 3.1.2.1), which were one of the reasons for introducing a common integration architecture. However, here we focus on the integration of two different architectures within one distributed application. Therefore, the implementation of a common integration architecture on the level of all individual components is out of scope. Instead, we are confronted with the different interaction mechanisms of both architectures as well as with the deployment of proxy components that map these mechanisms and, thereby, enable the communication of components between both architectures. For example, the machine component (C3) encapsulates in its domain-specific function a distributed ROS application that manages the collaboration of the different machine parts. The ROS nodes in this application communicate through different interaction mechanisms that the ROS architecture provides, e.g., ROS topics, or ROS services. These interaction means are not compliant with our common integration architecture, i.e., with the REST-based interaction and transport based on HTTP. Further communication mismatches may occur in the utilized transport protocol, the supported interaction patterns, or the methods for access and manipulation. The mapping of interaction mechanisms and enabling of data flows across the borders of architectures are challenging tasks that needs to be addressed.

4.1.2.4 Non-compliant Representation

Similarly to the challenge of Non-compliant Communication, we are also challenged with the problem of *Non-compliant Representation* of information. In particular, we face problems related to the information integration in a heterogeneous landscape of components. We are confronted with different ways of modeling data and, if at all, of including the semantic meaning of data, which the components bring together. For example, the ROS nodes in the ROS application of the machine component (C3), exchange information that adheres to a relatively simple set of data types and ROS messages, composed of these data types. The ROS messages are not compliant with our common integration architecture – with the RDF data model and with representation in one of the RDF serialization formats. In the context of integrating two different architectures into one distributed application, the mapping of information representations in the data flows that cross the borders of architectures is challenging.

4.1.3 Contributions

With respect to the challenges presented in Section 4.1.2 and advancing the current state of the art, we make the following contributions:

- In Section 4.2.2 and Section 4.3.2, we conduct two *Requirements Analyses* with respect to the identified challenges for both the optimization of interactions with respect to frequencies and the interaction mapping between domain-specific architectures and our integration architecture.
- We present our *Frequency-based Network Model and Optimization Algorithm* for the optimization of pull and push interaction patters between components of distributed applications in Section 4.2.3.
- With the *ROS Architecture Mapping*, we present in Section 4.3.3 mapping between the domain-specific ROS architecture and our integration architecture based on the REST and LD paradigms.
- In Section 4.4, we describe the ROS-REST Proxy (ROEST) as our implementation of the mapping between the domain-specific ROS architecture and our integration architecture.
- Finally, we conduct an *Evaluation of Frequency-based Interaction Optimization* by applying the network model and optimization algorithm to our scenario in Section 4.5

4.2 Approach for Frequency-based Interaction Optimization

Our approach for realizing a frequency-based interaction optimization is guided by a set of requirements derived from the problem areas introduced in Section 4.1.2. With these requirements, we restrict the space of factors, which may influence the realization of data flows between components of distributed applications, to a small set that provides sufficient characteristics to show our approach and at the same time ease the understanding of our view on distributed applications. In the following, we first briefly introduce the optimization scenario as a subset of our overall scenario.

4.2.1 Optimization Scenario

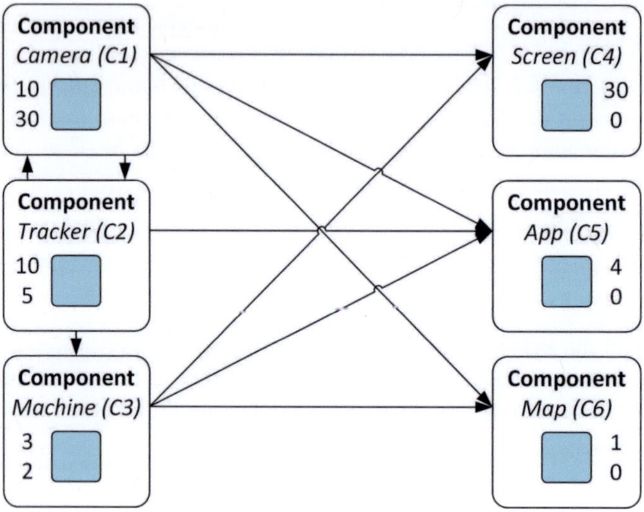

Figure 4.2: Optimization Scenario

The distributed application in our scenario is built out of a number of components that are connected to the same network and represent different devices and systems. In Figure 4.2, we show the relevant part of our scenario that includes all components, their in- and out-frequencies, as well as the data flows that they establish for their collaboration to provide the value-added function of the distributed application. In particular, the components on the left side represent a depth video camera, a tracker service at a low-cost computer, and a factory machine. On the right side, the components represent – a screen, a mobile app, and a map at a website, all of which visualize information for human users in different ways. Each component provides information for or consumes information from other components with different frequencies. In Figure 4.2, we annotate the components with the frequencies, with which they can consume data for their functions (number at the top) and the frequencies, with which components provide data based on their functions (number at the bottom). For the sake of simplicity, we use only processing components with stable time-based processing and limit the number of frequencies to one pair per component. However, our approach could also handle multiple pairs of frequencies per component – by treating these in distinct manner, and non-stable frequencies – by continuously reapplying our approach to the new situations.

4.2.2 Requirements

Based on the challenges that we introduced in Section 4.1.2, we derive a set of requirements for enabling interaction optimization.

4.2.2.1 Optimization of Interaction Patterns

Our first requirement, with respect to the challenges related to Interaction Inefficiency (c.f., Section 4.1.2.1), is the *Optimization of Interaction Patterns*. There are several factors that influence the efficiency of data flows between components, however, we focus in this approach on the pull and push interaction patterns. In addition, there are also several factors that influence the selection of these interaction patterns, and we focus on the frequencies, with which components can consume data from and provide data to other components. Therefore, we require that these frequencies are considered for the optimization of interaction patterns.

4.2.2.2 Provisioning of Metadata

Our second requirement, with respect to the challenges related to Interaction Inefficiency and Meta-interaction Patterns (c.f., Section 4.1.2.1 and 4.1.2.2) is the *Provisioning of Metadata*. As we pointed out, the optimization, e.g., of the interaction patterns between components in a distributed application, requires optimization-specific metadata, e.g., the in- and out-frequencies of components, that provides measures, which are required to perform these optimizations. While the optimization of a static integration scenario may be based on the specifications of components, we require the provisioning of metadata during runtime and the provisioning in adherence to the common integration architecture to enable optimization during runtime in scenarios with changing conditions. In addition, the provisioning of metadata should adhere to the integration architecture, i.e., respect the REST and LD paradigms.

4.2.2.3 Self-adaptation of Components

Our third requirement, with respect to the challenges related to Meta-interaction Patterns (c.f., Section 4.1.2.2) is the *Self-adaptation of Components*. In integration scenarios with changing conditions, in which the factors that influence the optimization change over time, e.g., changing in- and out-frequencies, we must re-adapt the initial configuration of pull and push interaction patterns to adjust existing non-optimal interactions. However, to be able to support this in an efficient way, these adjustments must be done by the components themselves. The SC approach provides the means for deploying interfaces, interactions, controlling logic, and processing triggers onto components at runtime and in adherence with the integration architecture. Thereby, the approach enables us to establish application-specific data flows between these components. However, the SC approach and architecture provide no optimizations with respect to the overall communication between components in domain-specific applications. Therefore, we are able to optimize communication a priori during the design of the applications but, by default, not during runtime after deployment. Therefore, we require the self-adaptation of components during runtime – the optimization of communication with respect to certain criteria through the adaptation of interfaces and interactions. The adaptation is done by the components themselves and is dependent on the available metadata, aiming to dynamically optimize the existing interaction patterns and, thereby, react on changing situations. In addition, this adaptation should adhere to the integration architecture, i.e., respect the REST and LD paradigms.

4.2.3 Frequency-based Network Model and Optimization Algorithm

In our approach, we treat a distributed application as a set of components. The components in this set take over specific functions, provide the means to access and modify their state and, thereby, provide access to this function or react to modified states. These components are integrated and collaborate through communicating over a network to provide the value-added function of the distributed application. This integration is established by transferring the states of components between the involved components – a component may require the state of another component, or other components may require the state of the component, or both at the same time. Which state transfers are required to provide a value-added function is heavily dependent on the specific distributed application.

During runtime, components repeatedly execute their function, access the state of other required components, and modify the state of dependent components. In accordance with the particular function, the rate, at which the state of components is modified may differ from the rate, at which the state of components is accessed, e.g., a component aggregates frequently pushed sensor information that is, subsequently, rarely requested by further components. We take this into consideration by distinguishing an in-frequency, at which components require the state of other components, and an out-frequency, at which components, triggered by their function, modify the state of other components. In addition, components may not require any states or they may not modify any states. In this case, the in- or out-frequency is zero.

The integration presumes that the representations of required states are transferred via the network between the collaborating components. We consider the push and the pull interaction patterns that can be performed by components to realize these transfers. Thereby, components may either pull state representations from remote components, or get these state representations pushed from other components. Analogously, representations of modified states can be pushed by the component to other components, or be pulled by these components.

The in- and out-frequencies of components, in combination with the different interaction patterns, raise the question – "When should state changes be transferred between components via pull interaction and when via push interaction?". In a pull interaction, outdated data may be pulled, while in a push interaction data may be pushed, which cannot be processed until the next push to the remote system. Given these characteristics, we provide a basic algorithm to improve the interaction between components by calculating the optimal interaction pattern for each data flow, based on the in- and out-frequencies of the involved components. By deploying the interaction according to the results of this algorithm, we prevent components from transferring state representation with information that will be discarded or was not changed, and thus minimize the overall data flow in terms of transferred state representations. The consideration of further parameters, e.g., the trade-off between bandwidth and latency, or processing and bandwidth limitation, is not discussed in this approach but can be incorporated.

We emphasize that our approach aligns well with our integration architecture, in particular, with the resource-oriented viewpoint of the REST paradigm. In the context of REST, components are integrated into distributed applications in a resource-oriented manner. For the transfer of state representations, these components expose REST APIs to the network. Depending on the particular use case, components represent such REST APIs as a collection of resources or as a single resource. A REST API enables remote components to pull state representations from or push state representations to a component. Thus, there might be components in the network, which do not provide a REST API but only pull or push states.

In the following, we introduce our model for describing the data flow in distributed applications, including the dynamics in terms of the in- and out-frequencies of components, and an algorithm for optimizing the interaction patterns.

4.2.3.1 Frequency-based Network Model

Model In Equation 4.1, we show our model for describing composite applications in terms of a network of components. The network model includes information about the number n of involved components, the existence of data flows F between these components, the in-frequencies I and out-frequencies O of components, and the interaction patterns P that these components use to establish the data flows.

$$\begin{aligned}
\{F\} \times \{I\} \times \{O\} \times \{P\} \\
F \in \{\text{true}, \text{false}\}^{n \times n} \\
I, O \in \{\mathbb{R}^{\geq 0}\}^{n} \\
P \in \{\text{push}, \text{pull}, \text{both}, \text{none}\}^{n \times n} \\
n \in \mathbb{N}
\end{aligned}$$

Equation 4.1: Network Model

$$F = \begin{pmatrix} \text{false} & f_{1,2} & \cdots & f_{1,j} \\ f_{2,1} & \text{false} & \cdots & f_{2,j} \\ \vdots & \vdots & \ddots & \vdots \\ f_{i,1} & f_{i,2} & \cdots & \text{false} \end{pmatrix}$$
$$f_{i,j} \in \{\text{true}, \text{false}\}; \quad i, j \in \mathbb{N}$$

Equation 4.2: Network Model – Data Flows

Data Flow In Equation 4.2, we model the data flow between the components, participating in an application, as matrix. Each entry in the matrix represents the data flow between component i and component j, i.e., in the case of $true$, the data flow between component i and j exists and, in the case of $false$, no data flow exists. The size of the matrix is the number of components n in the network. By default, data flows from components to themselves are not permitted, i.e., the diagonal of the matrix is set to $false$.

$$I = \begin{pmatrix} i_1 \\ i_2 \\ \vdots \\ i_i \end{pmatrix} O = \begin{pmatrix} o_1 \\ o_2 \\ \vdots \\ o_j \end{pmatrix}$$
$$i_i, o_j \in \mathbb{R}^{\geq 0}; \quad i, j \in \mathbb{N}$$

Equation 4.3: Network Model – In- and Out-Frequencies

Frequencies In Equation 4.3, we model the in- and out-frequencies of components as vectors. The pair i_n and o_n in the vectors I and O are indexed by the consecutive number of components n and represent the pairs of in- and out-frequencies of the components. The frequencies are measured in hertz (Hz), i.e., they are defined as events or cycles per second (s).

Interaction Patterns In Equation 4.4, we model the interaction patterns between components in the form of a matrix. Each entry in the matrix represents the interaction pattern that component i should execute with regard to component j, i.e., if component i should $pull$, $push$, pull and push ($both$), or execute no (*none*) interaction pattern with regard to component j. The size of the matrix is defined by the number of components n in the composition. By default, components cannot execute an interaction pattern on themselves, i.e., the diagonal of the matrix is set to *none*. The interaction patterns for specific scenarios are calculated by the basic algorithm that we present in the following.

$$P = \begin{pmatrix} \text{none} & p_{1,2} & \cdots & p_{1,j} \\ p_{2,1} & \text{none} & \cdots & p_{2,j} \\ \vdots & \vdots & \ddots & \vdots \\ p_{i,1} & p_{i,2} & \cdots & \text{none} \end{pmatrix}$$
$$p_{i,j} \in \{\text{push}, \text{pull}, \text{both}, \text{nonc}\}; \quad i, j \in \mathbb{N}$$

Equation 4.4: Network Model – Interaction Patterns

4.2.3.2 Frequency-based Optimization Algorithm

In Algorithm 4.1, we show in pseudo code the basic optimization algorithm for determining the optimal interaction patterns for all components participating in a composite application. In particular, the algorithm determines if a component should pull data from another component, push data to another component, or execute both pull and push patterns to send data in both directions. The algorithm requires as input the number of components n in the network, all in-frequencies I of components, all out-frequencies O of components, and the matrix F with the data flows between components. The constants $NONE$, $PULL$, $PUSH$, and $BOTH$ are placeholders for the corresponding interaction patterns. The algorithm returns as output the matrix of interaction patterns P that includes the interaction patterns for each component in relation to each of the other components. In Table 4.1, we list all decisions of the algorithm with their conditions and the derived interaction patterns. For readability, $NONE$-entries are not shown.

```
Require: n, I, O, F, NONE, PULL, PUSH, BOTH
Ensure: P
  function INTERACTION_PATTERNS(n, I, O, F)
     for c1 ← 0,n do
        for c2 ← 0,n do
           if F[c1][c2] ∧ O[c1] ≤ I[c2] ∧ F[c2][c1] ∧ O[c2] > I[c1] then
              P[c1][c2] ← BOTH
           else if F[c1][c2] ∧ O[c1] ≤ I[c2] then
              P[c1][c2] ← PUSH
           else if F[c2][c1] ∧ I[c2] > O[c1] then
              P[c1][c2] ← PULL
           else
              P[c1][c2] ← NONE
           end if
        end for
     end for
     return P
  end function
```

Algorithm 4.1: Optimization Algorithm for Interaction Patterns

4.2.3.3 Smart Component-based Interaction Adaptation

The network model and the optimization algorithm enable us to evaluate a composition of components with respect to the given in- and out-frequencies. Thereby, we can determine the optimal interaction patterns with respect to the minimal transfer of state representation needed to establish the required data flows. We can use the network model and algorithm a priori for the design of distributed applications or at runtime – for the subsequent adjustment of interaction patterns. Therefore, in situations, in which the in- and out-frequencies dynamically change over time, we utilize the SC approach to deploy the algorithm to the SCs participating in the composition and evaluate the selection of interaction patterns during every interpreter run. Thereby, we do not prescribe the way, in which metadata about the frequency of components is collected, but only require that it is provided, in the case of SCs, by the domain-specific function to the interpreter, and, in case of regular components, exposed as a resource at the network. Alternatively, the frequencies may be calculated by the interpreter, given an appropriate rule program.

Flow	Condition	Pattern $C1$	Pattern $C2$
$C1 \rightarrow C2$	$O(C1) \leq I(C2)$	$PUSH$	
$C1 \rightarrow C2$	$O(C1) > I(C2)$		$PULL$
$C1 \leftarrow C2$	$O(C2) \leq I(C1)$		$PUSH$
$C1 \leftarrow C2$	$O(C2) > I(C1)$	$PULL$	
$C1 \leftrightarrow C2$	$O(C1) \leq I(C2) \wedge O(C2) \leq I(C1)$	$PUSH$	$PUSH$
$C1 \leftrightarrow C2$	$O(C1) > I(C2) \wedge O(C2) > I(C1)$	$PULL$	$PULL$
$C1 \leftrightarrow C2$	$O(C1) \leq I(C2) \wedge O(C2) > I(C1)$	$BOTH$	
$C1 \leftrightarrow C2$	$O(C1) < I(C2) \wedge O(C2) \leq I(C1)$		$BOTH$

Table 4.1: Decision Table of the Optimization Algorithm for Interaction Patterns

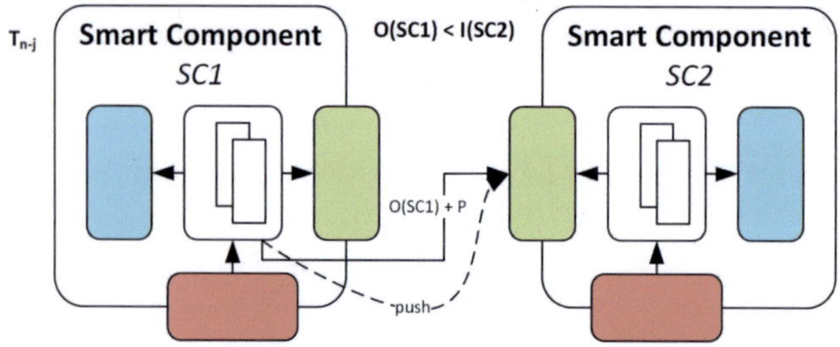

Figure 4.3: Smart Component-based Interaction Adaptation

In Figure 4.3, we give an abstract overview of the initial situation and in Figure 4.4 we show the adaptation from push to pull interaction between two SCs, based on the network model and our algorithm. The exemplary data flow leads from SC1 to SC2 and includes the out-frequency $O(SC1)$ of SC1 as well as the domain-specific payload P. SC1 exposes at its interface the payload P as a resource to SC2 or transfers the payload P via requests to SC2, depending on the state of a secondary resource. The request rule that is responsible for the push of P is conditional to the state of this resource. SC2 contains the algorithm as a rule program that evaluates the interaction pattern between SC1 and SC2 with respect to the out-frequency $O(SC1)$ of SC1 and the in-frequency $I(SC2)$ of SC2. The push interaction in step T_{n-j} holds as long as $O(SC1) < I(SC2)$ holds.

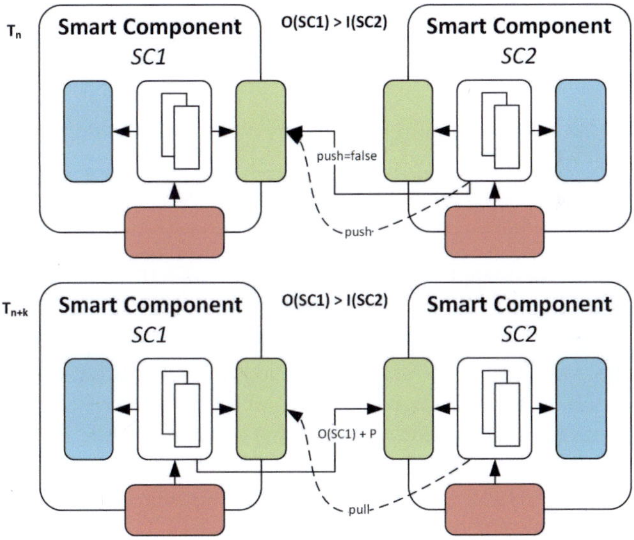

Figure 4.4: Smart Component-based Interaction Adaptation

In Figure 4.4, we show as an example the switch from push to pull interaction. In step T_n, the situation changes to $O(SC1) > I(SC2)$, i.e., the in-frequency of SC2 is now less then the out-frequency of SC1. In this case, SC2 establishes a data flow to SC1 that is represented by a single push interaction that changes the state of the secondary resource to $false$. Subsequently in step T_{n+k}, SC1 reacts by stopping to push and instead SC2 starts to pull the required information $O(SC1) + P$ from the interface of SC1, and does that as long as $O(SC1) > I(SC2)$ holds. The switch back to push interaction is handled in a similar way.

While the network model and algorithm are relatively simple, we show with this example the capabilities of the SC approach for enabling the adjustment of interfaces, interactions, and processing of components at runtime to incorporate the required behavior. The algorithm, the required resources, and the decisions to pull or push, can be deployed by adapting the SCs. Thereby, we establish the meta-interaction between the components that influences the way, in which the actual data flows are realized, i.e., determining the selection of the interaction patterns. In this particular case, we use a custom meta-interaction that cannot be classified as publish-subscribe or collect-subscribe (c.f., Section 2.3.4). However, realizing these classical meta-interaction patterns with our SC approach is also possible.

4.3 Approach for Domain-specific Architecture Mapping

Our approach for mapping domain-specific architectures to our integration architecture is guided by a set of requirements introduced in Section 4.3.2, that we derived from the challenges. With the help of these requirements, we focus on the main integration hurdles that need to be overcome when providing mappings to the integration architecture and its implementation. While these requirements hold for the integration of any domain-specific architecture, we focus, in particular, on the integration of the ROS architecture. In the following, we first introduce ROS and then briefly describe the mapping scenario as a subset of our overall scenario.

The Robot Operating System (ROS) [132] provides in the field of robotic and machine components means for the unified communication and for the efficient integration within modularized, distributed robotic systems. We give an overview of the important concepts, interaction mechanisms, data models, and data formats of the ROS architecture. In particular, the architecture provides a coherent way for identification and message transmission in distributed applications. These distributed applications are composed of *ROS Nodes*, which communicate with each other via *ROS Messages* by using *ROS Topics* and *ROS Services*, or by utilizing *ROS Parameters*. In the following, we describe these architectural elements in more detail.

The ROS architecture introduces the following concepts.

> **ROS Name** ROS names enable the identification of components in a distributed ROS system via a central hierarchical naming scheme. The naming is based on a slash-separated identifier for each resource in the ROS application, e.g., "/ns/node". Names start with an alpha character,

including forward slash and tilde, followed by alphanumeric characters, including forward slashes and underscores. The global namespace is identified by a forward slash and subsequent slashes separate different namespaces within an identifier. Resources may access other resources in or above their own namespace but only create resources in their own namespace.

ROS Node ROS nodes are the basic building blocks of the architecture and perform the computation in a ROS application. A ROS system may consist of several interconnected nodes, each handling the computation of a relatively narrow function, e.g., location tracking, or laser sensor operation. A node is uniquely identified by a name and all nodes in an application communicate via topics, services, or a parameter server. Each node has a node type, encapsulates its function, and provides a minimal API, which is exposed to the rest of the nodes. On file system level, within the package, the type of a node defines the name of the executable to be executed when the node is accessed.

ROS Master The ROS master provides a centralized name system and registration facility for nodes, for their published topics, and for their published services in the ROS system. It enables nodes to discover and locate other nodes, and tracks all subscribers and publishers of topics and services. The communication of messages between nodes over topics is, similarly to services, delegated to the nodes and not handled by the master. The function of the master is accessible through an API based on Extensible Markup Language Remote Procedure Call (XML-RPC).

The ROS architecture introduces the following data elements.

ROS Message ROS messages are simple data structures of typed fields, which are exchanged during the communication between nodes in a ROS resource graph. A message is typed by a message type, which defines the structure of the contained data. ROS packages may define these message types in simple text files, based on a set of built-in field types. Each message includes the version of the message type, which is based on the Message-Digest Algorithm 5 (MD5) hash of the underlying message type file. Only nodes with the same version of a supported message type, i.e., the same MD5 hash, are allowed to communicate messages of this particular message type.

ROS Bag ROS bags are a collections of serialized messages for persistent storage and later reuse, e.g., playback of messages. The original representation used by the ROS transport layer is utilized by bags as data format, which leads to efficient processing or replaying of messages.

Finally, the ROS architecture introduces the following means for interaction.

ROS Topic ROS topics provide an anonymous publish-subscribe meta-interaction mechanism for establishing interaction in a ROS system and enable unidirectional distribution of messages from a specific node to a number of interested nodes. A topic is identified by a name and is strongly typed for one kind of messages, i.e., the type of a topic is the same as the type of the messages to be distributed by the topic. Nodes receive messages of this message type only if they have subscribed beforehand to the topic.

ROS Service ROS services provide a request-response mechanism for the interaction in a ROS system. A service is identified by a name and supports a message pair, i.e., a request message and a response message. Similarly to topics, each service is strongly typed, based on a MD5 hash of the service file, which includes, in contrast to topics, the types of both messages. The interaction with a service is synchronous, i.e., a node sends a request message to a service and waits for the response message.

ROS Parameter The ROS server provides at runtime the parameter server as a shared dictionary of parameters for nodes in the resource graph. The server is not designed for high performance use cases but for rather static and low volume data, e.g., configurations. The identification of parameters follows the ROS name scheme. Single or tree-based access to the shared parameter storage is granted trough an API based on XML-RPC.

4.3.1 Mapping Scenario

In the following, we introduce in short our mapping scenario that is part of the overall scenario in Section 4.1.1. The distributed application in our scenario contains in its composition the machine component (C3), which includes as a domain-specific function the management of the actual machine, which is based on the ROS architecture. In Figure 4.5, we show the relevant parts of our scenario that include the component as well as a zoom-in on the details of the domain-specific function, i.e., the system based on ROS. However, we do not detail on every single element of this system.

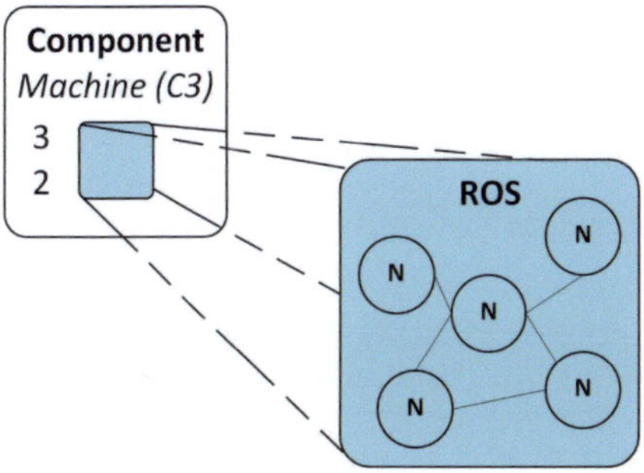

Figure 4.5: Mapping Scenario

In Listing 4.1, we provide a simple example of a ROS system, which we use to illustrate the elements of the ROS architecture. We also use this as a running example for describing our mapping approach. In particular, we modeled some details of the machine in an abstract manner as a set of ROS topics and ROS services that are provided by one or multiple ROS nodes.

```
Topics
/machine/engine/speed              > 0 - 1000

Services
/machine/start
/machine/stop
/machine/set_power                 < on | off
/machine/get_power                 > on | off
/machine/engine/set_speed          < 0 - 1000
/machine/engine/set_direction < 0 - 1
/machine/engine/get_direction > 0 - 1
```

Listing 4.1: Machine Topics/Services in ROS

Each line represents a ROS topic or a ROS service identified by a ROS name with input or output values, which are indicated by a left angle bracket for input and right angle bracket for output. The *start/stop* as well as the *set/get power* ROS services start and stop the engine. Via the *set speed* ROS service a new speed may be set and the *get/set direction* services are responsible for the direction, in terms of forward or backward movement. The ROS topic informs subscribed ROS nodes about changes in the speed of the engine.

4.3.2 Requirements

Based on the challenges that we introduced in Section 4.1.2, we derive a set of requirements for enabling interaction mapping. While we keep the mapping scenario in Section 4.3.1 simple, the scenario includes the most important means for communication in ROS that we intend to map to the integration architecture. Therefore, we derive in the following a set of requirements that an architecture and, subsequently, an implementation must fulfill for providing an effective mapping between the architectures.

4.3.2.1 Compliance with the Integration Architecture

Our first requirement, with respect to the challenges related to Non-compliant Communication and Non-compliant Representation (c.f., Section 4.1.2.3 and 4.1.2.4) is the *Compliance with the Integration Architecture*. While the mapping is challenging, we specify with this most basic requirement the adherence of the solution to the common integration architecture. The components that act as proxies to ROS may utilize arbitrary means for communication at the domain-specific side, but must adhere to the REST and LD paradigms at the side of the integration architecture. Therefore, the resource-oriented viewpoint on applications is determinative, URIs identify resources, HTTP is the transport and application protocol, RDF is utilized for the modeling of information, and RDF data formats such as Turtle, or RDF/XML serialize the representations exposed by resources.

4.3.2.2 Mapping of Interaction and Meta-interaction

Our second requirement, with respect to the challenges related to Non-compliant Communication(c.f., Section 4.1.2.3) is the *Mapping of Interaction and Meta-interaction*. Compared to the integration architecture, the ROS architecture imposes an alternative view on distributed applications, e.g., by permitting function-like calls, includes architectural elements without counterparts, e.g., a centralized authority for meta-interaction, and uses different transport protocols. However, the basic setup of having different components that collaborate in compositions of distributed applications, is very similar. With respect to interaction, the ROS architecture provides with the help of topics, services, and parameters, three different means for realizing the data flow between ROS nodes and the ROS master. To be able to establish the data flow between ROS nodes and components that adhere to the integration architecture, we therefore require the mapping of these architectural elements, as well as the interaction mechanisms, to HTTP and related technologies, while respecting the REST paradigm. In addition, the ROS architecture includes built-in mechanisms for meta-interaction, e.g., ROS topics, that must be handled appropriately.

4.3.2.3 Lifting and Lowering of Data

Our third requirement, with respect to the challenges related to Non-compliant Representation (c.f., Section 4.1.2.4) is the *Lifting and Lowering of Data*. Compared to the integration architecture, the ROS architecture relies on a relatively simple system of data types and ROS messages that include values of different data types. While not in the direct focus, we require the appropriate mapping of information that is serialized in ROS messages and that is communicated between ROS nodes, to the RDF data model. Thereby, the data can re-used as LD and may be subject to further processing, e.g., for data transformation, derivation, or subsequent requests in the case of SCs.

4.3.3 ROS Architecture Mapping

Our approach on integrating the ROS architecture with our integration architecture is based on two phases. First, the integration has to be realized on a conceptual and interaction level. With REST, we introduce a resource-oriented viewpoint on distributed applications. The basic concepts associated with REST and the corresponding implications on the interactions within the distributed application must be aligned with the particular ROS architecture. Second, the integration has to be realized on the semantic level, based on the meaning of the processed data, thus facilitating the unified handling of heterogeneous data formats and data sources. By introducing RDF as a way for formally specifying data models and LD for publishing and interlinking data, we provide the foundation for the integration of data, having different formats and coming from different sources. In the following, we provide a mapping between our integration architecture and the ROS architecture. In particular, we 1) map the concepts between both architectures, 2) map the interaction mechanisms utilized in the communication, and 3) indicate how the REST architectural style enables modeling of structural information and hypermedia, which is implicitly expressed in ROS.

4.3.3.1 Concept Mapping

In our integration architecture, we build on the REST and LD paradigms. The REST paradigm proposes the use of common Web technologies, e.g., URI, HTTP, and LR. The LD paradigm adds SWT, in particular, RDF, and, subsequently, the LDP specification to the set of technologies. In Table 4.2, we provide a mapping between the concepts of HTTP, i.e., REST, extended to LDP, i.e., RWLD, and the concepts of the ROS architecture.

For an architecture based on HTTP, we are able to identify the basic concepts, i.e., component, application, and resource. Any host capable of providing resources via HTTP at a DNS name or an IP address may serve as a component. A set of components, which collaborate through interaction via a network, composes a distributed application, which provides a value-added function. At the interfaces of components, HTTP resources expose relevant parts of their states to the network. In addition, we consider specific concepts for identification and transport. In particular, HTTP specifies also the underlying protocol for the transport of messages and for the interaction between components, as described in Section 4.3.3.2. Based on HTTP, we use URIs to uniquely identify resources. We are not obliged to adhere to a prescribed data model and representation format, since neither HTTP nor the REST paradigm specify a particular model. Any data format is permitted for serializing a representation of a state, although some specific data formats are frequently used, e.g., JSON, or XML. For supporting the differentiation of representation formats we can use mime types.

Concept	HTTP Concept	LDP Concept	ROS Concept
Component	Host	Host	Node
Application	Composition of Hosts	Composition of Hosts	Composition of Nodes
Resource	HTTP Resource	LDPR	Service, Parameter, Topic Subscriber
Represent.	XML, JSON, ...	Turtle, JSON-LD, ...	Message, XML
Data Model	-	RDF	Message Format, XML-RPC Schema
Identifier	URI	URI	Name
Transport	HTTP	HTTP	TCPROS, UDPROS
Interaction	HTTP Verbs	HTTP Verbs	Methods provided by Topic, Service, and Parameter

Table 4.2: Concept Mapping between HTTP, LDP, and ROS

Switching from an architecture adhering to the REST paradigm to an architecture that adheres to the LD paradigms, we introduce the respective concepts from the LDP specification that enables RWLD. As shown in Table 4.2, we use the more constrained definition of a LDPR and, subsequently, the derived LDP-RS, LDP-NR, and variants of LDPC. In addition, we close the gap of having a consistent data model by introducing RDF as a common, default data model. Several data formats exist for the serialization of representations adhering to the RDF model, e.g., Turtle, JSON-LD, RDF/XML, or N-Triples. However, we consider with LDP-NRs also other data models and formats, which are described in and linked from RDF representations.

Similarly to HTTP, we are able to identify the basic concepts in the ROS architecture. A distributed application based on ROS is a network of ROS nodes, which interact in order to provide a value-added function. The state of a ROS node is exposed by services, parameters, or indirectly by the subscribers of a topic. Therefore, different types of resources exist in the ROS architecture. In contrast to HTTP, ROS provides data models and formats for representation. The message format provides a simple model for messages exchanged via topics and services, serialized on the transport level in a ROS-specific data format. Representations of parameters adhere to the XML-RPC schema and are serialized as XML. The ROS architecture provides a global naming scheme for services, topics, and parameters, i.e., ROS names are unique identifiers for resources. With TCPROS and UDPROS the architecture provides two implementations of the abstract ROS transport protocol for the transfer of messages between nodes. Negotiation procedures transparently handle the optimal choice of the protocol implementation, based on the preferences of the involved nodes, and enable the extension with further protocols.

With the concept of resources, which expose a relevant view of the state of components to the network, and unique identifiers to identify these resources we allow a mapping, which is categorized as level one in Richardson's maturity model [165] for REST services.

4.3.3.2 Interaction Mapping

Derived from the resource-oriented view of the REST paradigm, our integration architecture has a fixed set of methods, which enable transport and interaction. In the simplest case, we can use some or all Create, Read, Update, and Delete (CRUD) operations on resources. In the case of HTTP, the HTTP verbs POST, GET, PUT, and DELETE map to these CRUD operations and in relation to resources, as shown in Table 4.3. In more detailed defined by the LDP specification (c.f., Section 2.2.3.1), we differentiate between regular resources

(LDPR, LDP-RS, and LDP-NR) and container resources (LDPC, LDP-BC, LDP-DC, and LDP-IC) for collections of resources, which provide a different behavior for some of these methods. In particular, resources are created or updated by executing HTTP PUT requests at a given URI, read by a HTTP GET request, and deleted by HTTP DELETE requests. In addition, we can create a new resource via a HTTP POST request to the URI of a container resource, that is subsequently provided at a server-determined URI and added to the collection represented by the container resource. We introduce the HTTP PATCH verb to complete the update methods. In contrast to HTTP PUT, the HTTP PATCH verb enables partial updates of resources.

Architecture	Res. Type	Create	Read	Update	Delete
HTTP / LDP	HTTP Res. / LDPR	POST / PUT	GET	PUT / PATCH	DELETE
ROS	Service	-	get*	set*	-
ROS	Topic Sub.	-	-	publish	-
ROS	Parameter	setParam	getParam	setParam	deletePar.

Table 4.3: Interaction Mapping between HTTP/LDP and ROS

We are able to identify different interaction mechanism in the ROS architecture, depending on the type of resource, i.e., specific interaction mechanisms exist for topics, services, and parameters. Depending on the type of resource, we partially map the mechanisms to the generic CRUD operations, as shown in Table 4.3. The subscribers of ROS topics provide, on a conceptional level, only one regular resource, which can be updated by topic publishers as a single, and thus distinct, CRUD operation. The creation and deletion of these resources provided by subscribers is not supported, i.e., the subscribers provide only one predefined resource for updates by publishers. In addition, these resources provide no read support for other elements of the ROS architecture, but nodes may expose their state, in turn, as topics or services. In contrast to topics, ROS services provide no support for distinct CRUD operations. In particular, the creation and deletion of services is not possible at runtime, i.e., services are a predefined, regular resources. Furthermore, services define a set of input and output ROS messages as RPC with custom processing between input and output message. While the creation and deletion of a service resource is not possible, in many cases the read and update operation are emulated by introducing getter and setter services (c.f., Listing 4.1). Finally, the ROS parameter is the only resource type in the ROS architecture that supports all CRUD operations in a distinct manner. The master node provides central access to all parameters and all interaction mechanisms for these parameters. In fact, the interaction with parameters is handled by XML-RPC but in a resource-oriented manner. A parameter may be created or updated by the "setParam" method, read by the "getParam" method, and deleted by the "deleteParam".

```
/machine/power                : on | off
/machine/engine/speed         : 0 - 1000
/machine/engine/direction     : 0 - 1
```

Listing 4.2: Machine Resources

In Listing 4.2, we show how the abstract machine, which we modeled in ROS in Listing 4.1, is mapped to a HTTP/LDP CRUD interface. For readability, we do not use full URIs in the listing but only their path parts for identification. By utilizing the convention of prefixing the ROS names of getter and setter services, we automatically map the ROS services "/machine/{set,get}_-power" and "/machine/engine/{set,get}_direction" to HTTP resources. The ROS topic "/machine/engine/speed" is combined with the ROS service "/machine/engine/set_speed" to a read-write resource. We can establish manual custom mappings for the start and stop services, which do not adhere to the convention and require neither input nor provide output, e.g., by mapping the combination of both services to HTTP POST requests at the parent resource.

With the mapping of a constraint set of interaction mechanisms, we enable a mapping, which is categorized as level two in Richardson's maturity model for REST services. We point out that the ROS architecture does not provide means for creating and deleting topics and services at runtime. Only ROS parameters, which we did not include our running example, are mapped completely as CRUD resources to HTTP. ROS topics are mapped to read-only HTTP resources, which only allow the HTTP GET method. ROS services allow automatic mapping to read-write HTTP resources by utilizing the convention of prefixing the ROS names of getter and setter services. In the case of other ROS services, custom mappings are required.

4.3.3.3 Resource Aggregation and Hypermedia Mapping

In our integration architecture, the REST paradigm is, in general, not limiting the granularity of resources, i.e., the granularity is a design decision, since there are no restrictions in terms of URI structure or representation formats. In this context, only the specification of the LDPCs adds some restrictions to the representation. In contrast, the ROS architecture only permits representations that are composed of basic data types, which leads to relatively fine-grained resources. As a consequence, a resource, which is modeled in REST as one HTTP resource, may be split over several fine-grained topics or services in ROS. In most cases, the ROS names of these topics and services contain structural information about resources. In addition, the REST architectural style proposes as a tenet the use of hypermedia to drive the state of applications, i.e., links connect resources, explicitly state the type of relation, and, thereby, relate states of the application.

```
/machine
linkrel          : start     ->  /machine
linkrel          : stop      ->  /machine
linkrel          : engine    ->  /machine/engine
power            : on | off

/machine/engine
linkrel          : machine  ->  /machine
speed            : 0 - 1000
direction        : 0 - 1
```

Listing 4.3: Machine Aggregated Resources and Link Relations

In Listing 4.3, we extend the CRUD interface of the abstract machine in Listing 4.2 to overcome these shortcomings. For readability, we do not use full URIs in the listing but only their path parts for identification. First, we aggregate fine-grained ROS resources as higher-level HTTP resources, i.e., as the resources "/machine" and "/machine/engine". For automation, we use the semantic information from the structure of ROS names, that now becomes obsolete. Second, we expose the application state, which is implicitly present in our ROS example, explicit by utilizing hypermedia, i.e., by linking the resources with typed links. These links, which drive the application state, are noted in Listing 4.3 as “linkrel” and point to the relative path of the target resource. The link “start” appears in the representation of a machine as long as the machine is not started. The link “engine” appears as long as the machine is started. The link “stop” appears as long as the machine is started and the speed of the engine is zero. An engine resource exists as long as the machine is started and its representation contains a link back to the machine. A client, capable of interpreting the link types, is directly able to use the machine system in the correct way by accessing a single URI as the starting point, which in this case the URI of the machine resource.

The ROS architecture does not provide means for creating complex resources and for relating these resources. By aggregating fine-granular ROS resources into higher-level HTTP resources and by adding hypermedia, we enhance the mapping and expose a ROS system as proposed by the REST architectural style, i.e., the service now adheres to level three of the Richardson’s maturity model. However, the mapping of the application semantics is currently still a manual task.

4.3.3.4 Smart Component-based Meta-interaction Mapping and Transformation

The integration architecture based on the REST and LD paradigms provides no means for specifying meta-interaction patterns such as publish-subscribe or collect-subscribe. In contrast, the ROS architecture provides with ROS topics built-in means for publish-subscribe meta-interaction. As presented before, we map these topics to regular resources that expose the newest pushed value of the topic at the network. However, by utilizing the SC approach, we enable the appropriate mapping of this meta-interaction. In Figure 4.6, we indicate this through the mapped ROS application as domain-specific function of the SC. In this case, the SC is actively processing, triggered by time or by received ROS messages. The SC enables us to map the meta-interaction by utilizing request rules in combination with lists of subscribers, e.g., by utilizing LDPCs, and to forward messages that are pushed by ROS topics in the ROS application to subscribed components in our integration architecture. In addition, we enable the transformation of information through rule programs. For example, generic vocabularies for the annotation of mapped ROS messages can be transformed to vocabularies that are appropriate for the specific application use case.

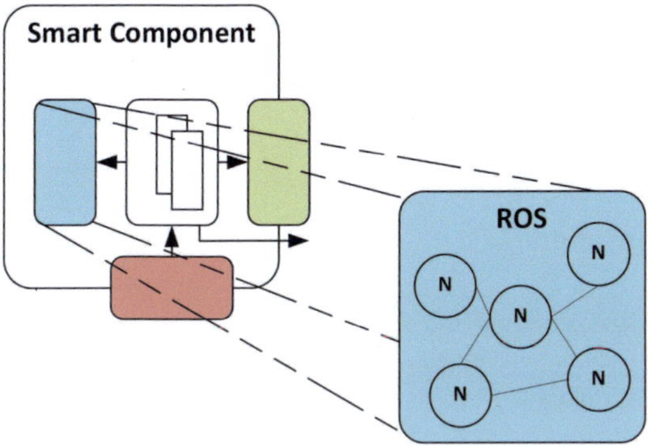

Figure 4.6: Smart Component-based Meta-interaction Mapping and Transformation

4.4 Implementation of the ROS-REST Proxy

In the following, we provide a short introduction to the ROS-REST Proxy (ROEST)[1], which is our proof-of-concept implementation of the mapping between the domain-specific ROS architecture and our integration architecture based on the REST and LD paradigms. In Listing 4.4, we show the definition of the ROS message "sensor_msgs/CameraInfo"[2], which we use as a running example throughout this sections.

As the most basic architectural element, we mapped the 14 datatypes that are supported by the ROS architecture, e.g., bool, int64, or time. The message definition in Listing 4.4 includes several fields of different data types, e.g., "uint32 height", or "uint32 width". The fixed set of data types in ROS allows us to provide a generic mapping for these data types. Therefore, ROEST maps these fields to literals in RDF that are annotated with the appropriate types of the built-in XSD datatypes, which are re-used by RDF. In addition to simple data types, ROS supports fixed-length and variable-length arrays as well as separate arrays for bytes and booleans. The message definition in Listing 4.4 includes different array fields, e.g., "float64[] D", or "float64[9] K". To keep the order of values within the arrays, ROEST maps these arrays to RDF lists [37].

[1] `https://rslv.link/ZSv7`

[2] `https://rslv.link/ZSvm`

```
std_msgs/Header header
  uint32 seq
  time stamp
  string frame_id
uint32 height
uint32 width
string distortion_model
float64[] D
float64[9] K
float64[9] R
float64[12] P
uint32 binning_x
uint32 binning_y
sensor_msgs/RegionOfInterest roi
  uint32 x_offset
  uint32 y_offset
  uint32 height
  uint32 width
  bool do_rectify
```

Listing 4.4: Definition of the ROS Message "sensor_msgs/CameraInfo"

As the second element of the ROS architecture, we map the instances of ROS messages that are transferred by reusing the simplicity of their structured definitions. This mapping of ROS messages consist of two parts. On the one hand, the information that is published by ROS topics or used as input and output of ROS services is serialized according to the definition of ROS messages. The definitions of ROS messages consist of fields that are identified by a name and are typed by a datatype. In contrast to ROS names, the names of fields in messages are not globally unique and, subsequently, their semantics are specific to the message definition. Therefore, the ROEST implementation maps these field names to predicates that link the message instances and the related literal values to URIs that are unique per combination of message definition and field name. Thereby, we ensure the unique identification of the type of linked literals, and enable the subsequent integration of semantics across several message definitions. In other words, the property of two mapped message instances is identified by the same URI if their message definition is the same and by different URIs if their message definition is different, even if the semantics are the same. On the other hand, message definitions can contain fields that are typed with other message definitions. This case is shown in our example in Listing 4.4 for the field "header" of the message type "std_msgs/Header" and for the field "roi" of the message type "sensor_msgs/RegionOfInterest". In the listing, we recursively show the definitions of these subordinate messages. ROEST reuses this recursive relation between message definitions and subordinate message definitions for linking superordinate instances of ROS messages with their superordinate instance. Thereby, ROEST maps one coherent RDF graph per transferred instance of a superordinate ROS message that includes all subordinate instances.

We can map the ROS topics, services, and parameters of a distributed ROS application partially or completely to the single interface of the ROEST implementation, which participates as a single ROS node in ROS applications and as a single component in compositions based on our integration architecture. In our proof-of-concept ROEST implementation, we limit this mapping of interaction mechanisms to ROS topics. ROS topics are identified by unique ROS names that are slash-separated strings. We reuse the ROS names as path parts in the URIs for resources that represent the mapped topics. In the proof-of-concept implementation, we provide no aggregation of fine-granular ROS topics, but represent every ROS topics with a single resource in the REST interface. Therefore, we cache the RDF representation of pushed ROS message instances for subsequent HTTP requests, i.e., we switch from push interaction in ROS to pull interaction in our integration architecture.

4.5 Evaluation of Frequency-based Interaction Optimization

In the following, we evaluate our approach for frequency-based data flow optimization, which we presented in Section 4.2, by calculating the optimal interaction patterns for our initially presented optimization scenario in Section 4.2.1 (c.f., Figure 4.7). First, we create our network model, which we presented in Section 4.2.3.1, based on the composition of components and data flows between the components. Subsequently, we apply our optimization algorithm, which we presented in Section 4.2.3.2, to determine the optimal interaction patters for every pair of components in the application.

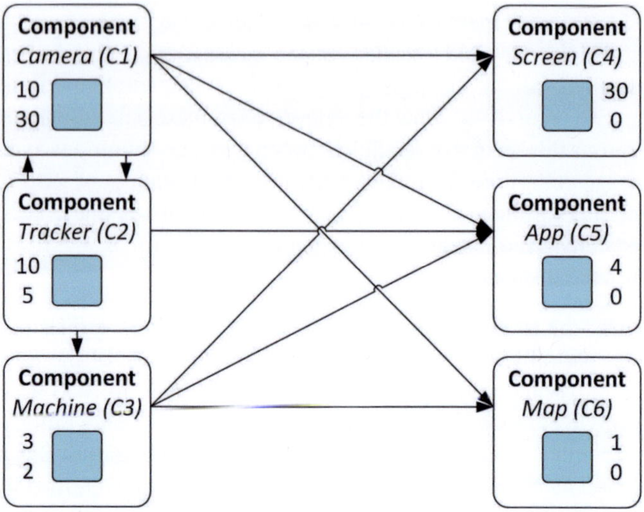

Figure 4.7: Optimization Scenario

$$F_s = \begin{array}{c} N \\ 1 \\ 2 \\ 3 \\ 4 \\ 5 \\ 6 \end{array} \begin{array}{c} \begin{array}{cccccc} 1 & 2 & 3 & 4 & 5 & 6 \end{array} \\ \begin{pmatrix} & \text{true} & & \text{true} & \text{true} & \text{true} \\ \text{true} & & \text{true} & & \text{true} & \\ & & & \text{true} & \text{true} & \text{true} \\ & & & & & \\ & & & & & \\ & & & & & \end{pmatrix} \end{array}$$

Equation 4.5: Network Model Evaluation – Data Flows

In Equation 4.5, we apply the modeling of the network of data flows to our scenario s. For readability, we list only *true* entries in the table that indicate a data flow between two components. The instance of the matrix depends on the integration of components in the distributed application. Therefore, every arrow in Figure 4.7 leads to a *true* entry in the matrix. In Equation 4.6, we apply the modeling of frequencies to our scenario s. The instances of the vectors depend on the properties of the components. In particular, every pair of in- and out-frequencies in Figure 4.7 is represented by a pair of entries in the vectors.

In Equation 4.7, we apply the optimization algorithm to the network model of our scenario s and calculate the matrix with optimal interaction patterns P_s. The algorithm is executed with the number of components participating in our composition $n = 6$, the vector of in-frequencies I_s, the vector of out-frequencies O_s, and the matrix of data flows F_s. The constants $PULL$, $PUSH$, $BOTH$, and $NONE$ are set to $pull$, $push$, $both$, and $none$. For readability, we omit $none$-entries in the matrix.

$$I_s = \begin{array}{c} \text{N} \\ 1 \\ 2 \\ 3 \\ 4 \\ 5 \\ 6 \end{array} \begin{array}{c} \text{Hz} \\ \begin{pmatrix} 10 \\ 10 \\ 3 \\ 30 \\ 4 \\ 1 \end{pmatrix} \end{array} \quad O_s = \begin{array}{c} \text{N} \\ 1 \\ 2 \\ 3 \\ 4 \\ 5 \\ 6 \end{array} \begin{array}{c} \text{Hz} \\ \begin{pmatrix} 30 \\ 5 \\ 2 \\ 0 \\ 0 \\ 0 \end{pmatrix} \end{array}$$

Equation 4.6: Network Model Evaluation – Frequencies

$$P_s = \begin{array}{c|cccccc} N & 1 & 2 & 3 & 4 & 5 & 6 \\ \hline 1 & & & & push & & \\ 2 & both & & & & & \\ 3 & & pull & & push & push & \\ 4 & & & & & & \\ 5 & pull & pull & & & & \\ 6 & pull & & pull & & & \end{array}$$

Equation 4.7: Network Model Evaluation – Interaction Patterns

In Figure 4.8, we visualize the solution for our optimization scenario that we calculated by applying the optimization algorithm. With dashed arrows between components, we imply, in contrast to the data flows in Figure 4.7, the direction of interaction and label these interactions with the corresponding interaction patterns. By deploying the interaction between components, the data flows are established and the amount of redundantly pulled or discarded pushed data is minimized. For example, the data flow from component $C2$ to component $C5$ is realized by a pull of the data from component $C2$ by component $C5$. Component $C5$ pulls data with an in-frequency of 4 Hz and will not receive redundant data, since the data at component $C2$ changes with an out-frequency of 5 Hz. During a push of data from component $C2$ to component $C5$ one out of five messages would be discarded by component $C5$.

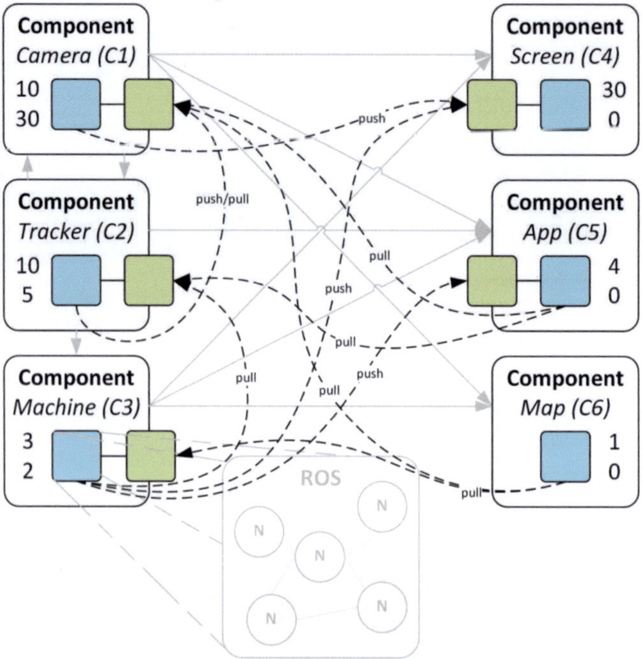

Figure 4.8: Optimization Scenario Solution

In Table 4.4, we list the aggregated estimate figures for the comparison of the optimized interaction patterns of our scenario solution to a push-only and a pull-only interaction for the same scenario. We included the accumulated overall frequencies for data flows in the composition of components, the accumulated redundantly pulled state representations, and the accumulated discarded pushed state representations. By adapting the derived optimized interaction patterns, our solution provides the lowest overall frequency and no state representations are transferred, which are redundant or discarded. In comparison, the push-only interaction causes the highest overall frequency and the most discarded state representations. The pull-only interaction provides, in this specific optimization scenario, an overall frequency, which is in between the two previous cases, and thus some state representations with redundant data are pulled. The frequency serves also as an indicator for bandwidth consumption between the different approaches. Nevertheless, the size of state representations has to be taken into account in order to be able to make statements about the technical bandwidth usage.

	Frequency	**Redundant**	**Discarded**
Solution	62	0	0
Push-only	141	0	79
Pull-only	97	35	0

Table 4.4: Comparison of Push-only, Pull-only, and Optimized Interaction

4.6 Summary

Recent years are marked by the widespread use and adoption of mobile devices and smart sensors as well as by the increasing modularization and distribution of formerly monolithic systems that accompany visions like the IoT, the WoT, and the SWoT. In parallel, new application use cases based on Web technologies emerge, which no longer involve mainly central servers and various clients but include several heterogeneous devices, that influence the evolution of the Web, the SW, and the WoD. While the devices become smaller and smarter, they reveal at the same time new and changed characteristics and trade-offs. On the one hand, the classical server and client roles become obsolete and it is common that the components participating in distributed applications own multiple roles, and, in addition, are complemented by diverse characteristics. Hereby, the efficient realization of data flows via interactions between the components becomes challenging. On the other hand, deciding on the trade-off between generic architectures, which provide increased independence of specific domains, and specialized architectures, that may be more efficient for domain-specific use cases, is challenging. In this context, we provide an approach for optimizing the interaction patterns that are used by components and provide an approach for mapping the architectural elements of the domain-specific ROS architecture to our integration architecture based on REST and LD. For both approaches, we point out the advantages of combining them with the SC approach. Furthermore, we provide a proof-of-concept implementation of our architecture mapping to and from ROS, and evaluate our network model and algorithm for optimizing interactions. While several different factors influence the efficiency of data flows and several domain-specific architectures exist, we see our approaches as specific contributions that directly provide solutions to the general challenges that arise with current developments that accompany IoT, the WoT, and the SWoT as well as the Web, the SW, and the WoD.

5 Distributed Benchmark Generation and Provisioning

In this chapter, we detail our work on generating and providing distributed benchmarks for LD. We focus on three main areas: 1) addressing the challenges of the LD setting with respect to benchmarks; 2) exploring the details and complexity of a domain-independent architecture for LD benchmarks; and 3) providing a solution for a domain-specific, scalable, and distributed LD benchmark.

In the following, we first introduce the context of our work on generating and providing distributed benchmarks and present a motivation scenario. Next we describe the specific challenges that we aim to address and provide a detailed problem analysis. We derive design requirements and provide an architecture for distributed environments that provide LD benchmarks. Based on our architecture, we present a specific distributed LD benchmark for our motivating scenario and detail on the implementation of the benchmark with respect to the different elements of our architecture. Finally, we conclude by presenting the performance evaluation of centralized and decentralized LD querying based on benchmarked environments that our implementation provides in different scales.

The content of this chapter is partially based on the publications by Keppmann et al. [104, 103].

5.1 Introduction

The development of LD has witnessed a rapid evolution and growth during the past years. Driven by the growing availability of data sources, solutions are constantly being newly developed or improved in order to support data exchange both in Web and enterprise settings. Thereby, LD is used in manifold integration scenarios – from the LODC [112], in which LD is used to expose datasets in semantically enriched and highly interlinked manner for public use, to the integration of devices that operate at high frequencies in the area of tracking, AR, and VR [142]. In such use cases, RWLD is utilized in specialized enterprise scenarios to overcome the heterogeneity in the interaction, representation, and semantics of information that is exchanged between devices from a multitude of independent manufacturers.

However, currently the choice whether to use LD in larger distributed application scenarios is, from a performance point of view, more an educated guess than a fact-based decision. Therefore, the provisioning of benchmarking tools and evaluation reports, which allow developers to assess the fitness of existing solutions, is key for pushing the development of better approaches and solutions, which are based on LD or, subsequently, RWLD. For instance, we evaluate the implementation of our SC approach, that we presented in Chapter 3, in a functional manner and the performance of the implementation at a single SC. To measure the performance of such approaches at different scales and to be able to evaluate different alternative solutions, we require benchmarks that are capable of providing truly distributed LD settings in a reproducible way. However, the support for the reproducible creation of distributed datasets as well as their setup and provisioning is challenging.

The LD setting (c.f., Section 2.2.3) is, on the one hand, characterized by datasets that consist of multiple distinct graphs and that are modeled in the RDF. Each graph is addressed by a different URI and is accessible via HTTP. The documents returned by hosts during requests at these HTTP URIs contain representations of these graphs in one of the RDF serialization formats, e.g., N-Triples, Turtle, or RDF/XML. Graphs may contain references to other graphs at different URIs. On the other hand, this LD setting exposes advanced requirements to clients beyond the capability of evaluating or querying RDF graphs. In particular, clients in the LD setting must be capable of handling remote documents. While, for example, RDF query engines enable the answering of queries against locally available graphs, LD query engines must retrieve graphs by requesting documents that contain graph representations via HTTP. Furthermore, these query engines must support resolving of links within received RDF graphs [85, 83]. In other words, query engines must support link following in the overall dataset of interlinked graphs during query answering.

In addition, in the RWLD setting, clients must be capable of combining the requirements of the LD paradigm with the more advanced implications of the REST paradigm in terms of interaction mechanisms.

However, current benchmarks [73, 35, 140, 36, 55, 93] in the area of SWT are focused on the generation of RDF graphs for local and mostly SPARQL-based evaluation, even if name-wise related to LD [55, 93]. While the generation of graphs is also important in the LD setting, the characteristics of typical LD integration settings go beyond the sole data generation. In particular, the generation of separated but interlinked graphs as well as their distribution at different hosts in a network, are substantial elements of the LD setting. Existing non-distributed benchmarks do not emulate these characteristics.

5.1.1 Scenario

In this work, we are not focused on the creation of specific benchmarking scenarios in terms of data generation, but on the interlinking and distribution of generated data as well as the deployment and reproducibility. Therefore, we base our scenario, the implementation of our architecture in Section 5.3, and the evaluation in Section 5.4 on an existing, simple, but established non-distributed RDF benchmark. In particular, the Lehigh University Benchmark (LUBM) [73]. However, the architecture of our approach, presented in Section 5.2.2 is, in general, independent of the specific data generators, which are exchangeable as long as they adhere to a limited set of requirements.

The LUBM scenario is derived from a university setting and includes information about universities, their departments, as well as the details of departments. Represented is the staff of the department, in particular, full professors, associate professors, assistant professors, and lecturers. In addition, undergraduate students and graduate students, courses and graduate courses, as well as publications are also represented. For each entity, a set of related properties is provided. In addition to the assignment of these entities to the department, several links connect the entities, e.g., authors of publications, courses taken by students, or courses give by teachers. In some cases, these links connect entities of a department to other departments. In particular, the degrees of graduate students, professors, and members of the staff are linked to other universities of the overall dataset. For evaluation, the LUBM benchmark provides a set of

14 SPARQL queries of different complexity, that take into account the information of a single department, the departments of a university, or information of several universities.

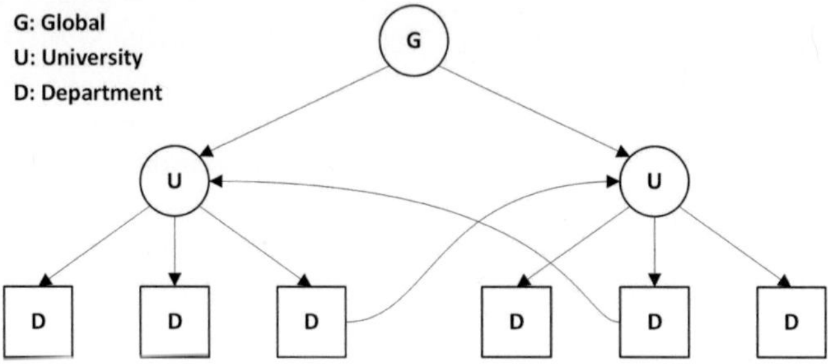

Figure 5.1: Distributed Benchmarking – Scenario

The LUBM benchmark is focused on the evaluation of SPARQL queries with respect to different complexity, but not on a LD setting. However, the benchmarking scenario can be intuitively mapped to a distributed setting, in which universities, departments, and probably even smaller groups of entities are provided by virtually or physically distributed hosts. In our distributed benchmarking scenario, visualized in Figure 5.1, we consider for the dataset separated graphs for universities, departments, which are interlinked with other universities, as well as a global graph, that links existing universities of the dataset. This setting enables different scaling.

- The size of the dataset can be scaled similarly to the original LUBM scenario. The more universities with related departments are generated, the bigger the dataset is and the more computing-intensive SPARQL queries become, depending on their complexity.
- The provisioning of documents that contain RDF graphs can be scaled. In the most distributed LD setting, the documents for each of these RDF graphs are provided by separate hosts. In the most non-distributed LD setting, the documents of all RDF graphs are provided by the same host.

These are scaling factors that an implementation aligned to this scenario must support. With this simply structured and well-known scenario, we intend to set the focus of our approach, architecture, and implementation for a distributed benchmark environment.

5.1.2 Challenges

The characteristics of distributed LD settings pose challenges to the design of adequate LD benchmarks. With respect to the generation and the distribution of datasets that form the benchmarking scenario, and to the provisioning of distinct but interlinked graphs as well as separated hosts, we face challenges that go beyond the features of current benchmarks (c.f., Data Generation in Section 5.1.2.1; Dataset Distribution in Section 5.1.2.2). Furthermore, the distributed nature of the LD setting imposes challenges on the actual deployment of benchmark datasets in a distributed manner. In addition, we face challenges with the reproducible generation, distribution, and deployment of datasets to enable comparability (c.f., Deployment Complexity in Section 5.1.2.3; Difficult Reproducibility in Section 5.1.2.4). In the following, we discuss these challenges in more detail.

5.1.2.1 Data Generation

With respect to the provisioning of the datasets in a LD setting, we are challenged with the problem of *Data Generation*. Existing benchmarks [73, 35, 140, 36, 55, 93] for RDF, including [55, 93] lack certain capabilities to cover major aspects of LD settings. In particular, benchmark data generators must be capable of generating datasets that consist of distinct but interlinked graphs. In addition to the artificial generation of data, benchmarks can also collect data a priori from real sources. The provided graphs must represent a subset of the overall generated information of the dataset and, in addition, must not prevent virtual and physical separation. Therefore, the graphs, which are provided at different URIs, must contain valid links to other graphs in the dataset. On the one hand, these links connect entities contained in the separated graphs, and, on the other hand, must be resolvable to retrieve the documents that contain the representation of the related graph in a LD fashion. For example, in our benchmarking scenario in Section 5.1.1, we may provide the dataset of different universities and their departments at different URIs that are probably hosted at different locations. However, the degree relations of people in departments to other universities must be represented by links that include the correct and resolvable URIs of those universities. In this case, we face a challenging mixture between data generation or data collection and the actual provisioning of data during the benchmark, that influences the actual configuration of URIs.

5.1.2.2 Dataset Distribution

Closely aligned with the correct interlinking of distinct graphs in a dataset, as described by the problem Data Generation, we are challenged with the problem of *Dataset Distribution* to provide truly distributed RDF datasets. Two characteristics of the LD setting, which distinguish the setting from pure RDF and SPARQL benchmarking, are the distribution of datasets in a network and accessibility of documents that contain RDF graphs through HTTP. In contrast, existing benchmarks for RDF focus on single evaluation engines and provide no support for distribution, as common for LD settings. Thereby, the distribution can be: not existing, i.e., local at a single system; in a local network; or at the intra- or internet. For example, in the one extreme LD is utilized to participate in the LODC [112] and in the contrary extreme LD is used in local applications or applications that use the local area network. From a technical point of view, these scenarios differ on the level of networks and computing resources, but not on the application layer.

5.1.2.3 Deployment Complexity

As a consequence of the problem Data Generation in combination with the problem of Dataset Distribution, we face a challenging problem of *Deployment Complexity*, in particular, in evaluation scenarios with large datasets that are highly fragmented and distributed. Due to the distributed nature of LD, we face complex deployments for the simulation of LD settings. While the deployment of all documents of a dataset at a single host is a valid benchmark scenario, we argue that the simulation of the LD setting includes besides distinct and interlinked graphs also the provisioning of these graphs by individual hosts that each implement the complete required Web stack and that are connected through a network. In addition, the time required for the setup of benchmarks, i.e., the data generation and provisioning, in particular, in larger benchmark scenarios, is significantly reduced if the utilized computing power is organized in a distributed manner. The deployment in such distributed manner includes several challenges, for example, the setup of multiple hosts, the distribution to and interlinking of graphs at these hosts, and the resolvability of links between graphs, which are provided by these hosts in certain network environments.

5.1.2.4 Difficult Reproducibility

The challenges above amplify the problem of *Difficult Reproducibility*. The reproducibility is a general requirement for benchmarks, as the goals of benchmarks are the performance measurement of a single or multiple solutions and the comparison of the same solution in different versions. Therefore, benchmarks must ensure that the problems presented to the solutions provide the same characteristics, in particular, being independent of time and locations of the benchmark executions. In contrast to RDF and SPARQL benchmarks, benchmarks for LD settings must provide reproducibility not only of the pure RDF generation but, with respect to the reliable generation of RDF graphs with the same characteristics, their correct separation and interlinking in the overall dataset, the resolvability of links with respect to the actual deployment, and the distributed deployment that provides the same characteristics. The setup of the same benchmark with the same parameters in different locations or at different times must result in comparable LD settings that share the same characteristics.

5.1.3 Related Work

With the growing proliferation of graph-based data, in general, and LD, in particular, benchmarking has become a prominent topic in the SW and database communities. Many benchmarks and data generators already exist, including LUBM [73], Berlin SPARQL Benchmark (BSBM) [35], SPARQL Performance Benchmark (SP2Bench) [140], gMark [12], Generating Random RDF (Grr) [36], or Waterloo SPARQL Diversity Test Suite (WatDiv) [3]. Furthermore, benchmarks have been developed in the field of RDF stream processors [47], including SRBench [169] and LSBench [110]. Still, the main focus of these benchmarks is on covering the main features of RDF and SPARQL, on query optimization, and not specifically on exploring the LD setting.

In general, the desirable characteristics of benchmarks [88], e.g., repeatable, fair, verifiable, and economical, are not always taken into consideration. Moreover, sometimes the specifics and requirements in RDF and graph data management are neglected, as pointed out in a series of benchmark surveys [51, 52, 166]. In this context, the Linked Data Benchmark Council (LDBC) [4] aims to establish benchmarks and benchmarking practices for evaluating graph data management systems. It proposes a "choke-point"-driven design of graph database benchmarks, which combines user input with input from expert systems architects.

We are also witnessing the development of benchmarks that cover specific domains. For instance, related to social network benchmarking, the LDBC developed the Social Network Benchmark (SNB) [55], which introduces a synthetic social network graph with three workloads: SNB-Interactive, SNB-BI, and SNB-Algorithms. Similarly, Facebook features LinkBench [7], a benchmark targeting the workload of Online Transaction Processing (OLTP) on the Facebook graph. LinkBench focuses only on transactions and uses a synthetic graph generator, which is unfortunately capable of reproducing very little of the structure or value correlations found in real networks. Finally, the BG benchmark [13] proposes to evaluate simple social networking actions under different Service Level Agreements (SLAs). Naturally, domain-specific benchmarks put emphasis on particular characteristics such as network structure and node correlations.

In summary, while there are a number of benchmarks supporting SPARQL features, including query optimization, and while there are also some benchmarks with focus on certain domains, what is still missing is a benchmark that targets specifically LD and not RDF in general. This is especially true for providing options for having virtually or physically distributed datasets, having valid links between graphs in these datasets, and, at the same time, being able to manage the deployment complexity of such a distributed setting.

5.1.4 Contributions

With respect to the challenges presented in Section 5.1.2 and advancing the current state of the art, we make the following contributions:

- In Section 5.2.1, we conduct a *Requirements Analysis* with respect to the identified challenges and derive high-level requirements for distributed LD benchmarking.
- We present the *Linked Data Benchmark Environment (LDBE)* in Section 5.2.2, including an architecture designed to cope with the requirements.
- We introduce the *Distributed LUBM (DLUBM)* as a specific implementation of our architecture in Section 5.3, including 1) a LD generator, 2) the integration with container-based virtualization and distribution technologies, 3) supporting tools for automatic composition and deployment, and 4) the reproducibility by through simple parametrization.
- In Section 5.4.1, we show the *Evaluation of Centralized Linked Data Querying* by utilizing DLUBM instances of different scales. These experiments have been conducted for comparability on computing resources of broadly available platform providers, in particular, in the Elastic Compute Cloud (EC2) provided by Amazon Web Services (AWS).
- In Section 5.4.2, we show the *Evaluation of Decentralized Linked Data Querying* at different scale by utilizing DLUBM instances integrated with SCAL. Similar to the other evaluation, these experiments have been conducted for comparability on computing resources of broadly available platform providers.

5.2 Approach for Linked Data Benchmark Environments

Our approach for realizing a truly distributed Linked Data Benchmark Environment (LDBE) is guided by a set of requirements derived from the problem areas introduced in Section 5.1.2. With these requirements, we ensure the broad applicability of our architecture and abstract away from specific implementation characteristics. Thereby, the approach itself is independent from domains and technologies but exposes explicit requirements for dataset generation, virtualization, and distribution technologies. Our DLUBM benchmark environment, described in Section 5.3, is one specific implementation. In the following, we present the guiding requirements and our benchmark architecture.

5.2.1 Requirements

Based on the presented challenges, we derive four groups of main requirements for an LDBE, each group covering one of the challenges.

5.2.1.1 Deployment-aligned Data Generation

Our first requirement, with respect to the challenges related to Data Generation is the *Deployment-aligned Data Generation*. Our goal is the creation of a truly distributed LDBE. Therefore, one requirement for our approach is the generation of RDF graphs that are distinct but interlinked and are suited to settings that adhere to the well-known LD [23, 33] principles. These LD principles indirectly impose requirements on the generation of graphs that can be used in a distributed environment. First, the data generator must support the generation of completely separate RDF graphs, e.g., split into different files. Depending on the deployment process of the distributed benchmark environment, the generation of subsets of the set of all graphs in the dataset is an advantage. Thereby, the distributed generation is improved by generating only the graphs that are relevant for provisioning at the hosts. Second, the data generator must support the correct interlinking of these graphs, with respect to the actual deployment of the distributed environment, i.e., the HTTP URIs within generated graphs must point to the correct related graphs, including their correct hostnames. Third, if SPARQL queries are dynamically generated along with the datasets, the generator must support the correct use of HTTP URIs in these queries with respect to the actual deployment of graphs in the distributed benchmark environment.

5.2.1.2 Network Layer Distribution

Our second requirement, with respect to the challenges related to Dataset Distribution is the *Network Layer Distribution*. For a distributed LDBE, an implication of the problem and, in addition, imposed by the second and fourth

LD principles, is the interlinking and lookup in distributed datasets, i.e., HTTP URIs in graphs of the datasets can be looked up to discover related graphs. While this can be achieved with a single host through distribution on the application layer (i.e., graphs identified and looked up by different HTTP URIs hosted at one server) simulating a realistic setting in the context of scenarios in the WoD, the IoT, the WoT, or the SWoT, can only be achieved if these graphs are distributed to different hosts at least at the network level. In addition, the provisioning of larger benchmark datasets at a single host may lead to performance bottlenecks, depending on the type and amount of expected requests. Therefore, the requirement guiding our approach is the distribution of interlinked RDF graphs at the network layer of the Open Systems Interconnection (OSI) model, in particular, by using different IP addresses or DNS records. Graphs must be provided by distinct hosts and be resolvable via HTTP. With respect to established cloud and emerging container-solutions, we neither require nor prohibit physically separate hosts.

5.2.1.3 Deployment Automation

Our third requirement, with respect to the challenges related to Deployment Complexity is the *Deployment Automation*. Hereby, we focus on the complexity, which accompanies the deployment of distributed applications. This includes, for example, the setup and networking of multiple hosts, the distribution to and interlinking of graphs at these hosts, and the resolvability of links in certain network environments. In addition, benchmark environments are not setup for long-term provisioning, but for experiments with different parameterizations and computing resources. Furthermore, benchmark environments must be flexible to be deployable at an appropriate scale. In smaller cases, the environment is deployed on limited development resources and, in larger cases, on computing resources of large-scale testing facilities. Our third main requirement for a distributed LDBE is, therefore, the automation of the deployments, thus reducing the complexity to a sufficient degree that renders the benchmark environments usable and enables temporary experimental settings on different scales. To enable the seamless scaling of the benchmark environment in terms of performance, the automation should be agnostic to the provided computing resources and enable the automatic deployment on single and multiple as well as virtually or physically separated systems.

5.2.1.4 Pervasive Declaration

Our fourth requirement, with respect to the challenges of Difficult Reproducibility is the *Pervasive Declaration*. Comparing different solution alternatives for the same problem area is one of the key goals of benchmarks. The same set of configuration parameters leads to the same set of resources, which are used to evaluate and compare different solutions for the same problem. The declaration of the same set of parameters must lead to generating the same datasets, distribution, and interlinking. In addition, the computing resources available for the hosts may be covered for greater comparability. The interweaving of LD generation and the actual distributed deployment, under different conditions, is especially challenging for reproducibility. Thus, for our approach, we distinguish between different types of parameters. On the one hand, we introduce parameters that influence the scale and granularity of the distributed LDBE. These may be global (e.g., the number of graphs and the size of overall datasets for scaling) or local, i.e., host-specific (e.g., the type of data to be generated in case of different granularities within the overall dataset). On the other hand, we introduce parameters that influence the interlinking of graphs. These are deployment-specific and enable the adjustment of generated data to the environment, in which the distributed benchmark is deployed (e.g., URI templates to generate correct links, according to the IP or DNS schema of the environment).

5.2.2 Linked Data Benchmark Environment

The architecture of our distributed LDBE is designed to fulfill the requirements. While the scope of reproducibility in RDF and SPARQL benchmarks is limited to the generation of equal graphs and queries, it is extended to the generation of distributed environments with equal characteristics in the case of LD.

- For the requirement of *Deployment-aligned Data Generation*, we build on LD-capable data generators or on established RDF benchmarks, that are extended to generate graphs for LD, e.g., as we present in our implementation in Section 5.3. In general, data generators are exchangeable in our approach, as long as they support the parametrized generation of datasets that contain distinct but interlinked RDF graphs, including the adjustment of links to the actual deployment.

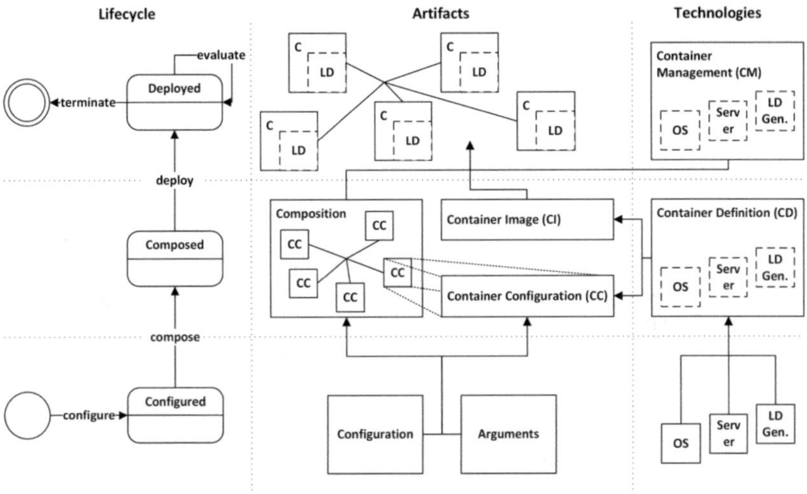

Figure 5.2: Linked Data Benchmark Environment – Architecture

- For the requirements *Network Layer Distribution* and *Deployment Automation*, we build on container-based virtualization technologies that, independently from the specific deployment platforms, enable the definition of hosts, networks, and other deployment-specific tasks.
- For the requirement of *Pervasive Declaration*, we build on the parametrization of the data generator, on the declarative configuration of containers, based on container definitions for the declarative setup of the included systems and software, and on the declarative composition of configured containers. Taking into account the computing resources that are provided for the deployment of a composition, we are able to achieve the reproducible creation of the overall distributed LDBE.

In our architecture in Figure 5.2, we distinguish between the lifecycle, the artifacts, and the technologies of the LDBE.

- We denote the lifecycle, similarly to a state machine, as a set of states and transitions that a benchmark environment passes through, starting with initialization and ending with termination.

- We show the artifacts that users or the LDBE tooling create for each state of the lifecycle.
- We introduce the technologies that accompany each state. Besides the technologies required for the LDBE, the transitions between states should be supported by technology to enable the increased deployment automation.

We also distinguish between the configuration phase, the composition phase, and the deployment phase, that group sets artifacts and technologies with a state of the lifecycle. With every phase, the set of required technologies is extended and, thereby, the details of the implementations are narrowed and further refined down. In addition, the evaluation phase represents the running and usable LDBE.

5.2.2.1 Configuration Phase

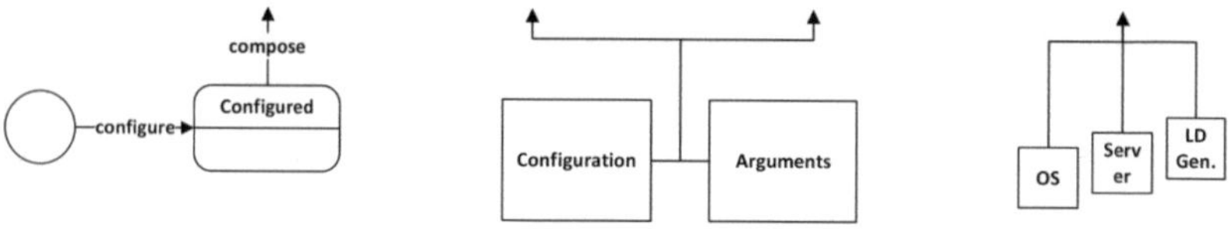

Figure 5.3: Linked Data Benchmark Environment – Architecture: Configuration

Lifecycle As shown in Figure 5.3, the *configure* transition leads from the initial state to the *Configured* state. In this state, the implementation of the architecture is independent from any specific virtualization technology or computing resources.

Technologies The technologies that accompany this state are technologies that are indirectly configured through the given parametrization of the LDBE, e.g., the operating system, servers, or the LD generator. In a later phase of the lifecycle, these technologies are set up in a declarative way via container definitions and are pre-assembled as container images. The images provide configuration parameters for the configuration during the initialization of containers, which are based on these images. By predetermining the setup of software in the containers in a declarative manner, we reduce the amount of variables in the overall system to only the parametrization of the LDBE.

Artifacts The artifacts generated or determined during the *configure* transition are limited to simple configuration files or program arguments. These configurations contain the essence of parameters that are required to define the characteristics of the distributed LDBE, which is then derived from these parameters in the following transitions.

5.2.2.2 Composition Phase

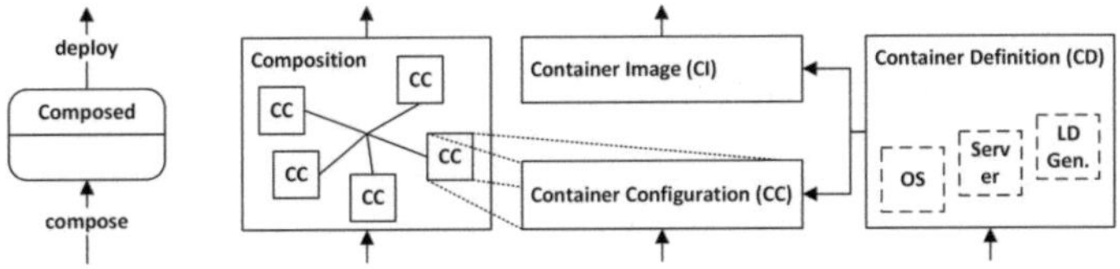

Figure 5.4: Linked Data Benchmark Environment – Architecture: Composition

Lifecycle As shown in Figure 5.4, the *compose* transition leads from the *Configured* state to the *Composed* state. In this state, the implementation of the architecture becomes specific to one virtualization technology but is still independent from computing resources.

Technologies The technologies accompanying this state are container-based virtualization technologies. First, these technologies enable us to define the detailed setup of systems in the form of container definitions, which include the setup of operating systems, applications, processes, and optional parametrization. From this container definitions, we can build container images that provide a pre-built setup of the complete system defined by the container definition. These images are utilized during the deployment to initialize an arbitrary number of similar containers that differ only in the parameters that have been specified in the container definition. Second, these technologies enable us to define the detailed setup of distributed applications in the form of compositions, including the container configurations for containers that should be part of the application, including their parameters, and the network connections between containers as well as to external networks. An implementation of the architecture must provide container definitions for the LD generation and provisioning. In addition, the *compose* transition should be supported by composition generators to expand the configuration of the LDBE.

Artifacts During the *compose* transition, we expand the benchmark-specific parameters of the configuration and create as artifacts the detailed composition, that is specific to the virtualization technology and includes the configuration of containers based on the provided container definitions. By utilizing the container definitions, in combination with the composition generator, we reduce the set of parameters in the overall benchmark environment to the aforementioned set of configuration parameters of the LDBE. These parametrize the composition generator and, thereby, the container configurations and, indirectly, the data generators as well. During this transition, we determine, for example, the correct amount of containers and the size of the generated datasets to fit scaling parameters, or the container-specific parameters to generate correct graphs and to generate correct links to other graphs, based on the host configurations in the composition.

5.2.2.3 Deployment Phase

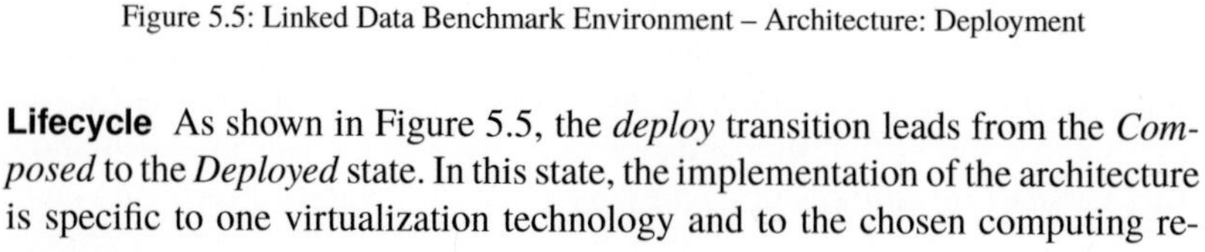

Figure 5.5: Linked Data Benchmark Environment – Architecture: Deployment

Lifecycle As shown in Figure 5.5, the *deploy* transition leads from the *Composed* to the *Deployed* state. In this state, the implementation of the architecture is specific to one virtualization technology and to the chosen computing resources.

Technologies The technologies accompanying this state are the container management of the container-based virtualization technology and the computing resources provided to this management. An important characteristic of these virtualization technologies is the platform-agnostic handling of standalone containers and compositions of containers, i.e., these virtualization technologies support the deployment on local computers, private clouds, or on Platform as a Service (PaaS) solutions. Our strategy behind decoupling the composition and the deployment platform is as follows: the broader the availability of the computing resources used for the benchmarking is, the more comparable the benchmarking results will be, e.g., by utilizing larger public or commercially available platforms. While custom local computing power or private clouds may be sufficient for development and test purposes, comparative benchmarking should be executed on detailed specified hardware settings and, ideally, run on broadly available computing resources. In this way, the benchmarking results become not only more comparable but also more reproducible.

Artifacts The artifacts generated during the *deploy* transition are the container instances that are set up according to the composition. These run on the chosen deployment platform, are connected by a network, provide correctly interlinked graphs, and expose the interlinked LD to clients. At this state, the LDBE is ready for use.

5.2.2.4 Evaluation Phase

Having reached the *Deployed* state, we indicate that the benchmark environment is in use via the *evaluate* transition. Experiments can repeatedly be performed to conduct evaluations by utilizing the deployed LDBE. After the completion of the experiments, the benchmark environment can be stopped (as indicated by the *terminate* transition to the final state). Furthermore, any reserved computing resources may be released.

5.3 Implementation of the Distributed LUBM

With the Distributed LUBM (DLUBM), we provide one domain-specific implementation of the architecture that we introduced in Section 5.2 and that realizes a distributed and interlinked LDBE. The implementation of the data generator component is derived from the well-known LUBM [73] benchmark and is an extension of the LUBM artificial data generator by Vesse[1] and, originally, by Guo et al. [73]. We support the same scaling and semantically same data but provide new contributions by adding new features that enable the generation of LD. In particular, we enable the generation of datasets of different size and granularity, as well as the correct interlinking of contained graphs with respect to the actual deployment.

Furthermore, we support virtualization based on the Docker[2] [113] ecosystem by providing DLUBM container definitions, i.e., Dockerfiles, container images, i.e., Docker Images, and the generation of compositions that enable the deployment of distributed multi-container DLUBM instances on standalone Docker engines or computing clusters managed by Docker Swarm on all supported platforms. In addition, the aforementioned container-based virtualization may be used with related container management systems like Kubernetes[3]. Our DLUBM implementation is configurable by a small set of parameters, is deployable with a high degree of automation on local computers, private clouds, or PaaS computing resources, and creates a domain-specific, reproducible, and truly distributed LDBE.

We developed different software components[4], which, integrated with existing technology, implement our architecture. In the following, we give in Section 5.3.1 an overview about the structure as well as the parameters of DLUBM and elaborate on the LD generator. In Section 5.3.2, we present the container definition and image and describe the generator for container compositions and queries. We briefly describe in Section 5.3.3 related container management solutions and computing resources for the DLUBM deployment.

5.3.1 Configuration Phase Implementations

To support the configuration phase of our architecture (c.f., Section 5.2.2.1), we describe in the following an overview of the structure as well as parameters of the DLUBM and provide the implementation of the DLUBM LD generator.

[1] https://rslv.link/ZSvh
[2] https://rslv.link/ZSvY
[3] https://rslv.link/ZSvH
[4] https://rslv.link/ZSvO

5.3.1.1 Structure

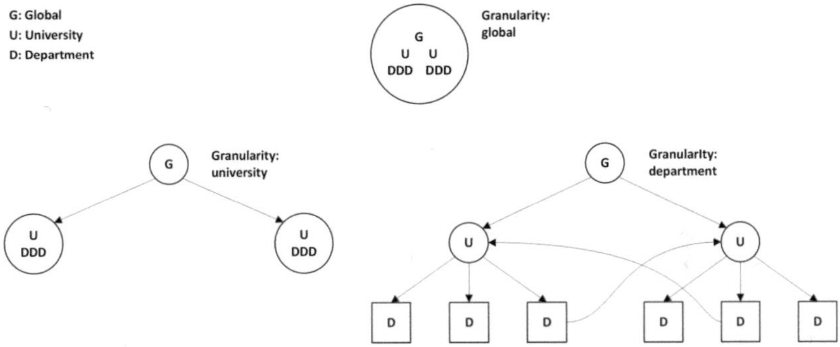

Figure 5.6: DLUBM – Structure and Interlinking

As shown in Figure 5.6, we provide parametrized support for different granularity levels that denote the structural level of detail, at which graphs about entities are provided by separate components of the DLUBM.

- In the most detailed *department* granularity, shown at the right bottom, the granularity level leads to separate components that provide the graphs of one or more departments as well as components for the graphs of one or more universities, and one component that provides a global graph. The global graph contains links to all universities, the university graphs contain links to all departments of the corresponding university, and the department graphs contain information about all other entities that partially contain again links to other universities.
- At the granularity level *university* (shown on the left side), the components at department level are not provided, but the graphs representing departments are provided at the university components, in addition to the graphs about universities.
- At the granularity level *global* (shown on top), all graphs are provided at a single components, i.e., no distribution of the dataset over several components is provided.

In addition to the granularity, the number of universities and departments per component is parametrized. Thereby, we support the scaling of DLUBM in terms of provided LD, i.e., the size of information, independently from the scaling in terms of distribution, i.e., the amount of components. For example, we may provide at the granularity level *department*, components at university level, that provide graphs with information about several universities, as well as components at the department level, which provide graphs with information about several departments. In this case, the correct interlinking of graphs is still guaranteed.

5.3.1.2 Parametrization

```
dlubm_instance = DLUBM(
    int seed,
    int granularity,
    int university_offset,
    int university_amount,
    int university_limit,
    int department_limit)
```

Listing 5.1: DLUBM – Function and Parameters

As indicated in Listing 5.1, we can describe the characteristics of a DLUBM instance as a function that is parametrized by a small set of global parameters. These parameters must be provided to the composition generator that derives the composition of containers for the DLUBM instance during the compose transition, including the local parameters for each container definition. Table 5.1 gives an overview of all important parameters that our DLUBM benchmark environment provides as global parameters for configuration or which are derived from these global parameters for supporting the automated configuration in later phases of the lifecycle.

The composition generator adds a container configuration for a fixed ontology URI to the composition, to prevent the dependency from external resources. Depending on the global parameter for the granularity level, the generator adds at the *global* level a single container configuration for the global component, or at the *university* level a container configuration for the global component

Parameter	Scope	Description
Seed	global	Seed of the data generator
Granularity	global	Structural level with distinct components
University Offset	global	Offset of the first university to generate
University Amount	global	Amount of universities to generate
University Limit	global	Limit of universities per component
Department Limit	global	Limit of departments per component
Host Depth	local	Structural level of the component
Host University Offset	local	Offset of the first university to generated
Host University Amount	local	Amount of universities to generate
Host Department Offset	local	Offset of the first department to generated
Host Department Amount	local	Amount of departments to generate
Ontology	deploy	URI for links to the ontology
University Template	deploy	URI template for links to universities
Department Template	deploy	URI template for links to departments

Table 5.1: DLUBM – Parameters

and multiple container configurations for the university components, or at the *department* level container configurations for components at all three levels. Every container is parametrized by the local parameters to generate and provide the correct graphs as part of the overall dataset. The last type of parameters is relevant for deployment, but not for the characteristics of the DLUBM instance. In particular, only the ontology URI and the templates for URIs to universities and departments must be provided in the container definition.

During the initialization of a container, the LD generator replaces template variables, e.g., path parameters for university and department indexes, and, thereby, generates resolvable links. The creation of these templates is taken over by the composition generator.

5.3.1.3 Linked Data Generator

We provide the DLUBM data generator[5] for generating distinct but interlinked graphs. Our extension includes several new features that enable the generation of graphs, which are suitable for a LD setting. In addition, the generator still supports the generation of the original LUBM dataset.

In particular, we extend the data generator to generate only a subset of the LUBM graphs. This feature is required to enable the distributed generation of datasets, thereby, reducing the resource usage of the individual components, and enabling faster overall LD generation at the distributed computing resources. Individual components, that are equipped with the data generator, may only provide a single graph or subset of graphs of the overall dataset. With this feature, we prevent the costly generation of the overall dataset at every component, in terms of required computing power and disk space, and the subsequent selection of the subset of graphs. For example, components that provide graphs with information about single departments are using this feature to generate only the single required graph.

Furthermore, we extend the data generator to generate graphs only at a specific granularity level. By adding this feature, we make the generator aware of the granularity levels that we require in order to enable different distribution scenarios (c.f., Section 5.3.1.1). In combination with the aforementioned generation of only a subset of graphs, we enable components to generate only the required graphs at a certain granularity level. For example, at the granularity level *university*, the data generators of components, which provide graphs with information about universities, generates, in addition, the graphs with information about related departments.

[5] `https://rslv.link/ZSvC`

Finally, we add the generation of correct links to other graphs in the dataset by utilizing URI templates. This feature is required to ensure the resolvability of links with respect to the actual environment, in which the components are deployed. As the LUBM utilizes artificial indexes for all kinds of entities, we support the substitution of related template parameters by these indexes. Thereby, we enable the customization of URIs in the generated graphs and the adjustment to the network environment, i.e., the adjustment to deployment-specific DNS records, hostnames, or paths, that are required to ensure resolvability.

5.3.2 Composition Phase Implementations

To support the composition phase of our architecture (c.f., Section 5.2.2.2), we provide in the following a container definition, a container image, and the implementation of a generator for container compositions and queries.

5.3.2.1 Container Definition and Image

We provide a container definition for the specification of the internal setup of components. In addition, we provide a container image that contains a pre-built setup, based on the container definition, that is used as the base for containers during their deployment. At the time of writing, the container definition and container image are specific to a virtualization technology. For DLUBM, we utilize the Docker ecosystem and provide as container definition a Dockerfile and as container image a pre-build Docker Image[6]. The Dockerfile defines in a declarative way the setup of an operating system, the setup of the LD generator, and the setup of a web server that provides documents that contain the representation of the generated graphs. In addition, the parametrization of the container (c.f., Section 5.3.1.2) as well as the handling of the supplied parameter for the correct control of the LD generator are specified. With the Docker Image a pre-built version of the defined system exists, ready to be used for a parametrized instantiation of containers in the Docker ecosystem, e.g., by utilizing the support for deploying compositions of containers (c.f., Section 5.3.2.2).

[6] `https://rslv.link/ZSqZ`

5.3.2.2 Composition and Query Generator

In addition to the container definition and the container image, the composition of containers and the included container configurations are also part of the composition phase. Similarly to the container definition and container image, the composition of containers is, at the time of this writing, specific to a virtualization technology. For DLUBM, we stay in the Docker ecosystem and utilize compose files[7] for the Docker Compose and Docker Swarm tooling. In contrast to the container definition and container image, the composition is not declared a priori, but derived from the individual parametrization of the LDBE, which is in our case the DLUBM. Therefore, we provide a generator for Docker Compose files, which is capable to expand DLUBM configurations to compositions of containers that specify the complete derived DLUBM instance in a declarative manner.

In Listing 5.2, we show an excerpt of a DLUBM composition file for Docker Compose, which contains as an example the container configuration of one DLUBM container instance that is part of a larger composition. The definition includes deployment-specific parameters, e.g., the redirection rules for a reverse proxy, as well as the previously presented DLUBM-specific deployment, local, and global parameters. Subsequently, the composition file can be utilized in the deployment phase of our architecture (c.f., Section 5.2.2.2) to instruct the container management, e.g., Docker, or Docker Swarm (c.f., Section 5.3.3.1), with the initialization of the containers and related infrastructure.

In addition to the generation of compositions, we support the generation of LUBM SPARQL queries that are aligned with the generated compositions. These SPARQL queries provide, in general, the same semantics as the queries provided by the original LUBM, but are tailored to the actual DLUBM instance in terms of URIs. These queries must be adjusted to the deployment, since the URIs in generated graphs are deployment-specific. However, the DLUBM LDBE does not limit the type of queries.

---

[7] https://rslv.link/ZSqv

```
[...]
d0_u0_dl1_ul1_uo0_ua5_gd_s0:
  deploy:
    labels: [traefik.docker.network=reverse_proxy,
        traefik.port=80, 'traefik.frontend.rule=Host:d0.
        u0.dlubm.local']
    placement:
      constraints: [node.role == worker]
  environment: ['DLUBM_ONTOLOGY=http://o.dlubm.local/univ
      -bench.owl', DLUBM_SEED=0, DLUBM_GRANULARITY=
      DEPARTMENT, DLUBM_UNIVERSITY_AMOUNT=5,
      DLUBM_UNIVERSITY_OFFSET=0, DLUBM_UNIVERSITY_LIMIT
      =1, DLUBM_UNIVERSITY_TEMPLATE=http://u{
      UNIVERSITY_INDEX}.dlubm.local/u#',
      DLUBM_DEPARTMENT_LIMIT=1, '
      DLUBM_DEPARTMENT_TEMPLATE=http://d{DEPARTMENT_INDEX
      }.u{UNIVERSITY_INDEX}.dlubm.local/d#',
      DLUBM_HOST_DEPTH=DEPARTMENT,
      DLUBM_HOST_UNIVERSITY_AMOUNT=1,
      DLUBM_HOST_UNIVERSITY_OFFSET=0,
      DLUBM_HOST_DEPARTMENT_AMOUNT=1,
      DLUBM_HOST_DEPARTMENT_OFFSET=0]
  image: dlubm:latest
  networks: [proxy]
[...]
```

Listing 5.2: DLUBM – Composition

5.3.3 Deployment Phase Implementations

To support the deployment phase of our architecture (c.f., Section 5.2.2.3), we introduce in the following the utilized container management solution and briefly describe the relation between the solution and computing resources.

5.3.3.1 Container Management

The Docker ecosystem provides several components that ease the management and deployment of large-scale container environments, which we shortly introduce in the following and refer to their documentation for further details. We use Docker Compose[8] for the deployment of compositions to local Docker instances. For the deployment of compositions to multiple Docker instances via a cluster managed by Docker Swarm[9], we use Docker Stacks[10]. In the latter case, the distribution and lifecycle of containers on multiple computing resources is dynamically managed. We use Traefik[11], a reverse proxy with support for local Docker instances as well as Docker Swarm environments. Hereby, the assignment of DNS records to containers and the corresponding routing of requests to these records is part of the composition and thus is automatically managed. In addition, alternative solution like Kubernetes[12] may be used for container management.

5.3.3.2 Computing Resources

By utilizing the means for container management mentioned above, we abstract away from the actual computing resources. The automatic container management enables us to deploy DLUBM instances on a local computer, a private cloud, or PaaS, e.g., AWS EC2. Hereby, we do not restrict the computing resources in any way but leave their selection and provisioning to the DLUBM users. Comparative experiments, however, should not only use the same parametrization of the DLUBM but also provide the same or comparable computing resources to the container management.

5.4 Evaluation

In the following, we evaluate our LDBE approach and the DLUBM implementation in two different evaluations:

- We evaluate the centralized querying of the DLUBM LDBE by a LD query engine in Section 5.4.1. In this evaluation, the DLUBM LDBE

[8] `https://rslv.link/ZSqq`
[9] `https://rslv.link/ZSqD`
[10] `https://rslv.link/ZSqN`
[11] `https://rslv.link/ZSq3`
[12] `https://rslv.link/ZSvH`

provides different LD scenarios in a decentralized manner. The LD query engine retrieves graph representations through HTTP, follows, if required, links to further LD resources, derives certain information, and evaluates the given SPARQL queries.

- We evaluate the decentralized controlled LD querying, enabled by SCAL in Section 5.4.2. In this evaluation, the components provided by the DLUBM LDBE integrate SCAL and, thereby, adhere to our SC approach. Subsequently, the retrieving of LD, the evaluation of SPARQL queries, and the aggregation of results are deployed in different scenarios by adapting the SCs.

5.4.1 Evaluation of Centralized Linked Data Querying

We evaluate our approach by utilizing our LDBE architecture and the DLUBM implementation in order to measure the performance of a LD query engine, which retrieves LD and evaluates SPARQL queries in a centralized manner. In the following, we first introduce the LD query engine, then describe the experimental setup, and finally discuss the results.

5.4.1.1 Linked Data Query Engine

For our experiments, we evaluate LD-Fu [156, 158] – a combination of SPARQL query evaluation engine and interpreter of N3 rule programs. LD-Fu is accompanied by the corresponding semantics for the interpretation of rules and supports separate handling of specific ontologies, e.g., the HTTP vocabulary[13] for execution of HTTP requests, or the Math ontology for providing built-in mathematical functions. During interpreter runs LD-Fu maintains an internal RDF graph that is enriched by RDF triples, which are given as part of rule programs, are derived by the interpretation of rules, or are requested via HTTP. The internal RDF graph can be queried via SPARQL. Thereby, LD-Fu enables requests to resources, link following, as well as querying of requested, aggregated, and derived data.

[13] `https://rslv.link/ZSqo`

5.4.1.2 Experiments

We provide a documentation[14] of our experiments, including guidelines, highly-automated deployment, experiment runs, and results.

Type	Operating System	Description	Amount
m4.xlarge	Ubuntu 16.04	Experiments	1
m4.xlarge	RancherOS 1.0.1	Docker Swarm Master	1
t2.small	RancherOS 1.0.1	Docker Swarm Worker	18

Table 5.2: Centralized Linked Data Querying – Deployment Platform

Deployment Platform We conducted our experiments on computing resources provided by AWS[15] EC2[16]. In Table 5.2, we give an overview of the 20 AWS EC2 instances of our setup. By limiting the number of EC2 instances to 20, we enable the usage of our documented experiments without requesting, at the time of writing, a limit increase for running more instances on AWS EC2.

In this setup, we reserved one EC2 instance for experiments and joined all other EC2 instances into a Docker Swarm instance for managing the compositions of containers. The instance for experiments is provisioned with the operating system Ubuntu[17] and all Docker Swarm instances use the Docker-centric operating system RancherOS[18]. The master instance of the Docker Swarm coordinates the provisioning of containers at all worker instances. At the master instance, a container including the Traefik[19] reverse proxy handles the mapping of incoming requests at a dynamically allocated DNS entry to containers managed by the Docker Swarm (c.f., Section 5.3.3.1). Thereby, the assignment of containers to hostnames can be declared in the composition. For the experiments, we restrict DLUBM containers to run only at worker instances.

14 https://rslv.link/ZSqn
15 https://rslv.link/ZSq8
16 https://rslv.link/ZSqA
17 https://rslv.link/ZSqJ
18 https://rslv.link/ZSqa
19 https://rslv.link/ZSq3

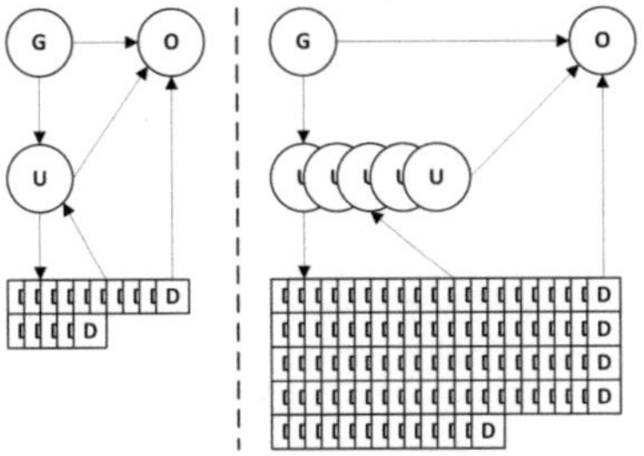

Figure 5.7: Centralized Linked Data Querying – Evaluation Scenarios

Linked Data Environment For comparability with the original LUBM benchmark results, we use two instances of our DLUBM environment with similar characteristics. In Figure 5.7, we visualized both setups. Both instances are configured at the department granularity for the generation of multiple components, i.e., one component per university/department. On the left side, the configuration *DLUBM(0, DEPARTMENT, 0, 1, 1, 1)* leads to 18 components.

- One component provides the LUBM ontology, which is linked by all other components.
- One component provides the global graph, which provides a link to a single university.
- One component provides the graph with information about the university.
- 15 components provide graphs with information about departments of the university.

The number of departments per university is determined by the algorithm of the original LUBM generator and is a pseudo-random number between 15 and 20. On the right side, the configuration *DLUBM(0, DEPARTMENT, 0, 5, 1, 1)* leads to 100 components that are structured as the first configuration, including 93 components that provide graphs with department information. Thereby, we maintain comparability of the query results with the results of the work on the original LUBM [73], which have been based, among others, on querying graphs that include information about one and five universities.

Queries For our measurements, we use the original 14 SPARQL queries of the LUBM benchmark, which are adjusted by our composition generator with the correct URIs for our DLUBM environment. In addition, we added the "DISTINCT" modifier to eliminate duplicate results.

Rules The LD-Fu interpreter is capable of evaluating N3 rules but without advanced built-in derivation capabilities for RDFS or OWL. Therefore, as part of separate experiments, we added entailment rule sets with RDFS and OWL-LD[20] entailment rules. In addition, in order to emphasize the modular approach of LD-Fu, in an extra run we add two custom rules to the OWL-LD rule set, which derive most of the still missing results for the LUBM queries.

5.4.1.3 Measurements

In the following, we present the results of the query evaluation, and also provide the different time and derivation metrics, measured during the evaluation of LUBM queries on both DLUBM configurations with LD-Fu.

Results We measured the evaluation of DLUBM queries without entailment rule sets, with every entailment rule set separately, and with the combinations of entailment rule sets. Due to space constrains, we show in Table 5.3 only the query results for the first DLUBM configuration *DLUBM(0, DEPARTMENT, 0, 1, 1, 1)* without entailment rule sets, with the RDFS entailment rule set, with the OWL-LD entailment rule set, and with the OWL-LD entailment rule set extended by two custom rules (Custom). Query 1, 3, and 14, contain simple selections and can be handled without entailment rules. For all other queries, we see an improvement with the RDFS entailment rule set, and even further improvement for query 11 with the OWL-LD entailment rule set, which supersedes the RDFS result. Finally, our two custom rules, which handle the derivation related to students and heads of departments, complement the OWL-LD entailment rule set in most cases (except for Q13).

Times During the experiments, we measured the different times for both configurations per query. We visualize for the first DLUBM configuration with 18 components – the overall runtime for query evaluation on the left side in Figure 5.8, the average request time for successful requests on the left side in Figure 5.9, and the average request time for failing requests on the left side

[20] `https://rslv.link/ZSqW`

in Figure 5.10. On the right side in each figure, we provide a visualization of the same measurements for the second DLUBM configuration with 100 components. Failing requests appear due to a hard-coded limitation within the original LUBM data generator, which generates links to universities with an index between 0 and 1000. These universities must not necessary exist, in particular, not for low number of university, as in our evaluation. Therefore, the diagrams in Figure 5.10 represent the average request times over several failing requests. The diagrams show in essence two noticeable details.

Q	A	None		RDFS		OWL-LD		Custom	
1	4	4	100%	4	100%	4	100%	4	100%
2	0	0	100%	0	100%	0	100%	0	100%
3	6	6	100%	6	100%	6	100%	6	100%
4	34	0	0%	34	100%	34	100%	34	100%
5	719	0	0%	719	100%	719	100%	719	100%
6	7790	0	0%	5916	76%	5916	76%	7790	100%
7	67	0	0%	59	88%	59	88%	67	100%
8	7790	0	0%	5916	76%	5916	76%	7790	100%
9	208	0	0%	103	50%	103	50%	208	100%
10	4	0	0%	0	0%	0	0%	4	100%
11	224	0	0%	0	0%	224	100%	224	100%
12	15	0	0%	0	0%	0	0%	15	100%
13	1	0	0%	0	0%	0	0%	0	0%
14	5916	5916	100%	5916	100%	5916	100%	5916	100%

Table 5.3: Centralized Linked Data Querying – Query Results and Completeness

First, the performance of the LD query engine is not only dependent on the performance of the engine itself, but has also to cope with a potential unpredictable network environment, which is out of its control. This is visible in the diagrams with average request times for failing requests for both DLUBM configurations. HTTP requests are, as far as possible, executed by the LD-Fu engine in parallel and are, therefore, considerably faster than in serial execution. However, if some requests are significantly delayed, e.g., indicated by the increased average request times, for example, during evaluation of query 1, 13, and 14 (Figure 5.10 – left), the engine has to wait for these requests to fail or to return a response. The delay caused by these requests is reflected in the overall runtime for the respective queries (Figure 5.8 – left).

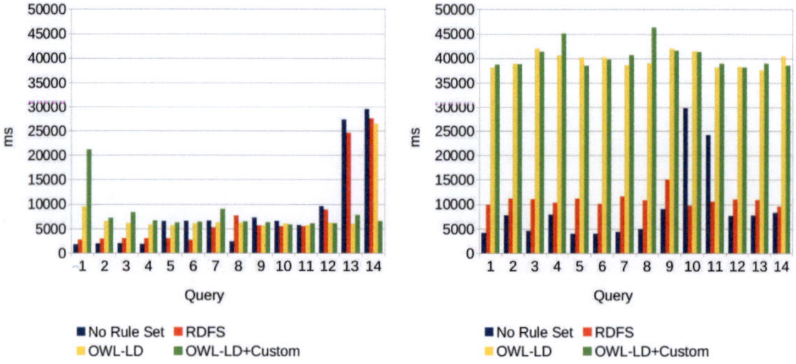

Figure 5.8: Centralized Linked Data Querying – Evaluation Results for Runtimes

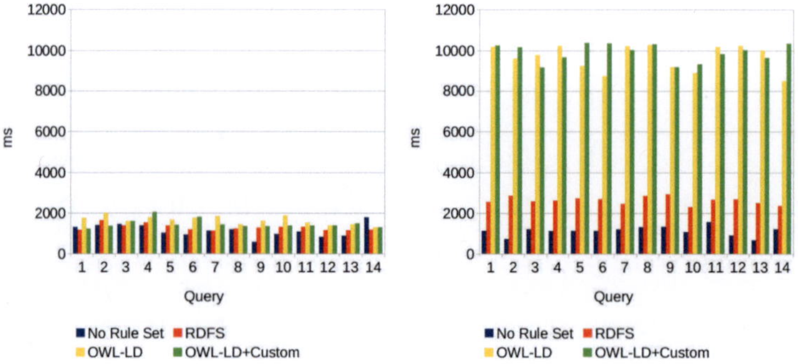

Figure 5.9: Centralized Linked Data Querying – Evaluation Results for Average Successful Request Times

Second, given the runtime measurements in Figure 5.8 – right, which show the query evaluation of the DLUBM configuration with 100 hosts, we can clearly see the impact of entailment rules. With the RDFS entailment rules, the runtime is already significantly higher, however, it increases even more for the OWL-LD entailment rules. Unclear, however, is the correlation with the average times for successful requests in the diagram on the right in Figure 5.9. Either the connection handling is slowed down by the processing power consumed for the evaluation of entailment rules, or the processing of the returned payload is slowed down for the same reason.

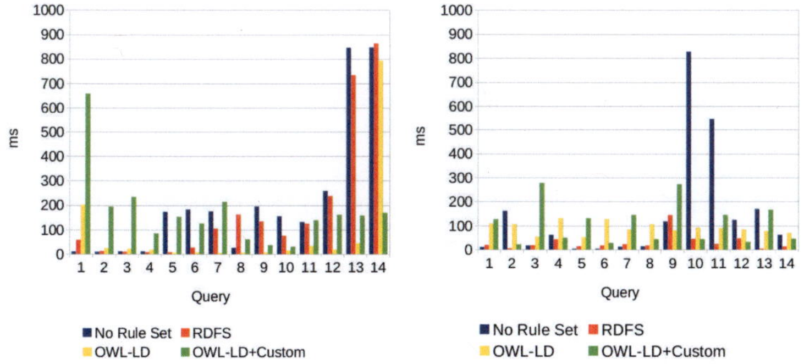

Figure 5.10: Centralized Linked Data Querying – Evaluation Results for Average Failing Request Times

Triples In Table 5.4 we show the triples that have been derived by the interpreter – in the different DLUBM configurations and with the different entailment rule sets.

Scenario	None	RDFS	OWL-LD	Custom
DLUBM(0, DEP., 0, 1, 1, 1)	0	115860	182949	184939
DLUBM(0, DEP., 0, 5, 1, 1)	0	700552	1115161	1127154

Table 5.4: Centralized Linked Data Querying – Derived Triples

5.4.2 Evaluation of Decentralized Linked Data Querying

Here we evaluate our approach by utilizing the Smart Component Adaptation Layer (SCAL) (c.f., Section 3.3.1) in order to integrate multiple components in a LD benchmarking scenario. In particular, we use the Distributed LUBM LDBE integrated with SCAL for Smart Component (SC) capabilities, deploy query evaluation in a centralized as well as two decentralized ways, and compare the query performance in these settings. In the following, we first introduce Distributed LUBM with decentralized control, then describe our experiments, and finally discuss the results.

5.4.2.1 Distributed LUBM with Smart Components

The DLUBM with decentralized control is realized through the integration of both SCAL and DLUBM implementations. In this case, we take advantage of the file system storage that is supported for persistence by SCAL and the generation of the correct subset of documents per component by DLUBM, which contain representations of RDF graphs in one of the RDF serialization formats supported by SCAL. These documents are provided by SCAL as LDP-RS of the LDP interface to the network. In addition, the LDP interface of SCAL provides all other SC capabilities, e.g., the deployment of AR like programs, queries, and runs, as well as the execution of interpreter runs. In this case, the provided DLUBM RDF graphs represent the domain-specific function of the SCs and can be used during evaluation steps of interpreter runs, or, in addition, be directly requested by other components. Thereby, we enable general access to the interlinked DLUBM datasets, while at the same time, provide adaptation capabilities directly at the DLUBM SCs. Analogously to DLUBM, we support the automation of the deployment for the integrated DLUBM SCAL LDBE through container-based virtualization. We provide container definitions in the form of Dockerfiles[21] as well as a Docker Image[22] that merges DLUBM and SCAL by replacing the default web server with our SCAL implementation.

[21] `https://rslv.link/ZSqB`
[22] `https://rslv.link/ZSqe`

5.4.2.2 Experiments

We provide a documentation[23] of our experiments, including guidelines, highly-automated deployment, experiment runs, and results.

Type	Operating System	Description	Amount
m3.large	Ubuntu 17.04	Experiments	1
m3.large	RancherOS 1.0.2	Docker Swarm Master	1
m3.large	RancherOS 1.0.2	Docker Swarm Worker	50

Table 5.5: Decentralized Linked Data Querying – Deployment Platform

Deployment Platform Similarly to the evaluation of the centralized LD querying, we conducted our experiments on computing resources provided by AWS[24] EC2[25]. In Table 5.5, we give an overview of the 52 AWS EC2 instances of our setup. Analogously to the aforementioned evaluation, we reserved in this setup one EC2 instance for experiments and joined all other EC2 instances into a Docker Swarm instance for managing the compositions of containers. The instance for experiments runs on the Ubuntu[26] operating system and all Docker Swarm instances use the Docker-centric operating system RancherOS[27]. The master instance of the Docker Swarm coordinates the provisioning of containers at all worker instances. At the master instance, a container, including the Traefik[28] reverse proxy, handles the mapping of incoming requests at a dynamically allocated DNS entry to containers managed by the Docker Swarm. Thereby, the assignment of containers to hostnames can be declared in the composition. For the experiments, we restrict the DLUBM containers to run only at worker instances.

[23] https://rslv.link/ZSq5
[24] https://rslv.link/ZSq8
[25] https://rslv.link/ZSqA
[26] https://rslv.link/ZSqJ
[27] https://rslv.link/ZSqa
[28] https://rslv.link/ZSq3

Linked Data Environment For our experiments, we used the second DLUBM configuration *DLUBM(0, DEPARTMENT, 0, 5, 1, 1)* of the centralized LD query evaluation, which leads to 100 components. In detail, this configuration initializes all data generators with a seed of *0*, the *DEPARTMENT* granularity leads to the generation of components on all three levels, the *university offset* lets the data generation start with the first university, the *university amount* limits the generation to five universities, i.e., the scale of the environment, and the *university limit* and *department limit* lead to provisioning of a single university or department graph per component. This DLUBM configuration equals the configuration visualized on the right side in Figure 5.7.

Queries Similarly to the evaluation of the centralized LD querying, we used for our measurements the original 14 SPARQL queries of the LUBM benchmark, adjusted by our composition generator with the correct URIs for our DLUBM environment. In addition, we added the "DISTINCT" modifier to eliminate duplicate results.

Rules In contrast to the evaluation of the centralized LD querying, we added only the RDFS entailment rules during the adaptations of the SCs to the LD-Fu interpreter. In addition, we added, depending on the adaptation for the evaluation scenarios, different request rules that enable the interpreter to request the required LD resources.

5.4.2.3 Measurements

In the following, we illustrate the results of the evaluation in terms of different time and query result metrics. We measured LUBM queries in both centralized and decentralized evaluation scenarios, with the integrated implementation of DLUBM and SCAL.

Adaptations We used our experimental setup to evaluate three different query evaluation settings. On the one hand, the queries are evaluated centralized at the global level and, on the other hand, decentralized, both at the university level and at the department level. In particular, we omit in our experiments the evaluation of queries by an external LD query engine but let the SCs take over this evaluation. For every query: 1) the components must get all relevant graphs that are required for the evaluation; 2) derive additional information with entailment rule sets, in this case the RDFS entailment rule set; 3) evaluate the query; 4) and provide a resource with the results that can be pulled by clients. The query evaluation is triggered on-request in order to allow measurement of the overall evaluation with respect to time. The adaptations are deployed at the LDP interfaces of components after the DLUBM SCAL environment is started. Due to space constrains, we do not list all adaptations of components in detail.

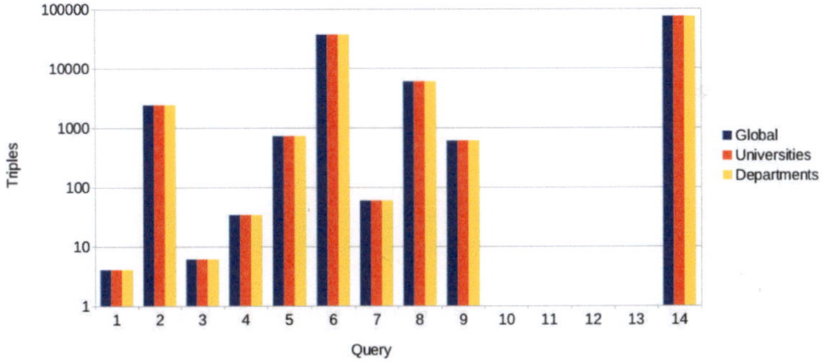

Figure 5.11: Decentralized Linked Data Querying – Evaluation Results

Results In Figures 5.11, 5.12, and 5.13, we provide an overview of the results of our measurements. We measured, with respect to all three evaluation settings (i.e., global, university, and department): 1) the overall evaluation time; 2) the average amount of triples added by request rules to the internal RDF graph of the interpreters; and 3) the number of results retrieved by a client. Starting with the number of results retrieved by clients – Figure 5.11, we see equal numbers of query results for all scenarios. This is a desired behavior, since in all scenarios the results must be the same, independently whether we have a global evaluating interpreter or merged results of the interpreters of several components. However, we need to note that the LUBM queries allow separate evaluation. The discussion of completeness is out of the scope of this work (c.f., Section 5.4.1), but due to the RDFS entailment rules, that are used by all SCs, we see results for all queries, except for the more sophisticated queries 10-13.

Times The overall evaluation time, however, differs significantly between the scenarios. The results, visualized in the diagram in Figure 5.12, confirm the expectation that splitting evaluation to multiple SCs of equal computing power leads to faster overall evaluation time. While the evaluation at the global component takes in average 30.29 seconds, we see significantly faster evaluation with 6.78 seconds at university level, and 3.19 seconds if queries are evaluated at department level.

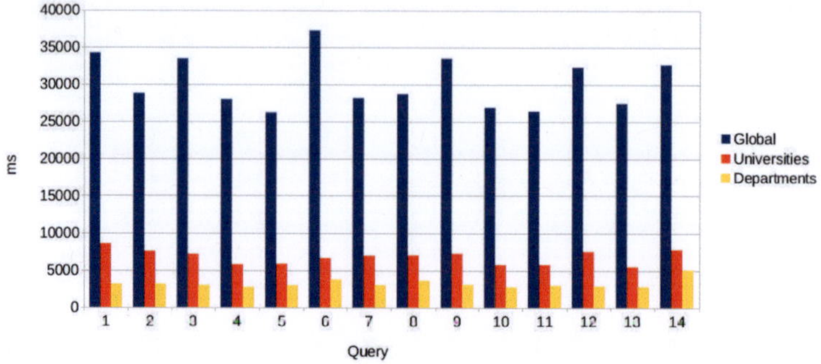

Figure 5.12: Decentralized Linked Data Querying – Evaluation Times

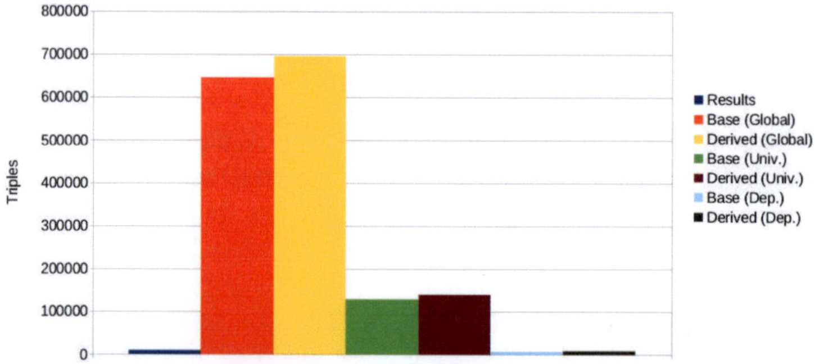

Figure 5.13: Decentralized Linked Data Querying – Evaluation Times

Triples The slower evaluation at a single global component is not caused by the requests that transfer all university and department data to the component, but is rather caused by deriving new triples with the RDFS entailment rules. This is visualized in the diagram in Figure 5.13, where the number of result triples and the average amount of requested (base) as well as the average amount of derived triples are compared. The more distributed the evaluation is, the fewer derived triples must be computed per SC.

Summarizing our experiments, we have shown that our approach and implementation enables different LD benchmarking scenarios, supported by the SCAL implementation for the adaptation of components. Furthermore, we have shown that our approach is scalable by deploying these integration scenarios as multi-component and heavily distributed applications to the computing resources of a PaaS provider. Finally, our performance analysis provides some insights about the implementation characteristics and shows some trade-offs between applications that are centralized and thus easier to manage, and those that are distributed but also more complex to deploy.

5.5 Summary

High-quality benchmarks and their evaluation results are essential not only for measuring the suitability of a certain technology or setup but also for pushing the development of better approaches.

We contribute to the evolution of LD technologies by introducing the DLUBM for creating reproducible and distributed benchmark environments for LD. While we extend the LUBM benchmark with features for generating LD, the approach itself is independent from a specific data generator, as long as the generator provides means for generating distinct graphs and provides means for adapting the links between these graphs to interlink the overall dataset. The substitution of components, e.g., the data generator, is possible due to our architectural approach as well as the introduced design requirements, which clearly separate the involved artifacts, the used technologies, and the current state of the system.

We demonstrate the practical use of DLUBM by evaluating a LD query engine via DLUBM with the original LUBM queries and different entailment rule sets. In addition, we demonstrate the adaptation capabilities of the SC approach by enabling centralized as well as decentralized query evaluation scenarios through the integration of DLUBM and SCAL.

6 Conclusion

In this thesis, we focused on the challenges that arise in relation to the emerging visions of the IoT, the WoT, and the SWoT as well as related visions such as the I4.0. These visions have the composition of distributed applications from a heterogeneous landscape of components in common. Besides the increasing modularization and the heterogeneity of components, also multi-stakeholder situations increases the complexity of integration. The development of these visions shows parallels to the development of the Web, the SW, and the WoD, which continue to evolve and provide means for Web-scale integration not only of information but also of applications. For their application in IoT-based solutions, we have to adapt the concepts and technologies from the Web and SW to the changed conditions in this new application scenarios.

In this context, we identified several challenges that we grouped in the problem areas of – integration of distributed components, unspecific development needs, control of distributed applications, interaction in distributed applications, integration of non-compliant components, data for distributed benchmarks, and provisioning of distributed benchmarks. In this context, we constructed the following hypothesis for approaching the problem areas and for finding solutions that cope with these challenges:

> *Web and Semantic Web concepts and technologies enable at runtime 1) the adaptation of components for their integration into distributed applications, 2) their control in centralized, decentralized, or hybrid manner, and 3) the deployment of this control.*

We believed that the combination and extension of established, standardized, and publicly available Web and SW concepts and technologies can pave the way for coping with the challenges that accompany emerging IoT, WoT, and SWoT visions. In particular, we aim to address the heterogeneous landscape of components and multiple involved stakeholders, thus counteracting the emergence of isolated, proprietary, non-standardized islands of components, which support only the integration of applications fitting the specific ecosystem.

From the challenges and our hypothesis, we derived three research questions, thoroughly investigated their implications, and contributed approaches for their solution, that include architectures, models, algorithms, implementations, and evaluations. With these approaches and their implementations, we showed the feasibility of our hypothesis. In the following, we briefly describe the contributions per research question and give an outlook on future work for each of the research areas.

6.1 Contributions

In this section we summarize our research contributions. We describe how they relate to the individual research questions and how they help to address the overall hypothesis of the thesis. Furthermore, we briefly discuss how each of the contributions was achieved, and what its general applicability and impact are.

Contributions to Research Question 1 With respect to the hypothesis, we ask the first research question:

> *How can we design an architecture for distributed applications, based on Web and Semantic Web concepts and technologies, that enables the adaptation of components at runtime, supporting both their integration and the deployment of control logic?*

In Chapter 3 on *Component Adaptation and Decentralized Application Control*, we presented the following contributions related to this first research question.

Requirements Analysis We performed a requirements analysis with respect to the identified challenges for the integration of components, the requirements of application use cases, and the decentralization of application control logic. First, we required the *Compliance with Integration Paradigms*. With this requirement, we enforce the REST and LD paradigms as well as broadly available and standardized technologies from the Web and SW as the basis of the approach. Second, we required the *Adaptability of Interaction and Processing*. With this requirement, we ensure that components must provide means for their adaptation to the specific requirements of the distributed applications. Third, we required the *Separation of Design, Adaptation, and Runtime*. With this requirement, we considered multi-stakeholder situations, in which different stakeholders are responsible for the development, provisioning, and integration of individual components.

Smart Component-based Integration Architecture We showed the details of our integration architecture, which incorporates the required broadly available and standardized technologies from the Web and SW. With this integration architecture, we enable the integration of arbitrary components that adhere to the REST and LD paradigms as well as components that follow our Smart Component approach. Depending on the specific application use cases, we can realize the required integration with only a subset of the Smart Components in their compositions.

Smart Component As the core of our approach, we introduced in detail the concept of the Smart Component as well as the Smart Component architecture. SCs adhere to the REST and LD paradigms, and thus support the communication with arbitrary components of the integration architecture. In addition, they support the adaptation of their interfaces, interaction, and processing at runtime. With this capabilities, we enable their integration in the composition of distributed applications at runtime, after deployment and without changing their initial design. Thereby, we provide support for different stakeholders that lead their development, provisioning, and integration. Furthermore, our SC approach enables the decentralization of application control logic. Depending on the application use case, we support the distribution of this application logic to the participating SCs in centralized, decentralized, or hybrid manner.

Smart Component Adaptation Layer With the SCAL, we provided a domain-independent implementation of our SC approach and architecture. SCAL supports the standalone deployment of centralized control for applications, the wrapping of existing components, and the programmatic integration as a software library. In all three cases, SCAL provides the adaptation capabilities of the SC approach.

Smart Component Adaptation Ontology For the description of adaptations, we introduced SCAO. This vocabulary provides the description of all concepts, required for adaptation in the SC architecture, as well as their relations. With SCAO, we enable the declaration of adaptations in the form of regular RDF resources at the interfaces provided by SCAL.

NIREST Smart Component Besides the domain-independent implementations of SCAL and SCAO, with NIREST we provided an implementation of a domain-specific SC. NIREST incorporates body tracking capabilities as its domain-specific function. Provided with the necessary hardware, the NIREST tracks the people, who are in range of its depth video camera, and provides the coordinates of their joints and the center of mass. This information is available during runtime and subject to further adaptations at the SCAL interface.

Evaluation of Function As the first of two evaluations, we evaluated the SC approach and architecture with respect to their function. In this evaluation, we check via testing several adaptations and re-adaptations, based on the NIREST implementation, the support for all capabilities of the SC approach. These capabilities fulfill the requirements of our requirements analysis.

Evaluation of Performance As the second evaluation, we evaluated the SCAL implementation with respect to performance. In this evaluation, we measure the overhead of the SCAL implementation on top of the NIREST domain-specific body tracking function. We compare the performance losses for the different adaptations of the functional evaluation. In these cases, the overhead of SCAL is within the lower range of milliseconds.

In summary, we showed that we can design an architecture for distributed applications, based on Web and Semantic Web concepts and technologies, that enables the adaptation of components at runtime, supporting both their integration and the deployment of control logic. The SC-based integration architecture enables the integration of SCs and arbitrary components that adhere to the LD and REST paradigms. The SC approach and architecture provide components that are adaptable at runtime in terms of their interfaces, interactions, as well as processing. Thereby, we enable the integration of components in compositions of distributed applications at runtime, after their design and deployment. As a consequence, we decouple the phases in the lifecycle of components and distributed applications, and support multi-stakeholder integration scenarios.

Contributions to Research Question 2 With respect to the hypothesis, we ask the second research question:

> *How can we enable the optimization of interactions between components, which are based on our architecture, and enable the integration of components, which are based on other specialized architectures?*

In Chapter 4 on *Interaction Optimization and Mapping*, we presented the following contributions related to the second research question.

> **Requirements Analysis** We performed the first of two requirements analyses with respect to the identified challenges for the optimization of interactions between components in distributed applications. First, we required the *Optimization of Interaction Patterns*. With this requirements, we narrow the optimization down to the optimization of push and pull interaction patterns used for the realization of data flows between components based on the frequencies for data provisioning and consumption. Second, we required the *Provisioning of Metadata*. With this requirement, we enforce the provisioning of metadata, which contains optimization-relevant information, directly at the components. Third, we required the *Self-adaptation of Components*. With this requirement, we consider application scenarios that exhibit dynamically changing

optimization-relevant factors, therefore, require re-optimization, and, consequently, the autonomous self-adaptation of components.

In addition, we performed a second requirements analysis with respect to the identified challenges for the mapping between domain-specific architectures and our integration architecture. First, we required the *Compliance with the Integration Architecture*. With this requirement, we enforce the REST and LD paradigms of our integration architecture. Second, we required the *Mapping of Interaction and Meta-interaction*. With this requirement, we ensure the realization of cross-architecture data flows. Third, we required the *Lifting and Lowering of Data*. With this requirement, we consider the preparation of data for the semantic integration between components of both architectures.

Frequency-based Network Model and Optimization Algorithm We provided a network model for capturing the properties of components with respect to the optimization goal. The network model enables the description of components in the compositions of applications with respect to the required data flows and the frequency of consumption and provisioning of data. We provided an optimization algorithm that optimizes, based on the network model, the push and pull interaction patterns for the data flow realization. In addition, we described the deployment of the network model and algorithm by utilizing our SC approach.

ROS Architecture Mapping For the mapping of architectures, we presented the mapping of concepts and interactions between the domain-specific ROS architecture and our integration architecture based on the REST and LD paradigms. We extend the mapping by resource aggregation and introduction of hypermedia, which exceeds the capabilities of the ROS architecture. In addition, we describe the support for meta-interaction mapping and data transformation based on the SC approach.

ROS-REST Proxy With ROEST, we provided an proof-of-concept implementation of the mapping between the ROS architecture and REST. ROEST supports the mapping of ROS topics to HTTP resources and the lifting of ROS messages to RDF. The implementation shows the feasibility of our mapping approach.

Evaluation of Frequency-based Interaction Optimization In our evaluation, we applied our network model and optimization algorithm to the initial optimization scenario. We compare the optimized interaction patterns with the pull-only and push-only realization of the scenario. The results show the optimization of the data flows with respect to pull requests, which contain redundant data, and to push requests, which transfer data that is not processed.

In summary, we showed that we can enable the optimization of interactions between components, which are based on our architecture, and enable the integration of components, which are based on other specialized architectures. The frequency-based network model captures the characteristics of components in the composition of distributed applications with respect to the frequencies, at which the components consume or produce data. The optimization algorithms determines the optimal pull and push interaction patterns to realize the required data flows. With both the network model and the algorithm, we provide one specific way for optimizing the interactions between components. With the ROS architecture mapping, we show, based on one domain-specific architecture, the means that are required for establishing cross-domain data flows. Thereby, we enable the participation of ROS nodes as components in distributed applications that adhere to our integration architecture.

Contributions to Research Question 3 With respect to the hypothesis, we ask the third research question:

> *How can we support the evaluation of distributed applications, based on our architecture, in terms of generating distributed benchmarks and in terms of providing these benchmarks as distributed environments?*

In Chapter 5 on *Distributed Benchmark Generation and Provisioning*, we presented the following contributions related to the third research question.

Requirements Analysis We performed a requirements analysis with respect to the identified challenges for the generation and provisioning of distributed LD benchmarks. First, we required the *Deployment-aligned Data Generation*. With this requirement, we ensure the generation of distinct but interlinked datasets. Second, we required the *Network Layer Distribution*. With this requirement, we ensure support for the distribution of the datasets on the network layer of the OSI model. Third, we required the *Deployment Automation*. With this requirement, we consider the complexity of large-scale distributed environments, which must be reduced through automation. Fourth, we required the *Pervasive Declaration*. With this requirement, we point out the comparative nature of benchmarks, which needs to be supported by guaranteeing the reproducibility of the same benchmark characteristics through simple parametrization.

Linked Data Benchmark Environment As the core of our approach, we introduced the concept of the Linked Data Benchmark Environment as well as the LDBE architecture. The LDBE provides a domain-independent framework for the development of specific LD benchmarks and considers in its lifecycle the configuration, composition, and deployment of the benchmark environments, as well as the repetitive execution of evaluations during its deployment. We realize these phases with container-based virtualization technologies that support extensive declarations of all required software components as well as capabilities for composition and deployment of components in distributed manner.

Distributed LUBM With the Distributed LUBM, we provided a specific implementation of our LDBE approach and architecture. The DLUBM provides the means for supporting domain-specific distributed LD settings at different scales. Thereby, we base the benchmarking scenario and our implementation on the well-known LUBM, which we extend with required features and accompany with additional tooling, to provide the benchmarking scenario as distributed LD.

Evaluation of Centralized Linked Data Querying As the first of two evaluations, we evaluate the LD-Fu query engine in a centralized LD query scenario. Thereby, DLUBM provides the benchmarking scenario at different scales on commonly available computing resources. In our experiments, we gain insights on the performance of the LD-Fu implementation and, indirectly, on the DLUBM implementation and deployment.

Evaluation of Decentralized Linked Data Querying In our second evaluation, we evaluate a decentralized LD query scenario. Therefore, we integrate the DLUBM implementation with the SCAL implementation of our SC approach. By utilizing the adaptation capabilities, we deploy the LD retrieval and the query evaluation directly at the distributed components of the DLUBM instance. In our experiments, we compare differently distributed query evaluations and show the use of SCAL in this context.

In summary, we showed that we can support the evaluation of distributed applications, based on our architecture, in terms of generating distributed benchmarks and in terms of providing these benchmarks as distributed environments. The LDBE approach and architecture provide a general framework for building distributed LD benchmarks. In the framework, we utilize container-based virtualization technology to cut down the complexity through automation and enable simple parametrization. With the DLUBM, we provide a specific implementation of the LDBE that supports the evaluation of distributed applications by providing reproducible LD settings at different scales.

6.2 Outlook

In the following, we provide an outlook on the future work that we see as open research opportunities and, at least partially, intend to investigate.

Component Adaptation and Decentralized Application Control
In Chapter 3, we presented our contributions related to *Component Adaptation and Decentralized Application Control*. We provided a comprehensive approach, including an architecture and a domain-independent prototypical implementation.

We intend to further stabilize the prototypical SCAO and SCAL implementations to provide a sound, reusable, and openly available software framework for our approach. This includes the extension of the embedded LDP server and further alignment with the LDP specification, the definition and implementation of reasonable processing triggers, as well as working out and extending the means for accessing and manipulating the state of interpreter runs.

The stabilization of the implementation extends to the efforts on the standardization of N3 and of the interpretation of rules, e.g., with respect to requests and mathematical operations. At the time of writing, different research contributions and community contributions to the W3C, but no formally established standards, define the N3 rule language and its interpretation. We also consider the evaluation of alternative rule languages with respect to their standardization, the RDF data model, the semantics of requests, and the fulfillment of other requirements exposed by the SC approach.

As an open research opportunity, we see the investigation of the self-adaptation of SCs by enabling embedded rule programs and queries, within other rule programs that, consequently, serve as adaptations of other components trough their appearance in request rules and their transfer in requests to these other components. Besides the conceptual and technical challenges, this research area has several implications on the composition of distributed applications and connects the approach even further with other research fields such as Artificial Intelligence (AI).

Interaction Optimization and Mapping In Chapter 4, we presented our contributions related to *Interaction Optimization and Mapping*. Due to the follow-up nature of these topics and the focus on the SC approach, we provided proof-of-concept implementations and application of the network model and algorithm, which can be further improved to provide more stable solutions.

We intend to implement the optimization algorithm as a combination of N3 rules and SPARQL queries, and also to support the deployment by utilizing the SCs approach and implementation. This implementation can be used for experimental evaluations of the data flow efficiency in compositions of SCs at different scales, and eases the consideration and the understanding of further factors that influence this efficiency.

The network model and optimization algorithm provide the basis for several potential extensions. For example, the inclusion of further factors that influence the efficiency of data flows, the consideration of trade-offs, e.g., between latency and bandwidth, or the consideration of interdependencies between data flows, i.e., the consideration of effects when components participate in multiple data flows at the same time and consume or produce information from several other components.

In addition to the extension of the proof-of-concept implementation to an more stable solution, e.g., by a consistent mapping to the LDP specification and the complete bi-directional interaction, the interaction mapping between architectures provides further research opportunities. For example, the integration of approaches for the mapping of information in structured data to the semantics provided by the RDF data model, the integration with the SC approach to enable, e.g., meta-interaction mapping, or the application of the general findings to further domain-specific architectures.

Distributed Benchmark Generation and Provisioning In Chapter 5, we presented our contributions related to *Distributed Benchmark Generation and Provisioning*. We provide a comprehensive approach, including the architecture of the domain-independent LDBE and the specific DLUBM implementation.

We intend to introduce further virtualization to the LDBE architecture by introducing container-based virtualization to the parametrization, generation of compositions, and the deployment process to computing resources, instead of using this virtualization solely for the deployment of LDBE. This pervasive container-based virtualization enables the use of LDBE Continuous Integration (CI) and Continuous Delivery (CD) pipelines as well as the further automation of experiments. We intend to extend the DLUBM implementation accordingly.

As a related research opportunity, we see the investigation of further LD data generators in combination with the LDBE framework for the provisioning of distributed LD benchmarks. These LD generators may artificially generate LD settings with different characteristics in their datasets or make use of real-world datasets. Their implementation within the LDBE enables alternative implementations in addition to the DLUBM.

Bibliography

[1] Adida, B., Birbeck, M., McCarron, S., Herman, I.: RDFa core 1.1 - third edition. Recommendation, W3C (2015)

[2] Al-Fuqaha, A., Guizani, M., Mohammadi, M., Aledhari, M., Ayyash, M.: Internet of Things: A survey on enabling technologies, protocols, and applications. Communications Surveys & Tutorials (2015)

[3] Aluç, G., Hartig, O., Özsu, M.T., Daudjee, K.: Diversified stress testing of RDF data management systems. In: Proceedings of the International Semantic Web Conference (ISWC) (2014)

[4] Angles, R., Boncz, P., Larriba-Pey, J., Fundulaki, I., Neumann, T., Erling, O., Neubauer, P., Martinez-Bazan, N., Kotsev, V., Toma, I.: The Linked Data Benchmark Council: A graph and RDF industry benchmarking effort. SIGMOD Record (2014)

[5] Antakli, A., Alvarado Moya, P., Brüderlin, B., Canzler, U., Dammertz, H., Enderlein, V., Grüninger, J., Harth, A., Hoffmann, H., Jundt, E., Keitler, P., Keppmann, F.L., Krzikalla, R., Lampe, S., Löffler, A., Meder, J., Otto, M., Pankratz, F., Pfützner, S., Roth, M., Sauerbier, R., Schreiber, W., Stechow, R., Tümler, J., Vogelgesang, C., Wasenmüller, O., Weinmann, A., Willneff, J., Wirsching, H.J., Zinnikus, I., Zürl, K.: Virtuelle Techniken und Semantic-Web. In: Web-basierte Anwendungen Virtueller Techniken: Das ARVIDA-Projekt – Dienste-basierte Software-Architektur und Anwendungsszenarien für die Industrie. Springer (2017)

[6] Aranda, C.B., Corby, O., Das, S., Feigenbaum, L., Gearon, P., Glimm, B., Harris, S., Hawke, S., Herman, I., Humfrey, N., Michaelis, N., Ogbuji, C., Perry, M., Passant, A., Polleres, A., Prud'hommeaux, E., Seaborne, A., Williams, G.T.: SPARQL 1.1 overview. Recommendation, W3C (2013)

[7] Armstrong, T.G., Ponnekanti, V., Borthakur, D., Callaghan, M.: LinkBench: A database benchmark based on the Facebook social graph. In: Proceedings of the International Conference on Management of Data (SIGMOD) (2013)

[8] Ashton, K.: That 'Internet of Things' thing. RFID Journal (2009)

[9] Atzori, L., Iera, A., Morabito, G.: The Internet of Things: A survey. Computer Networks (2010)

[10] Auer, S., Bizer, C., Kobilarov, G., Lehmann, J., Cyganiak, R., Ives, Z.: DBpedia: A nucleus for a Web of Open Data. In: Proceedings of the International Semantic Web Conference (ISWC) (2007)

[11] Bader, S., Wolf, A., Keppmann, F.L.: Evaluation environment for Linked Data Web Services. In: Proceedings of the Workshop on Services and Applications over Linked APIs and Data (SALAD) co-located with the International Conference on Semantic Systems (SEMANTiCS) (2017)

[12] Bagan, G., Bonifati, A., Ciucanu, R., Fletcher, G.H.L., Lemay, A., Advokaat, N.: gMark: Schema-driven generation of graphs and queries. Transactions on Knowledge and Data Engineering (2016)

[13] Barahmand, S., Ghandeharizadeh, S.: BG: A benchmark to evaluate interactive social networking actions. In: Proceedings of the Conference on Innovative Data Systems Research (CIDR) (2013)

[14] Barnaghi, P., Presser, M., Moessner, K.: Publishing linked sensor data. In: Proceedings of the International Workshop on Semantic Sensor Networks (SSN) co-located with the International Semantic Web Conference (ISWC) (2010)

[15] Beckett, D., Broekstra, J.: SPARQL query results XML format (second edition). Recommendation, W3C (2013)

[16] Behr, J., Blach, R., Bockholt, U., Harth, A., Hoffmann, H., Huber, M., Käfer, T., Keppmann, F.L., Pankratz, F., Rubinstein, D., Schubotz, R., Vogelgesang, C., Voss, G., Westner, P., Zürl, K.: ARVIDA-Referenzarchitektur. In: Web-basierte Anwendungen Virtueller Techniken: Das ARVIDA-Projekt – Dienste-basierte Software-Architektur und Anwendungsszenarien für die Industrie. Springer (2017)

[17] Belshe, M., Peon, R., Thomson, M.: Hypertext Transfer Protocol Version 2 (HTTP/2). Proposed standard, IETF (2015)

[18] Berners-Lee, T.: Information management: A proposal. Tech. rep., CERN (1989)

[19] Berners-Lee, T.: Universal Resource Identifiers in WWW: A unifying syntax for the expression of names and addresses of objects on the network as used in the World-Wide Web. Information, IETF (1994)

[20] Berners-Lee, T., Fielding, R.T., Masinter, L.M.: Uniform Resource Identifiers (URI): Generic syntax. Draft standard, IETF (1998)

[21] Berners-Lee, T., Fielding, R.T., Masinter, L.M.: Uniform Resource Identifier (URI): Generic syntax. Internet standard, IETF (2005)

[22] Berners-Lee, T., Masinter, L.M., McCahill, M.P.: Uniform Resource Locators (URL). Proposed standard, IETF (1994)

[23] Berners-Lee, T.: Linked Data (2006), `https://rslv.link/ZSqj`, retrieved January 22, 2018

[24] Berners-Lee, T.: Read-write Linked Data (2009), `https://rslv.link/ZSqt`, retrieved June 13, 2018

[25] Berners-Lee, T., Cailliau, R., Groff, J.F.: The World-Wide Web. Computer Networks and ISDN Systems (1992)

[26] Berners-Lee, T., Connolly, D.: Notation3 (N3): A readable RDF syntax. Team submission, W3C (2011)

[27] Berners-Lee, T., Connolly, D., Kagal, L., Scharf, Y., Hendler, J.: N3Logic: A logical framework for the World Wide Web. Theory and Practice of Logic Programming (2008)

[28] Berners-Lee, T., Fischetti, M.: Weaving the Web: The Original Design and Ultimate Destiny of the World Wide Web by Its Inventor. Diane Publishing (2001)

[29] Berners-Lee, T., Hendler, J.: Publishing on the Semantic Web. Nature (2001)

[30] Berners-Lee, T., Hendler, J., Lassila, O.: The Semantic Web. Scientific American (2001)

[31] Bizer, C., Heath, T., Ayers, D., Raimond, Y.: Interlinking Open Data on the Web. In: Proceedings of the Demos and Posters at the European Semantic Web Conference (ESWC) (2007)

[32] Bizer, C.: The emerging Web of Linked Data. Intelligent Systems (2009)

[33] Bizer, C., Heath, T., Berners-Lee, T.: Linked Data – the story so far. International Journal on Semantic Web and Information Systems (2009)

[34] Bizer, C., Lehmann, J., Kobilarov, G., Auer, S., Becker, C., Cyganiak, R., Hellmann, S.: DBpedia – a crystallization point for the Web of Data. Web Semantics: Science, Services and Agents on the World Wide Web (2009)

[35] Bizer, C., Schultz, A.: The Berlin SPARQL benchmark. International Journal on Semantic Web and Information Systems (2009)

[36] Blum, D., Cohen, S.: Grr: Generating random RDF. In: Proceedings of the Extended Semantic Web Conference (ESWC) (2011)

[37] Brickley, D., Guha, R.V.: RDF schema 1.1. Recommendation, W3C (2014)

[38] Brock, D., Schuster, E.: On the Semantic Web of Things. In: Proceedings of the Semantic Days (2006)

[39] Calbimonte, J.P., Sarni, S., Eberle, J., Aberer, K.: XGSN: An Open-Source semantic sensing middleware for the Web of Things. In: Joint Proceedings of the International Workshops on the Foundations, Technologies and Applications of the Geospatial Web (TC) and on Semantic Sensor Networks (SSN) co-located with International Semantic Web Conference (ISWC) (2014)

[40] Carothers, G.: RDF 1.1 N-Quads. Recommendation, W3C (2014)

[41] Carothers, G., Seaborne, A.: RDF 1.1 N-Triples. Recommendation, W3C (2014)

[42] Carothers, G., Seaborne, A.: RDF 1.1 TriG. Recommendation, W3C (2014)

[43] Carpenter, B.E., Hinden, R.M., Masinter, L.M.: Format for literal IPv6 addresses in URL's. Proposed standard, IETF (1999)

[44] Cerf, V.G., Kahn, R.E.: A protocol for packet network intercommunication. Transactions on Communications (1974)

[45] Cyganiak, R., Wood, D., Lanthaler, M.: RDF 1.1 concepts and abstract syntax. Recommendation, W3C (2014)

[46] Daga, E., Panziera, L., Pedrinaci, C.: A BASILar approach for building web APIs on top of SPARQL endpoints. In: Proceedings of the Workshop on Services and Applications over Linked APIs and Data (SALAD) co-located with the European Semantic Web Conference (ESWC) (2015)

[47] Dell'Aglio, D., Calbimonte, J.P., Balduini, M., Corcho, O., Della Valle, E.: On correctness in RDF stream processor benchmarking. In: Proceedings of the International Semantic Web Conference (ISWC) (2013)

[48] Dillon, T.S., Zhuge, H., Wu, C., Singh, J., Chang, E.: Web-of-Things framework for Cyber-Physical Systems. Concurrency and Computation: Practice and Experience (2011)

[49] Domingue, J., Fensel, D., Hendler, J.A. (eds.): Handbook of Semantic Web Technologies. Springer (2011)

[50] Domingue, J., Fensel, D., Hendler, J.A.: Introduction to the Semantic Web Technologies. In: Handbook of Semantic Web Technologies. Springer (2011)

[51] Dominguez-Sal, D., Martinez-Bazan, N., Muntes-Mulero, V., Baleta, P., Larriba-Pey, J.L.: A discussion on the design of graph database benchmarks. In: Proceedings of the Technology Conference on Performance Evaluation and Benchmarking (TPCTC) (2011)

[52] Duan, S., Kementsietsidis, A., Srinivas, K., Udrea, O.: Apples and oranges: A comparison of RDF benchmarks and real RDF datasets. In: Proceedings of the International Conference on Management of Data (SIGMOD) (2011)

[53] Duerst, M., Suignard, M.: Internationalized Resource Identifiers (IRIs). Proposed standard, IETF (2005)

[54] Duquennoy, S., Grimaud, G., Vandewalle, J.J.: The Web of Things: interconnecting devices with high usability and performance. In: Proceedings of the International Conference on Embedded Software and Systems (ICESS) (2009)

[55] Erling, O., Averbuch, A., Larriba-Pey, J., Chafi, H., Gubichev, A., Prat, A., Pham, M.D., Boncz, P.: The LDBC social network benchmark: Interactive workload. In: Proceedings of the International Conference on Management of Data (SIGMOD) (2015)

[56] Faulkner, S., Eicholz, A., Leithead, T., Danilo, A., Moon, S., Doyle Navara, E., O'Connor, T., Berjon, R.: HTML 5.2. Recommendation, W3C (2017)

[57] Fielding, R.T., Lafon, Y., Reschke, J.: Hypertext Transfer Protocol (HTTP/1.1): Range requests. Proposed standard, IETF (2014)

[58] Fielding, R.T., Nielsen, H.F., Mogul, J., Gettys, J., Berners-Lee, T.: Hypertext Transfer Protocol – HTTP/1.1. Proposed standard, IETF (1997)

[59] Fielding, R.T., Nottingham, M., Reschke, J.: Hypertext Transfer Protocol (HTTP/1.1): Caching. Proposed standard, IETF (2014)

[60] Fielding, R.T., Reschke, J.: Hypertext Transfer Protocol (HTTP/1.1): Authentication. Proposed standard, IETF (2014)

[61] Fielding, R.T., Reschke, J.: Hypertext Transfer Protocol (HTTP/1.1): Conditional requests. Proposed standard, IETF (2014)

[62] Fielding, R.T., Reschke, J.: Hypertext Transfer Protocol (HTTP/1.1): Message syntax and routing. Proposed standard, IETF (2014)

[63] Fielding, R.T., Reschke, J.: Hypertext Transfer Protocol (HTTP/1.1): Semantics and content. Proposed standard, IETF (2014)

[64] Fielding, R.T.: Architectural Styles and the Design of Network-based Software Architectures. Ph.D. thesis, University of California (2000)

[65] Gandon, F., Schreiber, G.: RDF 1.1 XML syntax. Recommendation, W3C (2014)

[66] Gershenfeld, N., Krikorian, R., Cohen, D.: The Internet of Things. Scientific American (2004)

[67] Gruber, T.R.: A translation approach to portable ontology specifications. Knowledge Acquisition (1993)

[68] Guinard, D.: A Web of Things Application Architecture – Integrating the Real-World into the Web. Ph.D. thesis, ETH Zurich (2011)

[69] Guinard, D., Trifa, V.: Towards the Web of Things: Web mashups for embedded devices. In: Proceedings of the Workshop on Mashups, Enterprise Mashups and Lightweight Composition on the Web (MEM) co-located with the International World Wide Web Conference (WWW) (2009)

[70] Guinard, D., Trifa, V., Mattern, F., Wilde, E.: From the Internet of Things to the Web of Things: Resource-oriented architecture and best practices. In: Architecting the Internet of Things. Springer (2011)

[71] Guinard, D., Trifa, V., Pham, T., Liechti, O.: Towards physical mashups in the Web of Things. In: Proceedings of the International Conference on Networked Sensing Systems (INSS) (2009)

[72] Guinard, D., Trifa, V., Wilde, E.: A resource oriented architecture for the Web of Things. In: Proceedings of the Internet of Things Conference (IOT) (2010)

[73] Guo, Y., Pan, Z., Heflin, J.: LUBM: A benchmark for OWL knowledge base systems. Web Semantics: Science, Services and Agents on the World Wide Web (2005)

[74] Gyrard, A.: Designing Cross-Domain Semantic Web of Things Applications. Ph.D. thesis, TELECOM ParisTech (2015)

[75] Gyrard, A., Bonnet, C., Boudaoud, K., Serrano, M.: Assisting IoT projects and developers in designing interoperable Semantic Web of Things applications. In: Proceedings of the International Conference on Data Science and Data Intensive Systems (DSDIS) (2015)

[76] Gyrard, A., Bonnet, C., Boudaoud, K., Serrano, M.: LOV4IoT: A second life for ontology-based domain knowledge to build Semantic Web of Things applications. In: Proceedings of the International Conference on Future Internet of Things and Cloud (FiCloud) (2016)

[77] Gyrard, A., Datta, S.K., Bonnet, C., Boudaoud, K.: Standardizing generic cross-domain applications in Internet of Things. In: Proceedings of the Globecom Workshops (GC Wkshps) (2014)

[78] Gyrard, A., Datta, S.K., Bonnet, C., Boudaoud, K.: Cross-domain Internet of Things application development: M3 framework and evaluation. In: Proceedings of the International Conference on Future Internet of Things and Cloud (FiCloud) (2015)

[79] Gyrard, A., Serrano, M., Atemezing, G.A.: Semantic Web methodologies, best practices and ontology engineering applied to Internet of Things. In: Proceedings of the World Forum on Internet of Things (WF-IoT) (2015)

[80] Gyrard, A., Serrano, M., Patel, P.: Building interoperable and cross-domain Semantic Web of Things applications. In: Managing the Web of Things. Morgan Kaufmann (2017)

[81] Hammer-Lahav, E., Nottingham, M.: Defining well-known Uniform Resource Identifiers (URIs). Proposed standard, IETF (2010)

[82] Harris, S., Seaborne, A.: SPARQL 1.1 query language. Recommendation, W3C (2013)

[83] Harth, A., Hose, K., Karnstedt, M., Polleres, A., Sattler, K.U., Umbrich, J.: Data summaries for on-demand queries over Linked Data. In: Proceedings of the International Conference on World Wide Web (WWW) (2010)

[84] Harth, A., Käfer, T., Keppmann, F.L., Rubinstein, D., Schubotz, R., Vogelgesang, C.: Industrielle VT-Anwendungen auf Basis von Web-Technologien. In: Proceedings of the VDE-Kongress – Internet der Dinge (2016)

[85] Hartig, O., Bizer, C., Freytag, J.C.: Executing SPARQL queries over the Web of Linked Data. In: Proceedings of the International Semantic Web Conference (ISWC) (2009)

[86] Hermann, M., Pentek, T., Otto, B.: Design principles for Industrie 4.0 scenarios. In: Proceedings of the Hawaii International Conference on System Sciences (HICSS) (2016)

[87] Hinden, R.M., E., D.S.: Internet Protocol, version 6 (IPv6) specification. Draft standard, IETF (1998)

[88] Huppler, K.: The art of building a good benchmark. In: Proceedings of the Technology Conference on Performance Evaluation and Benchmarking (TPCTC) (2009)

[89] Jackson, M.: Defining a discipline of description. Software (1998)

[90] Jacobs, I., Walsh, N.: Architecture of the World Wide Web, volume one. Recommendation, W3C (2004)

[91] Jara, A.J., Olivieri, A.C., Bocchi, Y., Jung, M., Kastner, W., Skarmeta, A.F.: Semantic Web of Things: an analysis of the application semantics for the IoT moving towards the IoT convergence. International Journal of Web and Grid Services (2014)

[92] Jara, A.J., Scarrone, E., Ladid, L.: Enabling a World-Wide Web of Things: An analysis and overview of the application semantics and standards for the IoT. Tech. rep., EU-China FIRE project (2014)

[93] Joshi, A.K., Hitzler, P., Dong, G.: LinkGen: Multipurpose Linked Data generator. In: Proceedings of the International Semantic Web Conference (ISWC) (2016)

[94] Kamilaris, A., Yumusak, S., Ali, M.I.: WOTS2E: A search engine for a Semantic Web of Things. In: Proceedings of the World Forum on Internet of Things (WF-IoT) (2016)

[95] Katasonov, A., Kaykova, O., Khriyenko, O., Nikitin, S., Terziyan, V.: Smart semantic middleware for the Internet of Things. In: Proceedings of the International Conference on Informatics in Control, Automation and Robotics (ICINCO) (2008)

[96] Keppmann, F.L., Käfer, T., Stadtmüller, S., Schubotz, R., Harth, A.: High performance Linked Data processing for Virtual Reality environments. In: Proceedings of the Posters and Demos at the International Semantic Web Conference (ISWC) (2014)

[97] Keppmann, F.L., Käfer, T., Stadtmüller, S., Schubotz, R., Harth, A.: Integrating highly dynamic RESTful Linked Data APIs in a Virtual Reality environment. In: Proceedings of the Posters and Demos at the International Symposium on Mixed and Augmented Reality (ISMAR) (2014)

[98] Keppmann, F.L., Maleshkova, M.: Towards pervasive Web API-based systems. In: Proceedings of the Research Workshop co-located with the Karlsruhe Service Summit (KSS) (2015)

[99] Keppmann, F.L., Maleshkova, M.: Smart components for enabling intelligent Web of Things applications. In: Proceedings of the International Conference on Intelligent Systems and Applications (INTELLI) (2016)

[100] Keppmann, F.L., Maleshkova, M., Harth, A.: Building REST APIs for the Robot Operating System – mapping concepts and interaction. In: Proceedings of the Workshop on Services and Applications over Linked APIs and Data (SALAD) co-located with the European Semantic Web Conference (ESWC) (2015)

[101] Keppmann, F.L., Maleshkova, M., Harth, A.: Towards optimising the data flow in distributed applications. In: Proceedings of the Workshop on Web APIs and RESTful Design Workshop (WS-REST) co-located with the International World Wide Web Conference (WWW) (2015)

[102] Keppmann, F.L., Maleshkova, M., Harth, A.: Semantic technologies for realising decentralised applications for the Web of Things. In: Proceedings of the International Conference on Engineering of Complex Computer Systems (ICECCS) (2016)

[103] Keppmann, F.L., Maleshkova, M., Harth, A.: Adaptable interfaces, interactions, and processing for Linked Data Platform components. In: Proceedings of the International Conference on Semantic Systems (SEMANTiCS) (2017)

[104] Keppmann, F.L., Maleshkova, M., Harth, A.: DLUBM: A benchmark for distributed Linked Data knowledge base systems. In: Proceedings of the On the Move to Meaningful Internet Systems Conferences (OTM) (2017)

[105] Keppmann, F.L., Stadtmüller, S.: Semantic RESTful APIs for dynamic data sources. In: Proceedings of the Workshop on Services and Applications over Linked APIs and Data (SALAD) co-located with the European Semantic Web Conference (ESWC) (2014)

[106] Koch, J., Velasco, C.A., Ackermann, P.: HTTP vocabulary in RDF 1.0. Working group note, W3C (2017)

[107] Kotis, K., Katasonov, A.: Semantic interoperability on the Web of Things: The semantic smart gateway framework. In: Proceedings of the International Conference on Complex, Intelligent, and Software Intensive Systems (CISIS) (2012)

[108] Krummenacher, R., Norton, B., Marte, A.: Towards linked open services and processes. In: Proceedings of the Future Internet Symposium (FIS) (2010)

[109] Lasi, H., Fettke, P., Kemper, H.G., Feld, T., Hoffmann, M.: Industry 4.0. Business & Information Systems Engineering (2014)

[110] Le-Phuoc, D., Dao-Tran, M., Pham, M.D., Boncz, P., Eiter, T., Fink, M.: Linked stream data processing engines: Facts and figures. In: Proceedings of the International Semantic Web Conference (ISWC) (2012)

[111] McCarron, S.: XHTML+RDFa 1.1 - third edition. Recommendation, W3C (2015)

[112] McCrae, J.P., Abele, A., Buitelaar, P., Cyganiak, R., Jentzsch, A., Andryushechkin, V.: Linked Open Data Cloud (April 2018) (2018), `https://rslv.link/ZSqP`, retrieved on 01.05.2018.

[113] Merkel, D.: Docker: Lightweight Linux containers for consistent development and deployment. Linux Journal (2014)

[114] Meroño-Peñuela, A., Hoekstra, R.: grlc makes GitHub taste like Linked Data APIs. In: Proceedings of the European Semantic Web Conference (ESWC) (2016)

[115] Mihindukulasooriya, N., Menday, R.: Linked Data Platform 1.0 primer. Working group note, W3C (2015)

[116] National Science Foundation: Cyber-Physical Systems Summit. Tech. rep., National Science Foundation (2008)

[117] Nielsen, H.F., Fielding, R.T., Berners-Lee, T.: Hypertext Transfer Protocol – HTTP/1.0. Information, IETF (1996)

[118] Nottingham, M.: Web linking. Proposed standard, IETF (2010)

[119] Nottingham, M.: Web linking. Proposed standard, IETF (2017)

[120] Nottingham, M., Sayre, R.: The Atom syndication format. Proposed standard, IETF (2005)

[121] Novo, O., Beijar, N., Ocak, M., Kjällman, J., Komu, M., Kauppinen, T.: Capillary networks – bridging the cellular and IoT worlds. In: Proceedings of the World Forum on Internet of Things (WF-IoT) (2015)

[122] Ostermaier, B., Elahi, B.M., Römer, K., Fahrmair, M., Kellerer, W.: Dyser: Towards a real-time search engine for the Web of Things. In: Proceedings of the Conference on Embedded Network Sensor Systems (SenSys) (2008)

[123] Overdick, H.: The resource-oriented architecture. In: Proceedings of the Congress on Services (Services) (2007)

[124] Patel, P., Gyrard, A., Datta, S.K., Ali, M.I.: SWoTSuite: A toolkit for prototyping end-to-end Semantic Web of Things applications. In: Proceedings of the Posters and Demos at the International World Wide Web Conference (WWW) (2017)

[125] Patel-Schneider, P.F., Motik, B.: OWL 2 Web ontology language mapping to RDF graphs (second edition). Recommendation, W3C (2012)

[126] Peon, R., Ruellan, H.: HPACK: Header compression for HTTP/2. Proposed standard, IETF (2015)

[127] Peterson, D., Gao, S., Malhotra, A., Sperberg-McQueen, C.M., Thompson, H.S.: W3C XML schema definition language (XSD) 1.1 part 2: Datatypes. Recommendation, W3C (2012)

[128] Pfisterer, D., Römer, K., Bimschas, D., Kleine, O., Mietz, R., Truong, C., Hasemann, H., Kröller, A., Pagel, M., Hauswirth, M., Karnstedt, M., Leggieri, M., Passant, A., Richardson, R.: SPITFIRE: Toward a Semantic Web of Things. Communications Magazine (2011)

[129] Postel, J.: Internet Protocol. Internet standard, IETF (1981)

[130] Presser, M., Barnaghi, P.M., Eurich, M., Villalonga, C.: The SENSEI project: integrating the physical world with the digital world of the network of the future. Communications Magazine (2009)

[131] Prud'hommeaux, E., Carothers, G.: RDF 1.1 Turtle. Recommendation, W3C (2014)

[132] Quigley, M., Gerkey, B., Conley, K., Faust, J., Foote, T., Leibs, J., Berger, E., Wheeler, R., Ng, A.: ROS: an Open-Source Robot Operating System. In: Proceedings of the Workshop on Open Source Software co-located with the International Conference on Robotics and Automation (ICRA) (2009)

[133] Rukzio, E., Paolucci, M., Wagner, M., Berndt, H., Hamard, J., Schmidt, A.: Mobile service interaction with the Web of Things. In: Proceedings of the International Conference on Telecommunications (ICT) (2006)

[134] Ruta, M., Scioscia, F., Pinto, A., Di Sciascio, E., Gramegna, F., Ieva, S., Loseto, G.: Resource annotation, dissemination and discovery in the Semantic Web of Things: a CoAP-based framework. In: Joint proceedings of the International Conferences on Green Computing and Communications (GreenCom) and Internet of Things (iThings) and Cyber, Physical and Social Computing (CPSCom) (2013)

[135] Ruta, M., Scioscia, F., Di Sciascio, E.: Enabling the Semantic Web of Things: Framework and architecture. In: Proceedings of the International Conference on Semantic Computing (ICSC) (2012)

[136] Ruta, M., Scioscia, F., Pinto, A., Gramegna, F., Ieva, S., Loseto, G., Di Sciascio, E.: A CoAP-based framework for collaborative sensing in the Semantic Web of Things. Procedia Computer Science (2017)

[137] Ruta, M., Scioscia, F., Pinto, A., Gramegna, F., Ieva, S., Loseto, G., Di Sciascio, E.: CoAP-based collaborative sensor networks in the Semantic Web of Things. Journal of Ambient Intelligence and Humanized Computing (2018)

[138] Sachs, J., Beijar, N., Elmdahl, P., Melen, J., Militano, F., Salmela, P.: Capillary networks – a smart way to get things connected. Ericsson Review (2014)

[139] Sahlmann, K., Schwotzer, T.: MOCAP: Towards the Semantic Web of Things. In: Proceedings of the Posters and Demos at the International Conference on Semantic Systems (SEMANTiCS) (2015)

[140] Schmidt, M., Hornung, T., Lausen, G., Pinkel, C.: SP2Bench: A SPARQL performance benchmark. In: Proceedings of the International Conference on Data Engineering (ICDE) (2009)

[141] Schreiber, G., Raimond, Y.: RDF 1.1 primer. Recommendation, W3C (2014)

[142] Schreiber, W., Zürl, K., Zimmermann, P. (eds.): Web-basierte Anwendungen Virtueller Techniken: Das ARVIDA-Projekt – Dienste-basierte Software-Architektur und Anwendungsszenarien für die Industrie. Springer (2017)

[143] Scioscia, F., Ruta, M.: Building a Semantic Web of Things: issues and perspectives in information compression. In: Proceedings of the International Conference on Semantic Computing (ICSC) (2009)

[144] Seaborne, A.: SPARQL 1.1 query results CSV and TSV formats. Recommendation, W3C (2013)

[145] Seaborne, A.: SPARQL 1.1 query results JSON format. Recommendation, W3C (2013)

[146] Shadbolt, N., Berners-Lee, T., Hall, W.: The Semantic Web revisited. Intelligent Systems (2006)

[147] Shelby, Z., Hartke, K., Bormann, C.: The Constrained Application Protocol (CoAP). Proposed standard, IETF (2014)

[148] Shelby, Z.: Constrained RESTful Environments (CoRE) link format. Proposed standard, IETF (2012)

[149] Soldatos, J., Kefalakis, N., Hauswirth, M., Serrano, M., Calbimonte, J.P., Riahi, M., Aberer, K., Jayaraman, P.P., Zaslavsky, A., Žarko, I.P., Skorin-Kapov, L., Herzog, R.: OpenIoT: Open Source Internet-of-Things in the cloud. In: Proceedings of the International Workshop on Interoperability and Open-Source Solutions for the Internet of Things (InterOSS-IoT) co-located with the International Conference on Software, Telecommunications and Computer Networks (SoftCOM) (2015)

[150] Speicher, S., Arwe, J., Malhotra, A.: Linked Data Platform 1.0. Recommendation, W3C (2015)

[151] Speicher, S., Arwe, J., Malhotra, A.: Linked Data Platform paging 1.0. Working group note, W3C (2015)

[152] Speiser, S., Harth, A.: Integrating Linked Data and services with Linked Data Services. In: Proceedings of the Extended Semantic Web Conference (ESWC) (2011)

[153] Sporny, M.: HTML+RDFa 1.1 - second edition. Recommendation, W3C (2015)

[154] Sporny, M.: RDFa lite 1.1 - second edition. Recommendation, W3C (2015)

[155] Sporny, M., Kellogg, G., Lanthaler, M.: JSON-LD 1.0. Recommendation, W3C (2014)

[156] Stadtmüller, S.: Dynamic Interaction and Manipulation of Web Resources. Ph.D. thesis, Karlsruhe Institute of Technology (2016)

[157] Stadtmüller, S., Speiser, S., Harth, A.: Future challenges for Linked APIs. In: Proceedings of the Workshop on Services and Applications over Linked APIs and Data (SALAD) co-located with the European Semantic Web Conference (ESWC) (2013)

[158] Stadtmüller, S., Speiser, S., Harth, A., Studer, R.: Data-Fu: A language and an interpreter for interaction with Read/Write Linked Data. In: Proceedings of the International World Wide Web Conference (WWW) (2013)

[159] Stirbu, V.: Towards a RESTful plug and play experience in the Web of Things. In: Proceedings of the International Conference on Semantic Computing (ICSC) (2008)

[160] Traversat, B., Abdelaziz, M., Doolin, D., Duigou, M., Hugly, J.C., Pouyoul, E.: Project JXTA-C: Enabling a Web of Things. In: Proceedings of the Hawaii International Conference on System Sciences (HICSS) (2003)

[161] Trifa, V., Wieland, S., Guinard, D., Bohnert, T.M.: Design and implementation of a gateway for Web-based interaction and management of embedded devices. In: Proceedings of the International Workshop on Sensor Network Engineering (IWSNE) at the International Conference on Distributed Computing in Sensor Systems (DCOSS) (2009)

[162] Verborgh, R., Hartig, O., De Meester, B., Haesendonck, G., De Vocht, L., Vander Sande, M., Cyganiak, R., Colpaert, P., Mannens, E., Van de Walle, R.: Querying datasets on the Web with high availability. In: Proceedings of the International Semantic Web Conference (ISWC) (2014)

[163] Verborgh, R., Steiner, T., van Deursen, D., van de Walle, R., Gabarró Vallés, J.: Efficient runtime service discovery and consumption with hyperlinked RESTdesc. In: Proceedings of the International Conference on Next Generation Web Services Practices (NWeSP) (2011)

[164] W3C OWL Working Group: OWL 2 Web ontology language document overview (second edition). Recommendation, W3C (2012)

[165] Webber, J., Parastatidis, S., Robinson, I.: REST in Practice: Hypermedia and Systems Architecture. O'Reilly Media (2010)

[166] Weithöner, T., Liebig, T., Luther, M., Böhm, S.: What's wrong with OWL benchmarks? In: Proceedings of the International Workshop on Scalable Semantic Web Knowledge Base Systems (SSWS) co-located with the International Semantic Web Conference (ISWC) (2006)

[167] Wilde, E.: Putting things to REST. Tech. rep., UC Berkeley: School of Information (2007)

[168] Wilde, E., Kofahl, M.: The locative web. In: Proceedings of the International Workshop on Location and the Web (LocWeb) co-located with the International World Wide Web Conference (WWW) (2008)

[169] Zhang, Y., Duc, P.M., Corcho, O., Calbimonte, J.P.: SRBench: A streaming RDF/SPARQL benchmark. In: Proceedings of the International Semantic Web Conference (ISWC) (2012)